A Life Both Public
and Private

A Life Both Public and Private

Expressions of Individuality in Old English Poetry

BRENT R. LAPADULA

McFarland & Company, Inc., Publishers
Jefferson, North Carolina

LIBRARY OF CONGRESS CATALOGUING-IN-PUBLICATION DATA

Names: LaPadula, Brent R., 1980– author.
Title: A life both public and private : expressions of individuality in Old English poetry / Brent R. LaPadula.
Description: Jefferson, North Carolina : McFarland & Company, Inc., Publishers, 2019. | Includes bibliographical references and index.
Identifiers: LCCN 2018047406 | ISBN 9781476673950 (softcover : acid free paper) ∞
Subjects: LCSH: English poetry—Old English, ca. 450–1100—History and criticism. | Self (Philosophy) in literature. | Difference (Philosophy) in literature. | Civilization, Anglo-Saxon, in literature.
Classification: LCC PR203 .L27 2018 | DDC 829/.1—dc23
LC record available at https://lccn.loc.gov/2018047406

BRITISH LIBRARY CATALOGUING DATA ARE AVAILABLE

ISBN (print) 978-1-4766-7395-0
ISBN (ebook) 978-1-4766-3347-3

© 2019 Brent R. LaPadula. All rights reserved

No part of this book may be reproduced or transmitted in any form or by any means, electronic or mechanical, including photocopying or recording, or by any information storage and retrieval system, without permission in writing from the publisher.

Front cover image of Old Medieval Church © 2019 zodebala/iStock

Printed in the United States of America

*McFarland & Company, Inc., Publishers
Box 611, Jefferson, North Carolina 28640
www.mcfarlandpub.com*

For Cathy

Without understanding yourself, what is the use of trying to understand the world?—Ramana Maharshi

Table of Contents

Preface   1

Introduction: Towards an Understanding of Identity and the Self: Meaning and Methodology   5

1. The Paradigm of Identity in Old English Literature: The Self as a Social Construct   31

2. Memory and Identity Formation: A Cognitive Construction of the Self in *The Wanderer* and *The Seafarer*   59

3. Living Vicariously and Identity Schema: The Multiple Selves of the Anglo-Saxon *Scop*   99

4. A Case for Female Individuality in *The Wife's Lament* and *Wulf and Eadwacer*   123

Conclusion   153

Chapter Notes   157

Bibliography   177

Index   189

Preface

The inspiration for this book grew out of my first couple years of graduate school, when our seminar group was tasked with reading some of the Old English elegies (*The Wanderer* and *The Seafarer*). As highly emotive verse, the elegiac genre spoke to me as representative of something special, perhaps unique, within the Old English corpus. The importance set on the narrator, the intimate language of introspection, and the thematic representations of the individual drove me on a quest to interrogate some of these poems with more intensity, and as I began to read, my eyes widened further. Reading as an impersonal exercise, where ancient characters often rear themselves inside an otherwise lucid critic's mind as bluntly painted ghosts on a tattered canvas, gave way to an image of these personae as not only displaying fidelity in action, but also in their thinking selves. They basically appeared more "real" than many other characters in the corpus, and I felt that it was because of this that a modern audience is more receptive to them than to other, more abstract characters. Thus as I read, a topos wherein identity in its varied facets and manifestations started to take shape, and it led me to inexorable, complementary questions: who were these people mentioned in these tales? Were they real or imagined? Were their inner expressions, fears, and desires something universal for the time? Were Anglo-Saxons really so psychologically dissimilar to a modern western audience? What composed the sense of self and the sense of identity for Anglo-Saxons? And what does all this mean for identity studies?

This work therefore seeks to answer some of these questions, with a particular emphasis on the concept of identity. Importantly, the central question will orbit the language of identity and self, both of which I outline and decode in the introduction and Chapter 1. Defining these terms and what it means for a study of Old English literature specifically, and the

Preface

Anglo Saxons as a group in general, will allow me to hone in on the concept of identity as the dominant interrogative pathway. While questions of identity and self are not so easily answered in any given modern framework, it is perhaps more difficult when affixing these questions onto a people who lived over a thousand years ago, and whose literature spanned roughly five hundred years. After all, we do not have the benefit of a psychological sample study of Anglo-Saxons, and of course we cannot question them in the traditional sense. Nevertheless, difficulty in the face of obstacle ought not be an impediment to the salience of the result, if the product of the result is of significant consequence to our understanding of human nature. It is to this maxim that I proceed with this investigation, and to this prospect that this work is inspired. I also asked myself if my sense of the question was something that had been broached to any significant extent before.

Indeed, I proceeded to spend time with the literature in the field, reading with an eye on identity and selfhood rather than looking at the various criticisms of overarching themes, linguistic quarks, or the historical realities of the characters in question. In my reading of the secondary material, which I outline in the coming pages, I found that there was a conspicuous absence of discussion regarding this idea of self or identity in the Anglo-Saxon period. To be sure, and to this I will acknowledge, a decent amount has been written on the nebulous concept of self or soul in the corpus, but very little on how I define the self. In other words, much of the literature in the academy has focused on what the soul is, how it is represented in the Old English, and its manifestation in verse and prose. Although meaningful in themselves, these studies nevertheless fail to identify "real" identity matrices within the characters and narrators. However interesting it is to contemplate the notion of the soul—particularly when taken in context with religious didactic verse, hagiography, and/or religious narrative—I find that the indeterminate nature of such theoretical approaches may be complemented by one that strictly defines its terms, its methodologies, and outcome(s).

Therefore, by looking at a representative sample of Old English poetry, this work questions the long-held notion that the individual, or personal-self, was not a reality in the western world until the Renaissance. This research makes use of a variety of recent and past methodological approaches to the self, so that we may apply these theories to a study of the individual in Old English literature, and by extension Anglo-Saxon

Preface

culture more generally. The four-chapter layout showcases how we may approach and answer the question of self in a variety of Old English verse—from elegies and didactic religious, to the heroic. Each study is unique yet complements that which precedes and follows it, so as to highlight how the study of self is really an inquiry of only *seemingly* disparate concepts. The outcome of this analysis demonstrates that the individual, or personal self-concept in Anglo-Saxon England was a reality, and consequently challenges past beliefs that the individual is a relatively modern notion. Thus opening the dialogue once more, this book ultimately asks how we may proceed with the question of self in different contexts, historical eras, and eclectic methodological avenues of inquiry, that we may further develop our understanding of one of the most important and ancient questions in humankind's story.

Introduction

*Towards an Understanding
of Identity and the Self:
Meaning and Methodology*

What is the self? It is a notion widely taken for granted, but in recent years there have been many theories about what it is, where it might reside in a person, and whether or not its genesis can be pinpointed to a particular historical era. This work explores some of the Old English poetry that deals with the concepts of selfhood and individuality in one form or another, and questions if we can identify selfhood and individuality in Anglo-Saxon personalities and therefore conclude whether the individual was a psychological reality in the Anglo-Saxon world. The result of this study will argue for the existence of a strong sense of individuality in Anglo-Saxon life, challenging past notions that the individual in the western world was an invention of either the twelfth or sixteenth centuries. To aid in this investigation, I incorporate a variety of modern methodological approaches to self-studies, many of which straddle different fields and academic subjects, showcasing how the question of self is diverse, both in its definition and discovery. This section begins with a brief outline that exhibits how the self has been approached through history, followed by some contemporary investigations of the self and the individual, including the many definitions that have been proposed by various researchers. Following this, I showcase some of the different methodologies used to understand the self and what others have said concerning the Anglo-Saxon self more specifically. Finally, I have included a chapter outline that details how this investigation proceeds with this line of inquiry, and the methodologies that I use in each chapter.

Indeed, owing to its complicated nature, the concept of the self has

Introduction

been the subject of philosophical discourse for millennia, and some would indeed argue that we are perhaps no closer today in answering these questions than our antecedent thinkers. What is clear, however, is that the number of thinkers and the methodological resources available for an understanding of the self in the post–Cartesian world have increased exponentially, while the fundamental problem of defining, finding, and understanding the self has remained constant.[1] One may then ask whether or not a philosophical, scientific, and folk-psychological consensus has ever been reached, and quickly dispensing with any anxiety on the issue I can say that it has not. In fact, the debate persists more lively than ever. Consequently, discussion surrounding this very human question continues to express itself in a variety of disciplines—including history, literature, sociology, psychology, philosophy, anthropology, and many empirical scientific fields. Indeed, interrogatives regarding the nature of the self and individuality and how it is reconciled with the establishment of groups and communities have only increased in the last hundred years or so, as the reality of globalism meets nearly all of us head-on, every day, and on nearly every level of existence. An attempt to answer questions of identity, then, is not only of academic interest, but universal to human understanding, for in its answer is found the source for the very ideas of human purpose, communities, politics, and the psychology of these mental influences through time in humankind's story. Therefore, my ambition is that this work will offer a snapshot of how self and personal identity operated in the Anglo-Saxon world, so that we may better understand the antecedents of this selfhood, and if/how it may have contributed to the modern concept of the self in the western world.

What Is the Self?

Depending on the respondent, the idea of the self will vary. For some, identification with a particular political philosophy will determine their "selfhood" or "autonomous identity," while for others, nationalism provides a banner under which people see themselves as independent and unique.[2] Perhaps yet another respondent will reply philosophically: "The 'I' that thinks that I am thinking is the self." Each answer is valid in each situation, and they are all open to criticism by what I call "situational-self protocols."[3] The first two responses are similar in that they are dependent on some-

Towards an Understanding of Identity and the Self

thing outside of oneself (a community) to be valid, and the latter is unique for its highly subjective, non-dependent outlook (i.e., nobody else is needed for this interpretation of self). So which one is most "accurate"? Which tells us what the self really is? Any answer, of course, will be subjective by its very nature, and thus hotly debated.

However nebulous and abstract defining the self has become, there have been, nevertheless, a plethora of attempts to field this question by academics from a number of disciplines. The anthropologist Clifford Geertz once defined the self as "a bounded, unique, more or less integrated motivational and cognitive universe, a dynamic center of awareness, emotion, judgment, and action organized into a distinctive whole and set contrastively both against other such wholes and against its social and natural background."[4]

Put more succinctly, in Lewis Hinchman's view individuals are "human beings understood as separate, discrete selves aware of themselves as such."[5] In both ideas we find a correlation between the inner world of the individual and how the concept of the self exists within the cognitive applications of the mind. Thus, Geertz's "dynamic center of awareness" is Hinchman's idea that each of us is aware that we are individual, set apart, unique. Similarly, another position holds that the self is simply "the existence of a world *within* [original emphasis] each being ... both physical character and inner reality"; thus, taken further, this view considers a subject/object viewpoint; that is, the first-person introspective account of self and the third-person objective view of oneself by other selves.[6] Yet another argument, both inclusive and modern, comes from Susan Harter, who says that the self "is both a *cognitive* and a *social* construction," but that it is "first and foremost, a *cognitive construction*" in that one's idea of the self develops before any influence of society, which in turn later helps to solidify a self-concept during early childhood and adolescence.[7] This idea is known as "cognitive developmental analysis," which states that the process of self-formation is more "continuous" than "discontinuous," implying that we develop a sense of self over time from early childhood into later stages of maturity. This developmental perspective coincides well with other empirical research that correlates societal influences with the formation of an individual identity. An interesting question is whether or not we continue to formulate an idea of self into adulthood and how this process operates. The topic of communal identity and self-development is discussed in Chapter 1, where I address the social constructionism of self

Introduction

and social identity schema, but it is important to note the two main themes discussed so far regarding what the self is and how it develops: that is, as an idea that one is different, unique, distinct from others—a concept which is formed by (1) an intrapersonal construct, taking place within the mind and independent of any outside influences, and/or (2) dependent on society, in that it receives influence from the direction of external sources.

Considering the main ideas posed so far, we need not subscribe to mutual exclusivity or favor one notion over another, and indeed, many are of the mind that the self is not so one-dimensional. For example, one suggestion allows for an understanding of the self as influenced by both intrapersonal and communal factors, albeit without taking a decidedly firm stance on either: the self is "an existential experience of one's own subjective being (which may or may not be culturally divergent), or a culturally constructed conceptual model through which people represent themselves to themselves and to others."[8] In other words, the self here may be either a deep notion that one exists apart from her community, or more abstractly, a persona, or mask (constructed externally to conform to societal standards) that one develops—consciously or not—to relate to the wider community and to oneself. Perhaps such a neutral stance gets us closer to the truth of how the self develops, if but somewhat indecisively, but we may confirm a few ideas from the discussion so far regarding selfhood in general. (1) Most commentators seem to think that the self is a construct that is either intrapersonal, communal, or a combination of the two—that relates the inner world of individuals to themselves and the reality outside of themselves in one form or another. (2) A rich discourse exists for the discussion of the self in a range of formats, e.g., the sociological self (i.e., self in society—to include anthropological studies)—critical discourse and the self (examples include Marxist, Foucauldian, and Nietzschean ideologies), the psychology of the self (Freudian theory), the philosophy of the self (which includes ontology and the philosophy of mind), and finally a fascinating modern discussion in the empirical sciences (e.g., neuroscience). Sadly, brevity must be a virtue here, as a thorough discussion of the theories of the self is well beyond the scope of this work. However, certain hypotheses—particularly self-schema, psychology and memory, and social constructionism, are explored more fully in the chapters below. These theories are put in to the context of Old English verse, so that our understanding of the Anglo-Saxon self may be more fully developed and, not inconsequentially, a representative sample of the ideas proposed by scholars since Descartes can be tested against the backdrop of the material in question in order to validate or otherwise confirm or question the utility of these notions. All of these ideas may be conflated to give us a comprehensive idea of the self, and consequently, they should all be respected and given due consideration, but it is to philosophical inquiry and neuroscience that we shall now briefly turn.[9]

As an inchoate formulation, the modern idea of the self developed out of an ontological philosophy, which was famously reflected by the seventeenth-century philosopher Descartes. The basic notion of his Cartesian/substance dualism can be simply understood in an analogy given by Jerome Shaffer, if a bit morbidly, when he states that when referring to a human carcass, we would normally say, "I found HIS body," not "I found him."[10] In this crude image, the expression that the self is distinct from the physical form is made clear. Thus the philosophy of Descartes makes a patent distinction between the physical and the mental, when he said, "I am, I exist, this is certain," but "only as long as I am thinking. I am therefore, speaking precisely, only a thinking thing [*res cogitans*], that is, a mind, or a soul, or an intellect, or a reason."[11] In fact, Descartes "held that the subject of consciousness is the *mind* ... [while the] body is a thing or entity whose essence (defining characteristic) is occupying space," so both the body and the mind (self) can exist independently from one another according to Descartes.[12] Strawson likewise sees the self as "a mental presence; a mental someone; a single mental thing that is a conscious subject, that has a certain character or personality, and that is distinct from all its particular experiences, thoughts, hopes, wishes, feelings, and so on."[13]

If we then see the self as a mental thing, as originating in our mental universe, then it quite forcefully *prima facie* tells us that we have the power to change our selves, our personalities, and by extension, how those around us will view us, by simply thinking our way out of old beliefs.[14] This is a powerful conclusion, and as we will see in both *The Wanderer* and *The Seafarer*, Anglo-Saxons were seemingly able to have done this very thing, but they also had to contest with strong societal influences. The protagonists in some of the poetry that I interrogate have changed their notion of self over a period of time, and this fact well argues the point that identity during this period could be changed and need not be under the complete influence of kin groups and community (of course, the motivations behind this change-of-self will be most important to consider, as well). Perhaps not surprisingly, then, this realization leads us into the question of whether or not introspection may help us to identify the self.

Many self-theorists have argued both for and against the idea that introspection alone naturally may lead to the discovery of the self. David Hume was against the notion of the introspective approach and said famously: "When I enter most intimately into what I call myself, I always stumble on some particular perception or other.... I never catch myself at any time without a perception and never can observe anything but the perception."[15] It would seem that Hume is concerned primarily with what he calls "perceptions," that is, put simply, thoughts or feelings in one form or another that act as a barrier to the access of the self. It should be noted that Hume did not believe that there is a self, which is independent of perceptions, however. This argument will necessarily lead to the conclusion, as it does for Hume, that humankind is nothing "but a bundle or collection of different perceptions, which succeed each other with an inconceivable rapidity, and are in a perpetual flux and movement"—hence, it is "the composition of these [perceptions], therefore, which forms the self."[16] Based on Hume, our conclusion could then be that the self is nothing but the accumulated perceptions that an individual has had and continues to have during his/her lifetime. Seen in this way, and taken further, the plausibility of the notion that our desires, beliefs, and knowledge of the world—all of which are directly influenced by our immediate communities—are *ipso facto* regulated and formed by those communities, gains momentum. This discussion in particular is addressed in Chapter 1, when I argue that the standard notion of identity in Old English poetry—that is, the way that Anglo-Saxons saw and "performed" their identities (what I call their self-schema) was a very communal one. Thus, the self is a communal formulation, in that it requires outside influences in order to individuate.[17] To be sure, however, arguments abound contra this argument, many of which rely heavily on the notion that a base consciousness exists that lies beyond perceptions—something that is immutable, unknowable, and without description.[18] One could argue that this idea of the self takes its cues from Plato's view that there is a soul which survives the body upon death, and "that we are really our souls, not our bodies," and that it is this entity, which "defines your identity as an individual person," and thus, "as long as it exists ... you exist."[19] But what of perceptions if the soul is the self? How are we to reconcile these two seemingly contradictory ideas?

Towards an Understanding of Identity and the Self

And how then did the self function for the Anglo-Saxons? Was it primarily an identity formed and developed by communal interaction, or was there some inner world apart from the group identity that was consciously or unconsciously the basis for how one conceived of her identity? What can the modern empirical sciences tell us about this, and how can these ideas all come together to give us a reliable critical pathway into understanding the world of the Anglo-Saxon self?

Empirical and Cross-Cultural Understandings of the Self

In recent years, empirical science and cross-cultural anthropological studies have contributed fascinating complementary data to our traditional philosophical understandings of the self, and these studies strengthen particular theories, thus providing us with clues as to how Anglo-Saxons may have thought about their selfhood. As we have already discovered, the idea of the self is generally put into one of two categories, or as often happens, an amalgamation of the two—that it exists and is developed interpersonally and/or as a societal construct. Developmental psychology may shed some light, as we find that the self is conceived of as a complex system of influences that begins from early childhood. For instance, in modern studies, infants have been shown to recognize similarities and differences in the self and "other," "readily distinguish[ing] their own actions from those of others early on," but ready to "imitate the actions of others in a flexible and goal-oriented manner, suggesting that infants represent the other as 'like me.'"[20] So it would seem that the early self is already highly independent. Further study strongly supports this, by showing that the ideas of "social roles and membership, reputation, [and] relationship to others" are established late in the developmental process, after the individual has first established an inner world of self-identity.[21] In fact, Decety and Sommerville see these studies as *prima facie* evidence that "individuality is possible only when comparing self to others."[22] This is not a contradictory point, however, as according to Decety, it is impossible for one to understand their own unique sense of self if it is not considered within the sphere of communal associations. Indeed, there can be no light without dark, good without evil, etc. Similarly, Burkitt posits that the "'I' and 'me' start to appear in early childhood, [whereas

Introduction

beforehand] there is only a protoplasmic consciousness, in which there is no awareness of others as distinct from self."[23] What can we make of these findings?

Interpretation of these data suggests that reasonable evidence exists to claim that the self is both an individual and social construction, the former developing first out of a state of "protoplasmic" thoughtlessness, the latter as a result of social interaction and influence. Two main questions then emerge. (1) Is this process of self-formation a human universal, irrespective of time and culture? (2) If this is so, may we then proceed to argue that since—according to studies by Decety, Sommerville, Burkitt, and others—human infants have a sense of personal identity outside of community, and that it is the relative power structure/importance given to the wider community of each particular culture which allows for the development of individual selves later on? Put another way: if it is human "nature" to have a sense of self, and human communal prerogative to affect the way in which that self will develop, can we argue that Anglo-Saxons had a similar "hybrid identity"? Was Anglo-Saxon self-identity more of a personally- or socially-constructed entity? We are not quite ready to make a firm conclusion, but looking at a few more scientific studies will take us further in establishing a framework for answering it.

"Self-Processing" and Social-Self Developmental Mechanisms

In the modern era, science searches for the answers to questions that have been posed by metaphysicians for thousands of years, often bridging the gap between the empirical and speculative, the personal and communal. For instance, Kelly et al. pose the question: "Is self-referential processing special in any way?"[24] In other words, is there something unique about how the brain operates when people think about themselves? Recent findings suggest that there indeed does appear to be "memory enhancement afforded to self-reference," and these findings argue for, and in fact support the theory that self-identification perhaps differs from identification with external ideas such as community.[25] Kelly's study had participants make "judgments about case adjectives" regarding "self-relevance," "other-relevance," or "case judgment" and found that "adjectives judged for relevance [to oneself] were remembered better than adjectives judged for relevance to a familiar other (President Bush in this case)."[26] Furthermore, this so-called "self-reference effect" did not show similar kindling in the brain that one would expect with an "ordinary extension of the levels-of-processing effect" (i.e., activity in the left frontal area of the brain), but indeed demonstrated a conspicuous lack of stimulation in the region, with the conclusion being that "these results argue against the notion that the self-reference effect is driven by ordinary memory processes."[27] We may conclude from these findings that not only do all of us seem to have within our brains the capability of recalling ideas about ourselves more clearly and with more certainty than we do for things outside of us, but we also appear to use a part of the brain that is separated from the area(s) generally utilized for referencing the external world. What this tells us, then, is that it may be physiologically "natural" to be somewhat self-centered (in the literal sense), considering that even our brains partition thoughts about ourselves from those of the external world. More research is needed in this field, but the implications are that a strong sense of personal identity and of partitioned self-referentiality is possibly a universal phenomenon, and from this it would follow that Anglo-Saxons, for instance, must have harbored an individual identity. Consequently, as an extension of this idea, we may now consider how the process of memory may help to form self-identity. This idea is given a proper treatment later on when I discuss *The Seafarer* and *The Wanderer*.

While I argue in Chapter 2 that memory is a prime mechanism that helped to form self-identity for Anglo-Saxons, it will benefit us to briefly look at one way in which this occurs differently than expected. When retrieving information about our selfhood, each of us will usually think of a past action or experience with which we can identify—in this way, we argue that we are one and the same person who experienced that which is in our memory.[28] However, memory may not be so simplified, as Klein et al. shows us. In a recent study of subjects who have suffered a period of amnesia, the researchers found that one participant could recall things of her past, even though she could not extract any particular memory of those things. An example of this included the fact that she knew she was a college student, but could not remember ever being in a classroom.[29] A similar example came from a man who "was unable to consciously bring to mind a single thing he had ever done or experienced, [but] was able to describe his personality with considerable accuracy"; the findings then suggest that semantic, not episodic, recall remained intact during the

Introduction

period of amnesia (both participants recovered).[30] Taken further, and as we saw with Kelly, semantic recall appears to be housed in a specific area of the brain that is not necessarily linked with the structures that keep memories. Do these findings suggest that a sense-of-self need not be found only in concrete memory, but that the *idea* of a person may also come from something else, through another mechanism entirely? This conclusion seems likely, as it is clear that one's self-understanding need not be completely dependent on memory, but on semantic references of the self independent of it. Hence, the researchers' comments on their findings bespeak their conclusions on self-referentiality during a phase of amnesia: (1) "while recollections of one's personal past appear to depend in an important way on the operations of episodic memory, trait self-descriptiveness judgments do not"; (2) "an awareness of what one is like is surprisingly well-preserved"; (3) "it was as though the trait self-judgment process had tapped into an island of lucidity in a sea of cognitive turmoil"; and finally (4) "at least some of the systems supporting self-knowledge are functionally independent of semantic and episodic memory."[31] The salience of this study for our purposes lies in its suggestion that the idea of the self—as I proposed from Decety and Sommerville's research earlier—may be a physiological human universal, and thus would be applicable to our understanding of the Anglo-Saxons. That is to say, the idea that we all have a self-concept, ostensibly independent of the wider world. While this work has wide implications for our understanding of the introspective self, we should also briefly consider how scientific research is being done cross-culturally as a way of understanding how self-concept is formed in different societies, as this is also relevant to the Anglo-Saxon world.

Scientific inquiry in this field of study has not been restricted to the individual, but has in fact made fascinating inroads in showing us how self differs in communities all over the globe, and this research often confirms for us how we generally understand the self today. It is a near-universal truth that the sense of self in the western world is highly valued, important to the structure of society, and a prime component to the life of most who live there. Indeed, the "general working hypothesis" is that this idea of the western self is "highly accessible," where "emotional life is grounded more on personal goals, desires, and needs," whereas the eastern self relies more on group-think, as the "interpersonal or social self [is] relatively more accessible ... [with] a greater value [placed] on it."[32] Further research by Kitayama suggests that some of what goes on in the brain is in fact different depending on the world region from which one hails. In one example, researchers found that native English speakers process arithmetic problems in a different area of the brain than that of Chinese speakers (the former showed activation in the left perisylvian cortices [known for linguistic processing], while the latter showed little activation in the area), "demonstrat[ing] that the same behavioral outcome is accomplished by different brain pathways" in people from different cultures.[33] It thus seems reasonable to suppose that the self—if it follows a similar pattern—could in fact "move" in the brain. That is to say, if part of how we identify our individuality with a self-concept occurs in the brain—as we saw with Klein et al. and Kelly when looking at self-referentiality—then it also stands to reason that this process is not universally located in the same part of the brain of individuals across cultures. We can only conjecture at this early stage as to what the implication may be from this. One possibility may be that even though different cultures use different areas of the brain for the same processes, the underlying concepts change little, if at all (i.e., it does not matter *how* or *where* one understands the self, but it is only important that we all *do*). Yet another way to look at this phenomenon of self-reference would see a fundamental difference in one's idea of the self based on how it is processed in the brain. The latter concept is most likely from my estimation and is based on what we see in anthropological studies highlighting the differences in self-concept from society to society, for example. This observation seems especially true with the idea of emotion, for example, where it has been discovered that localization in the brain with these processes can be associated with function. Thus, as a mental process as well, the functionality of emotion in the brain can also tell us something about how different cultures internalize a selfhood.

Oft cited as a key difference in individuality cross-culturally is the expression of emotion. Catherin Lutz says that the western view of emotion is "predicated ... on the belief that [it] is in essence a psychobiological structure and an aspect of the individual," where there is a "radical separation of the individual and the social in Western thought and the association of emotion with the former."[34] Murray supports this view and says that western selves consist of an amalgamation of "awareness, emotion, judgment, and actions that are in contrast to other individuals and the societies in which they live."[35] In other words, emotion is not only key to

Introduction

the psychology of a western person, but its expression is instrumental to the identification of oneself apart from other selves. It is thus in the outlet of emotions that we may find our individuality and selfhood—this is key when we look at Old English elegies, for instance. Indeed, modern cross-cultural studies confirm the view that emotions have the ability to define our selfhood and individuality, as in one study, Kitayama notes that "socially disengaging emotions" are felt more by Europeans and Americans (things like superiority, anger, frustration), while "socially engaging emotions" like friendliness, respect, guilt and shame are felt more by Asian societies.[36] Additionally, the same study found that some Asian communities "are far more likely to suppress their emotions"—so as not to "hinder ever-important social relations"—while the opposite effect was found in western countries.[37] These findings suggest not only that emotions are fundamental in identity cross-culturally, but also that the suppression of emotions (conscious or otherwise) may be interpreted as a certain suppression of the self, however subtle. That is, if Lutz's premise holds that emotion is an "aspect of the individual," and in fact some individuals censor their emotions in certain cultures, then it follows that there are a number of people in specific cultures who lack a particular aspect of their individuality. The question we must next ask ourselves is this: how similar was Anglo-Saxon society to that of today's western and eastern societies? My answer to this question is given in Chapter 2 on the cognitive construction of the self, and Chapter 1 on the social construction of identity in religious verse. Briefly, I will say that in general, I believe Anglo-Saxon culture was more similar to many of today's eastern cultures. That is, it was based on communal identity, where one's importance as a part of the whole took precedence over individuality and uniqueness. In verse such as *The Battle of Brunanburh* and *The Battle of Maldon*, we find strong associations between heroic individuals and their communal deeds/associations. However, I also explore and detail some fascinating data about this when we discover how Anglo Saxons were able to change their identities, seemingly at will—something which is unexpected from what we know of tribal cultures. I am here only introducing the concept before tackling it in detail. So, if we tie all of this together, it seems that the "patterns of connectivities among various structural elements of areas of the brain as well as parameters associated with such connectivities appear to be influenced substantially" not by basic anatomical structures but by culture itself.[38] Thus, the implications of how science, philosophy, and the various social sciences work in concert in the study of Anglo-Saxon literature and its interpretation are becoming manifest.

Methodology: A New Critical Approach and Its Implications

The study of the Middle Ages, and the Anglo-Saxon period in general, often has been the victim of anachronistic literary/cultural interpretations that have ostensibly aided scholars for hundreds of years; this situation is in need of remedy. Today's advances in medical science—neurological and biological—as well as the reworked and/or completely new philosophical and social scientific theories of the past two hundred years or so have given the modern scholar a repertoire of new tools in the study of the past—and particularly, the study of the self in society. My approach to the understanding of Old English literature, then, takes into consideration the imperative to look at antiquity through the lens of modernity. Thus, the relatively new and exciting field of cognitive cultural/literary studies/criticism, etc., will energize and be the primary critical pathway by which I will examine this material.[39] Various names have been conceived for this idea (i.e., the various methods by which we come to understand the human mind). However, I will use "cognitive cultural studies" henceforth to refer to the various methodologies in the social sciences that I use to analyze the material, but it should be noted that empirical sciences also fall under this banner. An example of this type of research is cited by Zunshine, when she comments on neuroscience's discovery of so-called "mirror neurons," which basically seem to exist in order to mimic behavior and emotion from external sources. That is, it seems that we are "hardwired" to be empathetic and communal in our outlook as a species, not self-centered or as "individualistic" as we have become. Thus, the empirical research often confirms what we discover in sociology, anthropology, and linguistics, enhancing the importance of studying the Anglo-Saxon period using such an approach. Indeed, the famous philosopher John Searle once said that he loved the Middle Ages, "because it is, in a sense, the childhood of our civilization"; similarly is cognitive cultural studies in its infancy.[40] Searle is also touching upon the very reason why this study of the self in the Anglo-Saxon world is so vital to our understanding of the English past and perhaps even our modern self-concept. For it is within this "infancy"

Introduction

of Anglo-Saxon culture that may lie the prototypical western concept of the "self" as individual, unique, and separate from society. This is one of the possibilities under scrutiny in this work. Thus, Old English literature can tell us much about how selfhood formed, was nurtured, and/or at times distanced from society. The understanding of this by way of modern critical discourse should bring us closer to knowing the individual Anglo-Saxon.

Several commentators have recognized the benefits of such a cognitive approach applied to the study of literature in recent years.[41] Jackson endorses this method by saying that "literary study can benefit from theories and practices that are more in line with the methods of science," since literary interpretation is usually not "falsifiable"; his idea lies in an approach that allows for "the *obligation* of falsifying the hypothesis"[42] we make when criticizing literature. This idea is somewhat novel in the arts and humanities, but if "Contemporary theories of literature and culture" continue to make "remarkable progress in demystifying traditional humanist and religious concepts of supposedly timeless categories, such as self, identity, and morality," then it ought to be held accountable in its interpretation of human nature.[43] It is not only for scientific fidelity that this approach need be used, either, since the ultimate purpose of practically all literary and historical interpretation is to come as close as possible to the truth of our assertions, thereby exposing the vérité of the past—in this case, the Anglo-Saxon self. So, my approach is not exclusively indebted to science or philosophy (after all, literary interpretation is just that—*interpretation*—at the end of the day), but I am relying on what Hart calls a "cognitive historicism," that is "trac[ing] the discourses on the brain and mind science through the literary and philosophical texts of earlier periods" to gain the most accurate representation of who the individual actually was in the Anglo-Saxon period.[44] Perhaps Jackson said it best: "Literature must have interpretation. Rocks or atomic particles or low-pressure systems or even economies do not depend on explanation in order to become what they most intrinsically are. Literature does."[45] Jackson goes on to question whether or not we can "make a legitimate use of the science without requiring literary interpretation to be judged by the criteria of [the] scientific method." This question is extremely insightful and must be asked. I believe that we absolutely can make such a use of the science without making our interpretations subject to scientific standards of falsifiability. That is to say, literature is not intrinsically anything other than how it is interpreted and used to formulate understanding. Literature, for instance, can have multiple meanings, more than one purpose, several salient facts about the society in which it was written, etc. Hence, using a more scientific discourse for the study of such a subjective field can only benefit our conclusions. Indeed, Palmer comments that "we do, in fact, understand fictional minds much better when we apply to them some of the work done on real minds by psychologists, philosophers, and cognitive scientists."[46] The reference here is to Evelyn Waugh's novel *Men at Arms*; however, this type of criticism may be used for any period, not just twentieth-century fiction. Indeed, it is perhaps more enlightening about a period for which relatively little is known. We will also need to discover how "fictional" the minds are in our corpus, as it seems likely that a lot of what we read in Old English came directly from life, because much of the literature highlights events and circumstances that were common at some point in Anglo-Saxon England (e.g., battles, lord-thane relationship, general kinship, etc.). It is in this vein that I have been inspired and proceed with this work. Now that we have discussed some of the philosophical/scientific/cultural ideas of what the self is and how it forms, it is time to turn to what others have said about the Anglo-Saxon self and how they have said it.

The Self in the Anglo-Saxon Period: Avenues of Inquiry

Perhaps unsurprisingly, some earlier scholarship has often approached the Anglo-Saxon self in a cursory, superficial way, investigating it as only a peripheral note to a wider study, and only desultorily approaching an understanding of the inner world of Anglo-Saxons. The reason for this comes from an assumption that the Anglo-Saxon self was in some way less developed than in today's world. However, in recent decades, a more direct investigation into this topic has found its way into the academy, questioning the multifarious ways in which Anglo-Saxons considered their inner world, and by extension, their sense of self. To date, the sample size is still quite small, but we may yet roughly demarcate the approach to this research into two general types: the abstract and the concrete.[47] The abstract thesis is to define the Anglo-Saxon self in strictly philosophical, nebulous terms—i.e., soul, mind, life force, etc. This discussion generally leaves out commentary regarding the particulars of personal identity. Con-

Introduction

versely, the concrete investigation focuses on the more tangible case for personal identity and individuality, asking what it is, how it works, and how it presents itself in Old English literature.[48] Naturally, then, as the scholarship honors diversity in methodology, so too do our definitions vary to a great degree within the discourse. Hence, this section will discuss elements of the self in recent scholarly inquests into the Anglo-Saxon self-concept, the methodologies of the research, and the many definitions that have been used. I should also note that this discussion is not meant to be all-inclusive, nor give an authoritative synopsis of the many ideas regarding the Anglo-Saxon self that present themselves in the discourse. My goal here is, however, to extrapolate the ideas of self-concept that we may reasonably infer from the scholarly material found to date and show the scholarly gap this work will address.

Presumably, the Anglo-Saxons, as members of the human family and not so temporally removed from modern humanity, exhibited many layers of selfhood and self-identification; and it is to this that Old-English literature acts as the primary witness. In particular, Old-English poetry is especially adept at revealing how the idea of self was seen during the Anglo-Saxon period.[49] The question is not easily addressed and the solution not so linguistically banal as to label all concepts of the self with a word, a phrase, or a series of words. In fact, we know that *sylf* in Old English (*OE*) did "not acquire the contemporary substantive connotation, 'individual identity' or 'ego' until much later [than the ninth century]."[50] So, to make a case for the self in this period is to look through the surface meaning of the literature and discover how the personal-self, or the individualized identity, functioned in society (i.e., what of the individual in the literature who is not abiding in trope, generality, or a communal-narrative momentum). This is not to say the Anglo Saxons did not believe that the elusive self resided in a particular place, or certain human or spiritual quality. For instance, Leslie Lockett has identified four primary elements of the human being in the Anglo-Saxon period that we find in the literature: body, mind, soul, and "transient life-force."[51] It is in each of these elements of the person that we may find particular qualities absent or apparent, and thus create an opening for inquiry that probes how the Anglo-Saxon self-concept functioned through specific, inherent faculties of the mind. For example, we may find and apply an example of this methodology in Lockett's observation that in much Old English verse, it appears that the emotional and mental components of the human being are not "in charge of the individual as a whole," but are just two of many elements that make up the individual *in toto*.[52]

This approach to the understanding of the self in Anglo-Saxon studies has been the standard analytical pathway for many years, and its virtues of accentuating an Anglo-Saxon conception of the self by peering through the literature at underlying cognitive systems is both nuanced and intriguing, and hence should not be underestimated or discontinued. We have learned, for example, that with the exception of one line in *Guthlac A*, the *sawol* in OE is almost always "excluded from efficacious mental activity" in the verse corpus, as it appears within the body at birth, leaves at death to participate in the afterlife, and "does very little in between."[53] The *ipso facto* supposition, then, would be that the self is not housed in the soul. Conversely, the lexical representations of the mind (*mod, hyge, sefa*, etc.) are not associated with this same level of inactivity during its life's sojourn. OE verse is in fact quite explicit in the references to the mind as an active agent in the life of the person (e.g., it is the center for thinking on morality and values, and it makes decisions based on those ethics).[54] *The Battle of Maldon (Maldon)* and *The Wanderer (Wan)* both confirm this observation, as the mind establishes emotional equanimity in the former, while it "travels from the breast while engaged in memory or imagination"—and is thus instrumental in the establishment and identification of individuality—in the latter.[55] Malcolm Godden would disagree with this assessment, however, noting that the mind appears "to be closely associated with mood and individual personality," not the self directly.[56] Similarly, Antonina Harbus "proposes an internal split between mind and self" in the poetic corpus, claiming that the self is "distinct from the soul, the body, and the thinking mind, though it acts in close concert with them in the folk conceptualization of the person."[57] Further complicating matters, Aelfric's idea of self is contained in his notion of the soul, as the soul incorporates just about every human mental activity and notion of selfhood imaginable (e.g., it reasons, wills, remembers, understands, knows, etc.).[58] Finally, Alexandra Ramsden says that the "spiritual soul is an essential carrier of human identity," but it is not necessarily the self.[59] We are now beginning to see the problem inherent in self-studies.

The self in Anglo-Saxon studies, then, has been said to either reside, or itself be, the mind, the soul, or a process combining the two. Hence, that ambiguity exists is to be expected in a discourse where there is a consensus of non-consensus regarding terminology, definition, or geography

Introduction

of the self. Because of the various hypotheses regarding the self, the scholarly debate contradicts more often than it balances the questions surrounding the self. However inquiry may fall short, it is yet fortunate that this debate is now open, as little attention was paid to the study of the self in the Anglo-Saxon period in years past, having been assumed that such a study was unimportant, uninteresting, and unsubstantial. For instance, social psychologist Roy Baumeister has claimed that "there is very little evidence that medievals engaged in introspection or experienced inner struggles," noting that theories of "selfhood in the Middle Ages in the West may have been far more collective than they are now."[60] Harbus also notes a number of other scholars who harbor similar beliefs, including the philosophers Hubert Dreyfus and Sean Dorrance, who relate to the commonly-held idea that people had a very little, if any informed, idea of the self before Descartes. Writings on the self in the twelfth century notwithstanding—which are substantial, with many seminal works included in the bibliography—my work questions this notion throughout its pages. A cursory examination of the Exeter Book elegies dissolves any validity to such a claim that inner contemplation on the part of Anglo-Saxons was not part of their intellectual repertoire, and in addition severely questions Baumeister's assertion that the collective self in the Middle Ages can be seen as generally more prominent in Anglo-Saxon society than it is in today's Western society (these observations are one of the goals of this work—i.e., the level of introspection and the role of community in the life of the individualized self). It should also be noted that similar sentiments are not exclusively the domain of non-specialists, as Alexandra Ramsden similarly espouses that there is "very little evidence in the extant corpus [...] that Old English poets conceived themselves, however divided and reflectively aware, as such fundamentally cognitive creatures."[61] This statement is contradictory, since "reflectively aware" peoples, by their very nature, must also consider themselves "cognitive creatures." Being introspectively reflective is a wholly cognitive task, although I grant that such peoples may not consciously consider themselves as such. Also challenging these assertions, Harbus lists Augustine's *Confessions*—and other pivotal texts—as primary to discount such generalities, as they are "entirely account[s] of the introspective struggle of coming to terms with knowledge, faith, memory and the self."[62] She also refers to King Alfred's redaction of Augustine's *Soliloquies* and Boethius's *Consolation of Philosophy*, both of which were copied in the tenth century and refer explicitly to an idea of the self and the introspective nature of early medieval people. These differences of opinion regarding the Anglo-Saxon self, however articulated and convoluted, are necessarily remedied when we consider and develop something more fundamental: the definition of self.

As the relationship of the self and its effects on the various cognitive systems in humanity are so varied and under academic scrutiny in a number of disciplines, so also are the definitions of self in the discourse diverse and multiform, and often need to be extracted from context. A defined self is nearly always implicitly expressed in the scholarship, which opens the doors to criticism and muddled interpretation. It is this aspect of the literature that would most benefit from a proper study into the Anglo-Saxon self, putting us on firm grounding for our research. For example, Ramsden defines the self "both as the central locus of experience and as the principle of action in human beings," which is on par with the "more general view of the self as a self-conscious subject of agency and experience in line with the increasingly prominent scholarly trend of moving away from a definition of the self as an essentially modern construct which emphasizes the unique and autonomous nature of the individual."[63] Later in her thesis, Ramsden more lucidly defines her term: "My approach to the self [...] suggests that personal identity in Anglo-Saxon thought resides precisely in what we are, what we do and what we experience," claiming that "inner aspects are essential elements of identity precisely because of their comprehensive agency." I take this definition to mean the totality of what we are as human beings; it is an all-encompassing definition that does not rely on a specific cognitive task or geographic location, but can be discovered as we witness actions, intentions, and the sum of human interaction (what I often call "actionable-identity"). Somewhat less inclusive is Harbus's definition of the self, which is "the basis of character or personal identity" but can still be directed by the mind, which is the "place of thought, perception, memory, emotion, and spiritual resolve."[64] In this view, the self is both subservient to and independent from the mind. Indeed, Harbus says that "the mind is part of the self and the self part of the mind" and that "the mind can direct the self." We can see this type of interaction in *Wan* and *Sea*, when the thinking mind brings memories of a past self to light, memories that are subsequently used to form a new self-concept We can see now that the self is at best a nebulous, and at worst, a completely irresolvable lexical puzzle to be debated in perpetuity.

The problem mostly stems from less-than-concrete characteristics

Introduction

of the self in the literature; hence, where this is clarified, an open discussion and debate is much more likely to occur. Whereas some scholars may interpret the self as incorporating very broad and general categories of human experience, and others stand on the theory that it is housed in a particular faculty or mental component, I see the Anglo-Saxon self as being best defined as somewhat in between these two traditions. For instance, similar to Ramsden's argument that the self is a "self-conscious subject of agency," and Harbus's identification of the self's passive-objective relationship with the mind, what I am most immediately interested in is action and not necessarily where, why or how, physiologically, that action occurs. This statement is not meant to discredit such work; indeed, neuroscience and cognitive psychology can tell us very important facts about physiological processes relating to the concept of the self. However, literature points to actions firstly, not processes, and the analysis of literature initially depends on the witnessing of such action, then to the underlying processes contributing to the action. E.g., that the wanderer felt compelled to find another community after losing the one he had is an example of an action predicated on a belief, a belief that is housed in the mind. So, action in this case could be said to stem from a cognitive system. That is, a sense of self here is defined by a cognitive structure, as Harbus has pointed out. The self then, is the aspect of a human being that one believes she is in her innermost thoughts. This is the externally observable, as well as the inner-observed sense-of-self that may variously be called ego, personality, or more generally, identity. This definition may incorporate an individualized sense of self (personal-self), or a more communally-based notion (communal-self). Thus, we are defining the self as something that is both influenced by inner notions of reality, and/or the outside group, and not making a case for the soul, higher-self, spirit, life-force, etc. In this way, we relate the question of individuality to something that is readily observable in the literature, and this opens up an investigation into Anglo-Saxon motive, belief, and possibly an understanding of selfhood via the cognitive processes of individuals—all of this leading to what I call "actionable-identity." This is different than saying, for instance, that the self *is* the mind or the soul. What I am referring to here is that outward identity, which here refers to the self that is predicated on one's role(s) and actions in society, can be understood by looking at mental faculties, in some cases. Chapter 2 deals exclusively with this, when I describe memory, via the mind, as one of the ways in which Anglo Saxons could define and redefine their sense-of-self over a lifetime. Ramsden offers a similar sentiment: "Notions of inner and outer in Anglo-Saxon thought about human nature, however, cannot be mapped onto dichotomies of spirit and matter, soul and body, or mind and body."[65] It is this sense of self that will give us the most workable model for interpreting of what the self-concept consisted in the Anglo-Saxon period, and in what circumstances particular concepts were most apparent.[66]

Actionable-Identity in the Anglo-Saxon World

As I just briefly explored, the Anglo-Saxon self is most easily recognizable when actors are performing outward expressions of identity, as these actions betray motive and are thus signposts to both the sovereignty and group-function of selfhood/identity. To be clear, nearly all human activities are examples of these expressions, since we act almost always only in reference to our sense of defined self. This study is interested in looking at actions and concepts cited within the literature as a way of defining different self-concepts throughout the Anglo-Saxon period. Indeed, the degree to which individuality is highlighted in actionable-identity is open for debate, but it appears that the former's existence in comparison with a communal self-concept is just that—an issue of degree. This argument is made more clearly throughout the book—particularly in Chapter 2, which deals with the idea of the communal self—since an individual self-concept is always (even in our modern world) a question of how far removed from communal norms it is, and does not imply a complete removal from society in any case. That is to say, even our modern, self-important sense of self still always exists within the realm of the society in which it was developed. Adding to this idea, for instance, Peter Clemoes has argued "away from a focus on individuality and personal uniqueness in its modern sense to suggest a sense of self which remained fundamentally entrenched in communal ideas, whether secular or spiritual."[67] And while I think that he is off the mark in moving away from the idea of a more individualized sense of personal-self in the Anglo-Saxon period, we may find examples of life in the period where there is a seeming paradox, where individuals harbor at once a strong personal self in association with a communal self-concept[68]; my research in Chapter 3 demonstrates that this is particularly true.

Introduction

A study of missionaries during this period, for instance, can tell us quite a bit about this dual nature of Anglo-Saxon identity. Martha Riddiford's work on social exclusion in Wessex takes into account the *peregrini pro Christo*, those who would renounce and "sever ties with their existing lifestyles [... including] contact with family friends and acquaintances."[69] Such individually motivated action at first seems highly autonomous and separate from one's communal identity, but we should also remember that these pilgrims had a "network of support" settlements en route to Rome that provided food, shelter, and camaraderie during the long journey, which "did not emerge accidentally" and thus promoted the "notion that no matter the distance or separation, all members were joined in spirit."[70] Considering this spirit reveals a case for both an individualized action that was outside the realm of normal activity and also a new communal identity.[71] These men and women often left their communities with a zeal for God, to whom they "devote[d] their exile, and along the way embraced a new community that offered homologous beliefs on salvation and the importance of personal, individualized action."[72] Although it may be true that these *peregrini* dwelt "outside normal social hierarchies and power structures," I should note that my research shows that the society which was left behind was in fact replaced with a new religious community with similar goals and values to the renunciant, however peripheral to the actual idea of individual selfhood for these seekers.[73] So, such a new society *became* a new source of identity for those involved, and as all "societies are aggregates of individuals," the identity of the group evolved out of a synthesis of personal, exilic identities.[74] It is in this example that we discover an intriguing question regarding the Anglo-Saxon self: what was the relative significance of personal versus communal selfhood for Anglo-Saxons seen in the corpus of Old English verse?[75]

It has been argued, for instance, that "every member of Anglo-Saxon culture was measured by his or her social bonds within the kinship networks of the community" and that even Alcuin, one of the most famous and prolific of religious writers of the Anglo-Saxon period, who would seemingly be little attached to a communal-self structure because of his deep devotion and extensive writing about individual faith, seemed still to abide by his society's notions of the community-identity paradigm. Specifically here I refer to Alcuin's admonitions, where we find examples of both "individual autonomy" and "cultural norms"; similarly, Alcuin shows to be a highly "self-aware social actor" who, by referring to his many contacts using nicknames depending on the situation, displayed how conscious he was of the sense of a communal self for these individuals, and indeed himself.[76] Thus, to a modern audience, Alcuin's actions betray his own views on a prevalent social consciousness of his day. We can see this in his writings; we can interpret this through his actionable-identity—this action being the act of writing on his society itself. Likewise, vernacular verse in the Anglo-Saxon period proves rich in this regard, exposing the different "layers" of self to be uncovered via actions or even non-action. Ultimately, this investigation will give us a better idea of what kinds of identity functioned in the Anglo-Saxon world, how and when it functioned in the ways that it did, and whether or not Anglo-Saxons were really all that dissimilar to us when it came to their idea of self, person, and identity.

Outline of This Work

In this chapter I have formulated my research question on individuality in Old English verse and discussed the ways in which the self has been understood in the past. I have also described some of the modern approaches to the questions of self and individuality within a variety of fields, introducing how these concepts may be applied to the study of the Anglo-Saxon world. This section also recognized some of the work done by Anglo-Saxonists over the past one hundred years and highlighted the methodologies used and the differences in the precise meanings of selfhood and the individual in this time. This discussion has thus preliminarily highlighted the lacunae in Anglo-Saxon scholarship relating to the self and individual. One missing element comes from an inconsistent or unclear terminology regarding what the self actually is (e.g., the abstract and concrete theses I examined earlier), and the second is a lack of consideration of a variety of methodologies and fields that all contribute not only to self-studies, but how we may apply them to the study of the Anglo-Saxon world. It is therefore clear from past scholarship that the concept of self in the Anglo-Saxon world is either approached suspiciously, without focus, or not at all.

This research therefore challenges past notions of Anglo-Saxon identity that make an umbrella statement suggesting an entirely communal existence, and utilizes a variety of interdisciplinary methodological approaches in order to uncover details about Anglo-Saxon inner worlds and their

Introduction

deepest ideas about themselves. Chapter 1 begins this process where I make strong use of the theory of social constructionism to demonstrate how the public, or communal, self-concept functioned in religious verse. My main focus is on *Genesis B* and *The Dream of the Rood*, through which I demonstrate how the discussion and argument for the personal-self in the following chapters is strengthened by seeing its opposite example considered. This first chapter highlights the differences between expressions of individuality and that of the communal, ultimately providing strong evidence that the former was a living reality for people in Anglo-Saxon society.

Chapter 2 details how the narrators in *The Wanderer* and *The Seafarer* use memory to assess, reassess, and ultimately change their sense of self over time, simultaneously highlighting the public and private spheres of Anglo-Saxon identity. I have included these texts as the focus of this chapter because they are highly emotive first-person narrations that speak of loss and lament, and this will give me the tools necessary to probe into the characters' sense of self. Particular importance is given to the personal-self and how and in what fashion it is displayed by the narrators over time. This examination also introduces my definition of self (personal-self, self-concept, and personal identity), and contextualizes these terms within my overall research question. Chapter 2 concludes by arguing that for some Anglo-Saxons, in certain situations, a strong individual identity existed, and was at least in some circumstances an entity not wholly unlike the autonomous individual we often speak of in our modern societies.

Chapter 3 looks at the general paradigm of Anglo-Saxon communal trope (what I call their schema of self) to uncover the individual self-concept within the *scopas* in *Deor* and *Widsith*. I have chosen these two texts because they are the only two poems narrated entirely by a *scop*, and this will allow me to concentrate on the identities of these characters. I demonstrate how these poets highlight both the public and the private notions of identity by their very function within their culture and their highly aware understanding of their own societies that includes Anglo-Saxon belief systems, their hopes and dreams, and that which they feared the most—the dissolution of their cultural identity. The discussion also offers a complex and subtle insight into the mind of several categories of individual in Anglo-Saxon life: namely, the scribe copying the poems into the manuscripts, the character of the *scop* within the poetry itself, and audience who would have been exposed to the stories. Finally, by showing

Towards an Understanding of Identity and the Self

how the characters display cognizance of their cultures, I am focusing on the ways that allow us to discover elements of high individuality and personal identity.

In Chapter 4, I argue a case for Anglo-Saxon women's experience of a personal-self. Specifically, I investigate the notions of "gendered" and "genderized" displays of the female voice in the corpus, comparing how the individual and communal are showcased in both, and using that as the basis for my conclusion that like men, women could have and did display elements of a personal-self in some Old English poetry. A brief comparison between *Wife* and *Wulf* ("gendered" narration) and several examples of "genderized" examples in the corpus exemplify the differences of focus between the individual and communal, forming the basis for my argument. My focus on *Wife* and *Wulf* is because they are the only examples of poetry narrated by a woman in the corpus, and this will allow me to compare these poems with other female narration.

This investigation, therefore, will demonstrate that appreciating the Anglo-Saxon self by giving it a new treatment with the use of eclectic methodological resources provides scholars with a different look at the self in the Anglo-Saxon period, while I argue that people living over a thousand years ago in Britain had a sense of personal identity that in many ways parallels our own. Consequently, a reassessment of the Anglo-Saxon self naturally leads us to a re-evaluation of the point of origin for the concept of identity in the Western world more generally. That is, by arguing for individual identity in Old English poetry we are also considering the validity of arguments that are dedicated to the proposition that the individual simply did not exist until much later in our history. Thus, this research reopens discussion that has seemingly been closed for some time within the academy and opens new avenues for inquiry of how the concepts of self and individual may be understood within a literary—and ultimately historical—context.

= 1 =

The Paradigm of Identity in Old English Literature
The Self as a Social Construct

My investigation in subsequent chapters will highlight the argument that Anglo-Saxons did not have simple, static identities, but that many had rather rich inner lives and a sense of personal self that correlates remarkably well with modern identity theory. The dearth of positive examples in the corpus, however, confirms that this was the exception rather than the rule—at least as it is documented in literature—and the innumerable instances of Anglo-Saxon identity functioning primarily in relation to ones communal roles and associations is a testament to this claim, and hence should not be ignored. The scarcity of the evidence does not detract from what the evidence will show, which is that Anglo-Saxon identity could be very individual, personal, and intimate. To this add what we know of identity in simpler, tribal societies, and it is not hard to see why most scholars associate Anglo-Saxons with basic identities born from the necessity to survive rather than an autonomous will sans significant communal influence. Indeed, Peter Burke and Jan Stets similarly argue that "the premodern self was generally simpler than the postmodern self," and because of this such societies saw "more sharing of cultural meaning and expectations" than we do today. The implication here is that by having fewer affiliations, one would have fewer identities. It is also important to note that although less complex, peoples in pre-modern societies could still harbor diverse identities in certain situations. Additionally, a society need not be simple and exhibit these traits. Jean-Pierre Vernant's research into the ancient Greek concept of the cogito between the eighth and fourth centuries BCE demonstrated that the notion of self during this time was "neither bounded nor unified, without introspection, extroverted

A Life Both Public and Private

rather than introverted, with an existential rather than a reflexive self-consciousness."[1] It is for this reason that I have chosen to begin this investigation with a foray into the most commonly seen form of identity that we find in Old English poetry—the communal type. This need not raise concern with the argument that a layered and private identity *did* in fact exist in the Anglo-Saxon period, however, and so by showcasing what type of identity was commonest in Old English literature (i.e., a communally-constructed one) in this chapter, the better able we are to contrast this with the evidence that follow in Chapters 2, 3, and 4, which will help prove the latter's significance even further.

Therefore, and as with the chapters to follow, special attention is given to narration, with the role community had on the maintenance of identity featuring as a particular focus. Modern methodological resources featuring a social constructionist argument of identity will also play a key role in concluding my findings. Coupled with the contrasted predominance of the individual uncovered earlier, this chapter will demonstrate two distinct but complementary Anglo-Saxon identity types—the public and the private—while simultaneously providing discursive grounds for why the former seems to be more prevalent in the literary evidence. Given the scope of this study, the Old English texts included for analysis here are only representative forms of narration in religious poetry.[2] The limited choice of texts is simply a reminder that the question of identity in Old English literature permeates all genres and topical patterns, encouraging further research. I have chosen these specific texts because they showcase strong elements of narration like the elegies do, but do not result in the same conclusions of the self when investigated in the same way. Therefore, the texts under consideration here will demonstrate that not all narration in Old English poetry provides any kind of paradigm for the argument of the personal self. I have also chosen these texts specifically because they offer examples of first-person narration similar to the verse in the following chapters. However, these texts demonstrate that, even though narration is in the first-person and highly emotive (similar to the poetry I look at later on), these selections demonstrate a social construction of the self and a communal identity of the characters. The inference being that not all first-person emotive narration demonstrates a strong personal-self, and therefore that this kind of self—however rarely seen—is *indeed* evident in a select few texts. The conclusion of this chapter will therefore show that because descriptions of the social element of the self predominates in

1. The Paradigm of Identity in Old English Literature

Anglo-Saxon poetry, we are hence better able to look for its opposite when it occurs and thus prove that the Anglo-Saxon self was not a simple matter of group-think, as many scholars have imagined.

Society and Identity

Any study of self or identity must perforce incorporate a discussion of reciprocity between the self and the society in which it functions. For the self—personal or otherwise—never exists in a vacuum, but is born from, maintained and nourished, and given substance by its association with a wider community. Indeed, "the self is both individual and social in its character," where the nature of our characters is often formulated by language and other symbolic interactions.[3] Most actions, for instance, represent physical manifestations of identity in conformity with common goals. The ring-giver is not just a person who gives gifts, for example, but he is a paradigmatic schema for the assertion of dominance, a person who is asserting his communal identity over his constituents, and a being thus maintaining social order by concretizing the personal identity of each person in relationship with him. In this way, "all human identities are, by definition, *social* identities," where we use the "discourses available to us" in an unconscious social dance that both forges and reinforces our sense of self.[4] Hence, the self is a multilayered conglomerate of identities based on social relationships. However, this is not to say that a peeling away of these layers—accidentally or otherwise—does not reveal an identity that becomes less and less centered on the social and more on the personal. Indeed, this study will argue that such a statement would be false in reference to the Anglo-Saxon period. We are, in fact, dealing with layers of identity and degrees of communal influence that instantiate that identity. Lee and Urban have referred to this process as a "cultural constitution of the self," which includes the most basic "subjective awareness," and moves all the way to "personal pronouns" and beyond.[5] In fact, it has been shown that the "mere perception of belonging to a social category is sufficient for group behavior"; and so the individual need not necessarily exhibit "cohesive interpersonal relations" with other persons in order to fully integrate into a group.[6] Therefore, it is easy to recognize literary tropes in Old English that are imperative to group identity. In other words, heroic language in literature is one of many ways in which the personal is incorporated in the communal. Consequently, in order to fully appreciate personal identity, it is imperative for us to understand how the self and community function together.

The self is a semiotic marker, a "sign system we use [that] must rely on memory," and "culture itself is memory."[7] This is to say that in all of its forms, the self is an encoded entity, which interacts with culture and from this influence coalesces into an identity. But the type of identity that correlates to this process still often hinges heavily upon degrees (mostly of the major sort) of communal influence. Again, this is not to say that a nascent, or close-to-nascent personal identity cannot be discovered, which has a minimum of societal traces. Indeed, contemporary identity theory holds that it can, and our modern introspective experience further makes this a certainty (the question of whether peoples in Early Medieval English society exhibited such an identity will of course be the focus of the next three chapters).[8] But again, the focus of this chapter is to show how society informs the self in Old English poetry, and further evidence of this interplay appears in social psychology. For example, the "Social Cohesion" (SCM) and "Social Identification" (SIM) models stress how individual and culture interact to form group conduct. In the SIM specifically, we find that "group membership has primarily a perceptual or cognitive basis," where members "structure their perception of themselves and others by means of abstract social categories, [and] that they internalize these categories as aspects of their self-concepts," which ultimately generates "group behavior."[9] In other words, existing in a group membership informs one's sense of self by a mixture of subjective referencing of the relationship and how all the members of the group act in accordance with that membership. A cursory examination of any number of characters in Old English demonstrates how this process worked in Anglo-Saxon society—at least ostensibly if art is in some way an imitation of life. This process by which the self is informed by society is known collectively as social constructionism.

The Social Construction of Identity

At its most basic level, social constructionism implies symbioses between a person's identity and the community of which they are a part. Thus, identity work "is always a social activity" and can either be focused

1. The Paradigm of Identity in Old English Literature

on benefiting the "needs of the individual" or the group as a whole.[10] The salience of this understanding for my purposes comes from the fact that identity work allows one to be "functionally recognizable" in society, precisely because it involves "any act that reflects a desire to signify one's qualities to others, and thereby define one's self as a social object."[11] Such signifiers may have taken any number of forms in Anglo-Saxon culture, from holding a place of esteem as the *scop* of an Anglo-Saxon lord, to performing actions that demonstrate clear subordination to someone in a higher social position—such actions would have encouraged a recognition and maintenance of one's communal identity by conforming to social positioning and hierarchy. Therefore, at its most complex, "the self is at some level a social construction," whereby "we define our selves through our past, present, future, and imagined involvements with people and things."[12] John Searle argues that there are things which are "*intrinsic* to nature and those features that exist *relative to the intentionality of observers, users, etc.*" (original emphasis). He also claims that social reality is ontologically subjective and is distinct from intrinsic features of reality like "mental states themselves." In other words, personality and the communal aspects of the self would be ontologically subjective, as they are not intrinsic to nature. This is a critical understanding of the self, since it shows that identity is "tacked on," as we exist within a complex array of social relations.[13] Of course, identities are never static nor simplistic, and any normative blanket statement that would have all identities fall under one category would fail to account for the complex nature of the self.

In fact, personal identity and the self are highly malleable, exists in multiple realms of introspective and extrospective interchange, and are readily subject to change based on circumstance. For instance, Jonathan Culler perceptively argues that "the self is dissolved as its various functions are ascribed to impersonal systems which operate through it."[14] The implication here is that discovering/identifying some kind of inchoate self, unadorned by "impersonal systems" such as personal history, communal memory, and societal obligations becomes an onerous task more useful for philosophical debate than in literary/historical analysis. Any semblance of an inherent, more "natural," or archetypal self is thus covered by the various influences to which a human being is exposed from birth. These influences contribute to the creation of a human personality, which shifts, mutates, and can even be lost partly or completely over the course of a lifetime; the characters in *Wan* and *Seaf* demonstrate this explicitly, for instance. It is therefore Levi-Strauss to whom we must nod, as his famous statement "The goal of the human sciences ... is not to constitute man but to dissolve him" proves particularly apt here, as the taking apart of a wholly communal notion of self would give us true insight into a more embryonic nature of the person.[15] However, finding evidence of such a scenario—particularly in past and/or tribal cultures—is a challenging prospect, since a majority of the evidence we have showcases community rather than individuality. For instance, there are cultural norms in some codified law that view the person as residing not only within the body, but indeed within her "social network," and that all of this evidence is taken into consideration when determining the issue of culpability, which demonstrates how "the notion of responsibility connects the individual to a web of persons."[16] In this way, the self can be seen as an entity that is "inseparable from existing in a space of moral issues, to do with identity and how one ought to be" within a community where other selves exist in relation to one another.[17] In one way, then, "the self is not a thing on its own account [...] nor can it be reduced to a relation of identification with the psychological body."[18] Thus, we need to be around other people for the semiotics of identity to work. The concept of self is therefore often highly dependent on a web of social relationships, cultural norms, and semiotic markers that outwardly display a type of self that is in harmony with the group and its collective idea of identity, and because of this, revealing actual examples of how the self functions in a group environment is quite easy.

The manifestation of self in a social setting occurs in a variety of ways, and each can tell the story of the influences and dynamic associations that helped create it. For instance, Thomas Shaw argues that culture aides in identity construction in two primary fashions.[19] He refers to these as "solidarity" and "loyalty," where we find "gestures and styles that index membership in a status category," delineating and defining the self in "local moral worlds."[20] For a study of the Anglo-Saxons, for example, we would want to highlight the actions and motivations (gestures and styles) that would inform the communal self.[21] In semiotics, there is the concept of iconicity, where we "produce signs that stand in some direct simulative relation to their referents" and that "the iconic mode of representation is the relation of the sign with its referent through replication, simulation, imitation, or resemblance." In other words, we can pick out a personality or personal-self because all of us together replicate our sense of selves simultaneously and thus create a normative understanding of identity as

1. The Paradigm of Identity in Old English Literature

a collective group; and so any deviation from this—especially in simpler societies—allows us to make a case for individualism. This idea was coined "iconicity hypothesis" by Marcel Danesi. Indeed, foregrounding cultural norms in literature—such as celebrations in the mead-hall or stating one's fealty to a lord—could act as positive examples of how this process worked in the real world.[22] In this theoretical model, the self is dependent on its cultural surroundings for its instantiation and continuation, where "consistency of self-experience is preserved by shared standards of self-worth within local moral worlds, [and] the consistency of these standards and their preservation in subcultural meaning systems can be traced to the intergroup relations."[23] It follows from this model that a self which had lost association with its "moral world" would then be at risk of breaking down—and this would especially be true in a society where such worlds were fewer than in the contemporary west.[24] Dependence on social relations in such cultures to sustain one's notion of identity would thus be nearly absolute, lest self-dissolution and its attendant identity crisis follow. Indeed, there are some cultures today that have a "sociability based on overhearing and incorporating the other into one's self," where "distinct selves are understood to be the same" and the "boundaries of the self are extended to encompass others."[25] Of course, we cannot make authoritative statements on the similarity between the Anglo-Saxons and modern indigenous societies of Brazil—nor should we—but like all cultures, both of these societies display the self as socially constructed and informed; and as we have seen, social constructionism would have the self as "an "outreaching identity" that connects feelings, thoughts, and actions of one individual with those of others through the processes of semiotic communication."[26] As I discussed in the introduction, we may more simply refer to these sign systems as "actionable-identity," and they can take a number of forms.

As my investigation so far has sought to uncover identity from decomposing what is written on the page, so too does Culler agree that to use semiotics is to "make explicit the implicit knowledge which enables people within a given society to understand one another's behavior."[27] Likewise does Gergen say that "constructionism will inevitably confront strong resistance within psychology more generally," since it sees our understanding of the self from a "psychological state or process" with that of "persons in relationship." Taken as an absolute statement, individualism would in some way be dependent on others.[28] Semiotic identity markers are thus far from abstract, but provide clues into the psychology of the person who acts them out, which in turn may give us a better understanding of how culture influences the self and how the self is reflected outwardly back into society. In society, these markers become "patterns of behavior" that we use to enact identity to either conform or deviate from a local group code.[29] Again, such symbols are to be found in actions performed by the person, in a process of encoding and decoding between one and another. Beowulf's accolades and reverence for Hrothgar upon entering his court is an example of this playing out, as it exemplifies the externalization of identity via the laudation of a person in authority. Crucially, then, outward expressions of identity appear in all forums that represent human interaction—from real to fictional universes. Consequently, the symbols of communication that we use to reveal the self are often seen in "cultural narratives" and all forms of stories, which exist "as part of a cultural 'tool kit' ... deployed in social settings to accomplish social objectives."[30] Literature, of course, is rife with such treatment of identity, and offers a plentitude of ways in which to uncover it. One example comes from Emile Benveniste's discussion of the three types of "we" in literature, and describes how it relates to identity. The Democratic, Editorial, and Royal uses of the first person plural pronoun correlate to the user's state of mind and thus describe how her sense of identity includes the community as a whole. The Democratic and Royal "we," for example, "include the speaker and ... addressee," which is something scholars see in nearly all Old English poetry.[31] This naturally raises the question of "whether a social consciousness and a collective identity is being expressed analogous to the expression of an individual consciousness and a personal identity by the use of 'I.'"[32] Thinkers such as Pierce, Royce, Mead, and Cooley all say yes—as well as this author.[33] But of course, expressions of identity in literature are not only demonstrable by linguistic markers.

The Social Self in Literature

The study of literature offers many avenues of inquiry to reveal how social-selves function in any given society, and with respect to narrative, discourse in the form of dialogue, communal memory, and the reader/audience, we are given particular insight into this complexity. Regarding narrative and discourse, and from a sociolinguistic perspective, Schiffrin

1. The Paradigm of Identity in Old English Literature

has shown that "we verbally place our past experiences in, and make them relevant to, a particular 'here' and 'now,' a particular audience, and a particular set of interactional concerns and interpersonal issues."[34] Another way of looking at this is that such "past experiences" are frequently stories, which are often orally transmitted through culture, and carry an obvious lesson and/or salience to a contemporary culture. How the present "interrupts" the fidelity of the story often appears as changes to the narrative to account for current social norms, beliefs, or concerns. In this way, narrative that is disseminated in culture "serve[s] to legitimate a present social order," as much as it appears to produce a shared past for the benefit of nostalgia.[35] Examining, for instance, any historical/mythical narrative in Old English (like *GenB*) offers rich analysis of this kind of reading, since many of the tropes and schemas would have been updated to account for contemporary social norms and concerns. And so these discourses serve to aid in the "construction and display of our sense of who we are," while simultaneously showing how our current experiences are "largely depend[ent] upon our knowledge of the past."[36] The narrative past thus informs our present, helps us to identify with a shared memory, and sustains our notion of self within a communal framework. This framework is the same in all societies, but it is more manifest in simpler social milieus. Anthropological studies of Amazonian tribes, the Zuni, areas of Polynesia, and even modern American cultures, for example, have showcased this process. In fact, some tribal societies even consider inherited songs as being the "singer's own experiences," with the attendant suspension of disbelief suggestive that the past and present person are so similar as to be indistinguishable.[37] We find an obvious literary example of this in *Widsith*, as the *scop's* travels ostensibly span hundreds of years, and in different geographical regions. The significance of his tale for us, however, is detailed in Chapter 3 and shows how the *scop's* position in society and keen understanding of his peers is demonstrative of a complex identity that was informed by both the communal and the individual. Therefore, the most salient feature of these findings is the notion that past stories— whether orally transmitted or in manuscript form—do not function entirely in order to faithfully record a distant experience, but in fact hold substantial implications for the present within the culture to which it refers and is recorded/rerecorded. As we have seen, the most important of these implications concerns how the past impresses upon the present and informs the identity of the singer and the participants, further "function[ing] to sustain a sense of stability and predictable understanding of the world."[38]

I have already shown how Anglo-Saxons could use individual memory to inform and even change major aspects of personal identity, but when we look at how the social aspect of memory works in literature, we find that much more commonly it functions to solidify group identity and the social construction of the self.[39] Memory acts as a spearhead leading to the self, and we often rely on it to tell us who we are. Similarly, the collective memories of a culture as a whole—often appearing as produced and reproduced histories, fables, and creation stories—work in an analogous way. In fact, literature—like history—asks of recipients to "take account of conscious and unconscious selection[s], interpretation and distortion," in order to define reality and the sense of self, and hence is not done individually, but is socially qualified.[40] Members of a social group thus agree upon the elements of the story that will provide for them a sense of belonging and collective agreement. Ron Eyerman and Jeffrey Olick correlate collective memory and identity in a similar way when they claim that "memory provides individuals and collectives with a cognitive map, helping orient who they are."[41] Interestingly, this process of identity construction and sustainability within a group setting is the very thing that allows us to discover high individuality, since any deviation from the former model would produce obvious departures from normal behavior and/or beliefs.[42] The authors refer to this as a "counter-story," and this is why to study individuality one must study society and its effects on identity. In this case, the authors have used this to study oppressed and minority groups in contemporary societies, but it works exactly the same way when we try to discover irregularities in self-identification in Old English literature.[43] And although we may certainly discover elements of individualism within the communal literary environment, it is far more common that we see its opposite in Old English literature. Part of the reason for this is because of the Anglo-Saxons' close connection with a shared past that relied on a strong oral tradition of storytelling. Even in the tenth century, when much of the extant Old English literature was documented on vellum, there would have been some connection with that past, even if the practice of oral transmission had died out. Therefore, Old English literature, in all of its forms, "contain[s] information on the archaic past—the deepest layer of memory"—and this is essential for preserving identity through multiple generations.[44] This would be especially true if elements

1. The Paradigm of Identity in Old English Literature

of performance contemporaneously coexisted with scriptoria or royal courts in the latter period, even if less pervasive than centuries past, since a story exists within "a performer and is actualized only when orally performed and communicated," whereby the performers are "individuals [but also] member[s] of the community, sharing the memory common to the community as a whole, memory which is the source of its cultural identity"; indeed, a story does not *necessarily* require a physical performer who works with a live audience, I would argue, since such an appellation could also apply to a monk who was simply writing down a story that had been hitherto only orally recreated. The monk in this instance would therefore *be* a performer similar to a *scop*, since narrative embellishment and flourish would similarly most likely be colored to conform to contemporary concerns, anxieties, or norms.[45] Even Bede, in his *Historia*, discussed the importance of communal memory on the actions and psychologies of men, which demonstrates that even before Bede's time, a common memory shared by society was an influencing factor in how groups acted.[46]

Communal memory therefore assists in self-identification within a group structure, allowing for a self-construct that is in harmony with the zeitgeist of a given society. Memory, however, does not remain static, nor does it simply imperfectly reflect historical data, but through the process of remembering memory "becomes present through symbolic interactions, through narrative and discourse."[47] In other words, stories from our past are often reshaped and reinterpreted through a contemporary lens to propagate a specific type of identity that is in accord with the social constructionist model of identity. Indeed, memory becomes a "collective framework [...] to reconstruct an image of the past which is in accord, in each epoch, with the predominant thoughts of the society," whereby "the images of the past commonly legitimate a present social order."[48] Milton Singer agrees that the past is accommodated to concerns in the present, but takes this idea a step further. He argues that personal identity "extends to 'social consciousness,' the consciousness of living others with whom one is in sympathetic communication," and also to a "spiritual consciousness," "the consciousness of others who are no longer living but whose ideas and feelings are still present among the living."[49] These two elements create symbioses between the personal and the collective, the past and the present, homogenizing to form an identity-soup of communal norms and societal engagement. This is not to say that this process is a conscious act on the part of the participants, however, but quite the contrary. In the majority of cases, reimagining stories and histories in each cultural present in order to help form the identity of the group and the individual takes place as an intuitive act inside each person. The intuitive nature of this process has been called "iconic otherness," or the "basic stuff of culture [where] patterns of action and representation of the world [...] are adopted unconsciously and without reflection."[50] That is, for survival we create and sustain our identities to be in league with the predominant social order. This of course would have been especially important to the Anglo-Saxons, as many scholars have noted that death was preferable to exile, and therefore to maintain one's identity within a social network meant stability, security, and prosperity.[51] And while all members of society contribute to this collective identity formation, it is for the narrator/writer/reader—the frontline interpreters of cultural stories—to whom we may apply special significance.

This tripartite system represents those participants who have the distinct function of encoding and decoding the symbols within a story and then sharing it with their communities, and they have held this role in all cultures where story has been told. In contrast to modern society, these positions offered much more esteem in the Anglo-Saxon world, since the influence of the interpreter within society affected people from all walks of life and social hierarchy. Readers, for instance, act as a "center," a "virtual site" to serve as the location where semiotic markers are interpreted.[52] Just as in modern society, in the Anglo-Saxon period the reader or audience would be those who were either reading or hearing the story aided either by the performance of a *scop* or as the reader of the text. Interpretation and revision would thus be in constant flux, depending on the historical era, signifying personal identity by way of social interaction.[53] Turner speaks of this interaction as the way in which an "individual internalizes some form of social categorization so that it becomes a component of the self-concept," which ultimately confirms one's status in society, since it positions the person within a social hierarchy.[54] The Anglo-Saxon *scop*, for instance, is a role that would form part of this categorization. The *scop's* identity would then be based on this categorization, which would further reflect on others within and outside of this social unit.[55] Consequently, a complex mirroring of society takes place when an interpreter shares their findings with the wider community, and this assists in the establishing of a social identity, and because "elements of a text do not

1. The Paradigm of Identity in Old English Literature

have intrinsic meaning as autonomous entities" they must be understood by interpretation, which often includes "isolating fundamental oppositions."[56] What this means in practice is that by comparing opposites in a narrative, we may learn why particular themes are salient in culture[57]; and by disseminating to society the norms of her culture, the unconscious role of the narrator/writer/reader is to perform this function.

Similar to readers, speakers also perform a role that provides clues to how societies view the self and others. For instance, the concept of the theatrical "I" is well studied in scholarship and demonstrates how speakers in cultures where oral narration is common take on the identity of the person(s) whom they are representing, speaking "through the character" as it were.[58] This process enables an audience to suspend their disbelief while allowing the narrator to "become" the subject of his representation. During this process, communal identity and social concretization are occurring on two levels. The first comes from the speaker, since she is becoming the character in the story and thus setting in her mind the notion of identification with a person from society's past. Secondly, this transfers to the audience as they collectively recognize and agree that the person to whom they are listening is in fact a character that represents their aggregate sense of self and community. Indeed, in some traditions, speakers take a specific interest in the response(s) from the audience during and after using the first-person pronoun.[59] This suggests that the speaker often caters the delivery to the needs of the listeners, which further exemplifies how this role is a complex interchange between the past and present. Such an interaction also displays how an individual takes specific steps to consider his delivery in a social system, which entails formatting the narrative such that the individual is indeed responding to communal schemas and tropes. This process is especially seen in "myth narrative," where the "I" is observed in a number of ways, to include a speaker reflecting a past society as a whole and transmitting that identity to his audience.[60] The salience of these analogies stems from the fact that we do not know as much as we would like about the Anglo-Saxon *scop*. For instance, we do not know precisely how often the practice of singing stories of the past occurred, neither do we understand exactly how important the esteem of the *scop* was before the Conquest, nor do we know how common was their role after the great manuscripts were copied in the tenth century.[61] Our inadequate understanding of these questions requires that we look to other cultures that hold the professional singer in esteem similar to what we believe the Anglo-Saxons did, and then make a comparison based on what we see in the literature and what we know of modern sociological studies. And although our knowledge of the Anglo-Saxon self is limited, there is much that we may confidently conclude when we look at the literary evidence.

The Social Self in Old English Poetry

The literature of the Anglo-Saxons provides the best evidence for how the self functioned in their society, and the prevalence of heroic imagery in Old English has been well documented by scholars for many years. As the majority of poetry demonstrates a sharp focus on the communal aspects of Anglo-Saxon society, we have some of the best descriptions of how society influenced identity during this time. Such descriptions prove so common that they appear little more than poetic trope. For example, imagery of the "dispensing of drink in the hall," which was such a "great symbol of communal joy and security" is easily recognizable as one of the most explicit models of communal identity.[62] However, this common scene carries with it significant markers that enable us to uncover the importance community had on personal identity. It has, for instance, been long recognized that the hall represented security from the dangers of the world, by its housing of thanes and warriors with a joint goal of revelry and a common dedication to one's lord. Magennis has argued that "the individual is shown ideally as engaged in a communal enterprise," and that "individualism itself can bring community into danger." In communities with strong kinship associations, it is only natural that individualism is often seen as a threat to the status quo, the extended kin group concerns, and the social construction of identity more generally.[63] We can see how this played out in Anglo-Saxon culture, as the hall became "the focus and centre of people's communal being," providing a space for camaraderie, group solidification, and identity sustainability.[64] Consequently, the imagery of the hall should not be taken for granted as simply another heroic literary device, but in fact a semiotic marker that allows us to investigate the psychologies of groups of people who lived over a thousand years ago.

Within the framework of the hall, as well, we read descriptions of the presence of the *scop*. Similar to the hall, the character of the *scop* and the

1. The Paradigm of Identity in Old English Literature

situations in which we find him furnish us a map for "reading" Anglo-Saxon identity.[65] The Anglo-Saxon poet had a number of functions and held a place of esteem in his lord's court. To say that the image of the *scop* is a simple description of a professional role during this period would be a vast understatement. As Chapter 3 goes over in detail, the *scop* not only related stories to a contemporary audience, but also in his duties "perform[ed] an inestimable service in ensuring the continuation of cultural life" for his peers.[66] That is to say, the social construction of identity is made manifest in a scene where the *scop* is telling a story to his audience. This occurs in at least two ways. For one, his position in society is continually reinforced, as his audience gives him the attention he deserves. And secondly, the stories that the *scop* tells additionally provide communal images that undoubtedly conformed to the heroic world of group solidarity and kinship. The interchange between storyteller and audience is thus demonstrative of the reciprocal nature of identity formation in the social construction model. Indeed, for drama and performance to work, "spectators must draw on their own experience or imagination to round up its concretization in their minds."[67] In other words, an audience co-creates the stories that they are told, in that they give more importance to some details than to others. This helps explain why each recitation of a story in oral societies almost invariably differs from the last, and particularly over different ages. In a sense, the audience and speaker are negotiating what is salient in their culture, and hence their collective identity, by highlighting particular tropes and norms. Such norms are commonplace in Old English poetry—both in the situations the verse describes and the characters it develops. All of this confirms the importance and the norm of community on personhood in the Anglo-Saxon period in general.

Genesis B

The Old English *GenB* provides numerous examples of characters displaying how identity and society mixed to formulate a sense of self that was often heavily reliant on group systems. All of the primary figures in *GenB* adopt beliefs and attitudes that are based on heroic society and its norms; Satan's character, for example, is no exception. Satan's actions and motivations have often been noted to showcase his relationship with God and the fallen angels as being akin to the trope of retainer, lord, and fealty.

A Life Both Public and Private

With Satan specifically, however, his immediate persona—exemplified via his conflict with God and accompanying banishment from heaven—is that of a disloyal retainer to God his lord.[68] Many scholars have noted that Satan's disobedience and "subsequent punishment of being an outcast from heaven was a fate [that ... removed the] þegn from his natural place in his lord's hall."[69] This description of Satan early in the poem conforms to the heroic tenets of group loyalty, þegn and lord relations, and communal identity, which would have been appreciated by a contemporary audience. In fact, "the ideal of loyalty [...] is at the core of the ethical system by which the behavior of the characters [...] is judged," and hence Satan's "pride become[s] the violation of the social hierarchy."[70] As the audience would have been familiar with these ethical systems, so too would they be immediately obligated to disapprove of Satan's actions, opposed to his plan of naming himself autonomous, and hence fiercely against his motivations. In contrast, the poet offers a description of the kind of characteristics Satan should have displayed in acting out his identity as a good thane:

>   Lof sceolde he drihtnes wyrcean,
>   dyran sceolde he his dreama on heofonum, and
>   sceolde his drihtne þancian
> þæs leanes þe he him on þam leohte gescerede [256b–258a].[71]

The dichotomy is thus set up to showcase the identity of a loyal retainer on the one hand, with a character in exile for challenging his lord on the other. The question then becomes one of understanding Satan's identity after his exile has occurred. After all, I have already shown that to lose one's place in heroic society commonly equated to losing one's sense of communal self, creating a vacuum of primary identity, and giving one scope to develop and exhibit an individuality not commonly seen in the literature. But is Satan's character similar in this way? After his expulsion into hell, Satan's actions prove that the answer is no.

Immediately after being exiled from heaven, Satan quickly gets to work on creating for himself a new comitatus, giving himself the position of ring-giver. It is at this stage, where his brief foray into self-pity rebounds, as he "ceases to regard himself as an exile and reassumes the role [...] of a [leader in the] heroic world."[72] Satan's communal identity thus remains intact, which would conform to the expectations of identity held within the contemporary Anglo-Saxon audience. Indeed, Cherniss makes a very insightful observation when he asks whether the *GenB* poet consciously

1. The Paradigm of Identity in Old English Literature

"rather than instinctively" acted when he portrayed in the poem "a society and a spirit congenial to [his] own Germanic cultural heritage."[73] From what I have shown earlier, I believe the answer must be that it was largely unconscious—particularly in regards to general tropes of community and loyalty. Satan's own words betray his motivation for ostensible autonomy, while simultaneously conforming to a system of communal interchange and group preservation:

> Hwy sceal ic æfter his hyldo ðeowian,
> bugan him swilces geongordomes? Ic mæg wesan
> god swa he.
> Bigstandað me strange geneatas, þa ne willað me æt
> þam stride geswican [282b–284b].[74]

The key features that lend to understanding Satan's identity at this stage come from Satan's comments on his new supporters, demonstrating his reliance on them to carry out his plan to ruin humanity and thus turn humankind from God. In fact, Satan's supposed autonomy is further questioned during an inner monologue, where he pronounces his body useless to his plans, since he remains shackled in fetters, unable to escape:

> Wa la, ahte ic minra handa geweald
> and moste ane tid ute weorþan,
> wesan ane winterstunde, þonne ic mid þys werode—
> Ac licgaþ me ymbe irenbenda
> rideð racentan sal [368b–372a].[75]

Satan may have plans of his own, which initially suggests a form of individuality via personal independence, but that independence is predicated on the assistance of a new troop, and a new relationship with loyal retainers who will do his bidding. In this way Satan's identity is once again fully integrated within communal norms and practices of Anglo-Saxon society, not in opposition to it.

There is an irony not lost on scholars regarding Satan's seeming contradiction in his insistence and dependence on his followers' loyalty, while he himself has shirked his own duty to God.[76] With particular attention given to social constructionism, we now see how Satan's primary communal identity has simply shifted from one heroic value system over to another, similar one. In other words, Satan's "loss of self" has been so brief almost as to be unregistered by the audience. Unlike *Wan* and *Seaf*, where an identity vacuum was not immediately filled by the presence of a new human lord or comitatus, Satan's identity quickly retained its structure, as a new system of loyalty filled the void. Consequently, Woolf's claim that Satan should not be seen as merely a victim of his self-loathing, but "flushed with the exhilaration of defiance," and by extension reintegrated with a strong communal self, is particularly appropriate here.[77] This reintegrated identity is even more apparent when we notice the descriptions of the Fall, where emphasis is given to "Satan's spiritual distance from God" and the "memory of where he was"—not where he ends up—as being the most painful experience.[78] The poet makes this clear when he tells us that as Satan was tossed from heaven, he experienced that as the *ealra morðra mæst* ("greatest of all torments"), not the subsequent physical detriments of hell. Soon afterward, Satan's regrouping of the fallen angels and his promise of treasure to the one who could aid him in deceiving humanity confirms his new communal role:

> Se þe þæt gelæsteð, him bið lean gearo
> æfter to aldre, þæs we her inne magon
> on þyssum fyre forð fremena gewinnan [435a–437b].[79]

In Satan's character, therefore, we find substantial and overt references to the importance he continues to give to the heroic ideals of loyalty and fealty, while ostensibly displaying personal autonomy. Ultimately, his brief individualism is supplanted by a new but familiar self that requires his comitatus' aid in order to make it function, which allows him to maintain an identity familiar to the tenth-century audience of *GenB*. In Satan we find exemplified ideals of society and self, overshadowing an abbreviated attempt at individual expression; however, for Adam and Eve, there is no such duality.

Images of the social self within the situational elements and narration of Adam and Eve's characters showcase the standard identity trope in most Old English literature. Whereas for Satan an argument could initially be made for a weak individuality, for Adam and Eve, no such contrast is evident. For instance, scholars have given particular scrutiny to Eve's actions and motivations. Eve's decision to convince Adam to heed the serpent's promise of power, and hence cause them and the rest of humanity to fall from grace, especially showcases how her identity is fully ingrained within a societal framework. Instead of placing blame or a duplicitous motive on Eve's actions, scholars—and the poet especially—note that Eve acts "out of loyalty to Adam" when persuading him to eat the fruit.[80] Indeed, the parallels between her actions and the ideals of queenship have not been lost on commentators.[81] Langeslag claims that Eve's decision "is done with a noble motive" and that she "is the prototype of true Woman-

1. The Paradigm of Identity in Old English Literature

hood, selfless and self-sacrificing."[82] The poet himself makes this clear, while also hinting at Eve's complex identity structure:

> Heo dyde hit þeah þurh holdne hyge, nyste þæt þær
>   hearma swa fela,
> fyrenearfeða, fylgean sceolde
> monna cynne, þæs heo on mod genam
> þæt heo þæs laðan bodan larum hyrde,
> ac wende þæt heo hyldo heofoncyninges
> worhte [708a–713a].[83]

Represented here is Eve's "double loyalty," as it were. Simultaneously loyal to both Adam and God, Eve acts in accordance with heroic values of kinship and duty. Her decision was not made in ignorance, nor was it made to deceive or to hurt, but she was in fact taking in all available evidence and making the decision she thought best to appeal to her communal status. The messenger's words further exemplify this, as his appeal to her duty is made to entreat her to decide in his favor. After approaching Eve, the messenger takes advantage of Eve's dedication to God and Adam, by saying *Gif þu þeah minum wilt, / Wif willende, wordum hyran* (Yet if you, a willing woman, will listen to my words).[84] The Old English *willende* (willing/wishing) has also been translated "compliant" by Bradley, and so has the connotation of duty-bound self-determination in an action.[85] By specifically asking Eve if she will be "willing" or "wishing" to listen to the messenger's words, he is in effect asking her if she is willing to show her loyalty to God. The messenger thus knows of Eve's dedication to God, and takes advantage of it, as he believes that by convincing her that he was sent by the Lord of Heaven, she will do all she can to remain loyal to him. Eve expresses this loyalty and concern with their retainer-status when she eventually approaches Adam with the messenger's proposal:

> Hwæt scal þe swa laðlic strið
> wið þines hearran bodan? Unc is his hyldo þearf;
> he mæg unc ærendian to þam alwaldan,
> heofoncyninge [663b–666a].[86]

Here, Eve likens insubordination to the messenger as defiance towards God, while also appealing to Adam's duty of fealty. Importantly, Eve believes that the messenger is an intercessor for God, and so in the absence of any direct communication with the latter, they feel that they are forced to follow the former.

Although initially reluctant, Adam eventually agrees with Eve to eat

A Life Both Public and Private

the fruit. As its sourness aches in his heart, both know of their mistake, and Adam expresses his apathy to serve the world and fear of exile in candid speech:

> Nis me on worulde niod
> æninges þegnscipes, nu ic mines þeodnes hafa
> hyldo forworhte [835b-837].[87]

It is important to note that Adam's fear of losing God's favor mirrors Eve's earlier concerns with following the messenger's request, since both are fully concerned with maintaining a social order in which they were accustomed and secure. Adam believes that his fealty has been rent and fears the consequences of living a life of exile and depravity.

> Nys unc wuht beforan
> to scursceade, ne sceattes wiht
> to mete gemearcod, ac unc is mihtig god,
> waldend wraðmod [812b-815a].[88]

For Adam, knowing that they have erred against God offers the possibility of losing their security and place in the world, which would result in a subsequent loss of primary identity. Adam even describes his situation as something that affects both of them collectively—and by extension, humanity as a whole—when he criticizes Eve:

> Hwæt, þu Eue, hæfst yfele gemearcod
> uncer sylfra sið [791a-792a].[89]

The dual pronoun indicates Adam's state-of-mind and belief system regarding his social positioning and self-identity. He not only feels as though he has lost out, but that both of them have suffered together, taking joint responsibility. Their lament does not last long, however, since the "disruption of their society with each other and with God" is brief, highlighting an important difference between Satan and Adam/Eve.[90] Ericksen's position is that Satan's physical exile from heaven places him "irreparably in the land of unlikeness, while Adam and Eve can [...] dwell in the land of unlikeness and still restore their likeness to God through penance."[91] This "unlikeness" is another way of stating that Adam, Eve, and even Satan have been stripped of their primary identities and thrown into a mental world of "unlikeness," or identity disassociation, while they embark on developing their sense of self. However, the process proves so brief as to barely require any treatment, since this vacuum of identity lasts only shortly and does not inform the rest of the poem's narrative.[92] Mckill

1. The Paradigm of Identity in Old English Literature

likewise notes that Adam and Eve's supposed exile seems to signify a new beginning, since "God as a loving father [is] unwilling to abandon his child."[93] Satan fares not so well, but as I have already noted, his social self is ultimately preserved in his reestablishing of the comitatus in hell. Both parties, it would seem then, continue their personal lives within their respective communal structures, catering to a contemporary Anglo-Saxon audience and reflecting the status quo of the self as primarily represented as communally dependent during this period.

This brief discussion on *GenB* highlights ample imagery and narrative tropes that would have aided in informing group identity in tenth-century England. In this way, and ironically perhaps, theology in *GenB* appears to "play [...] a minimal part" in the poem, giving room instead to foreground "life in the secular world."[94] This is not surprising, considering what we have discovered about the role of stories in the development and sustaining of identity. The narration in *GenB* was thus "speaking" to the audience, helping to maintain in them their communal associations and sense of self. Therefore, "an Anglo-Saxon poet could only arouse [...] comprehension in his audience by the use of imagery drawn from contemporary society."[95] This is why imagery of the communal self is so widespread in the literature, and also why the scholar is more easily able to discern kinds of identities that always previously or later became more individualistic and autonomously self-reflected. Indeed, the poet seems to have a word of warning for the would-be individual, as shortly after Eve approaches Adam to consider the messenger's proposal, the audience is given a maxim concerning the dangers of being "too individualistic":

> Bið þam men full wa
> þe hine ne warnað þonne he his geweald hafað! [634b-635b].[96]

The Dream of the Rood

Similarly to *GenB*, *The Dream of the Rood* (*DrR*) provides valuable insight into the communal structures of Anglo-Saxon identity, while also masterfully incorporating narrative from the seemingly disparate identities of the dreamer, the Rood, Christ, and the wider community. Although often viewed as essentially religious in tone, *DrR* is also characterized by deep heroic values and rules of the secular world. In fact, the poet seems to have taken care to create a narrative of Christ's passion that seamlessly includes both the religious and the secular, as it is "consonant with the world [...] whose cosmos is the spiritual and celestial kingdom and society."[97] As with the poet of *GenB*, it is important to recognize that the first character to whom we are introduced in *DrR*, the dreamer, is "a contemporary of the poet and of his audience," which as we have seen has wide implications for how the intended audience was provided with the self-paradigm that they would have identified with.[98] This paradigm highlights structures of communal identity that would have been salient to a tenth-century audience, and is exhibited by each character in the poem.

The opening of *DrR* presents the dreamer narrating a dream vision, where he meets the Cross used to hold the crucified Christ, and is then told a story of the Passion from the perspective of the Cross. These two narratives are seamlessly woven into each other and provide excellent illustrations of how both secularity and religiosity in Old English poetry exemplify the communal aspects of Anglo-Saxon identity, with complementary effect. Similar to *Seaf*, *DrR* begins with a narrator's desire to share a personal tale with the audience. Immediately, we are struck by the analogous tone of separation and isolation:

> "Hwæt! Ic swefna cyst secgan wylle,
> hwæt me gemætte to midre nihte,
> syðþan reordberend reste wunedon!" [1a-3b].[99]

The first-person pronoun and the description of the physical separation from the wider community both work together to emphasize the dreamer's ostensible isolation from society, as he has effectively "separated himself from the rest of men."[100] This isolation is only apparent, however, as we find that the dreamer's communal identity is not lost throughout the poem.[101] For instance, soon after the opening lines, the dreamer's sight connects with the vision of the Cross, which is battered with the memory of violence to which it was subjected. We are told that *Eall ic wæs mid sorgum gedrefed* ("I was completely beset with sorrows") when the dreamer's thoughts moved to what must have transpired for the Cross and Christ.[102] This lamentation may be trope, but it also effectively connects the dreamer with a contemporary (and historical) Christian audience, who would have mourned collectively for the martyred Son. With these simple words the dreamer associates himself again with a known community, and he is acting within that schema of identity. This is not unlike the female mourner at Beowulf's funeral, who similarly acts as a communal voice of pain and sorrow. Thus, the dreamer's lament and

1. The Paradigm of Identity in Old English Literature

sharing of his vision ultimately allow him to become "fully a member of the community of those to whom he is sent," while he simultaneously is "in community with the rood." Indeed, Brit Mize says that releasing what is in one's mind can be seen as "community forming and [a] stabilizing force," arguing that this is just as powerful as the ring-giver in its communal importance. Consequently, "the idea of the mind holding something tightly can also have unfavorable associations, because the inaccessibility to others of valuables stored deep in a person's mind can threaten community and the cooperative responsibility to gather, preserve and pass down a cultural treasury of wisdom."[103] Additionally, the dreamer fails to lose his primary identity since he still lives in "anticipation of the honorable status which he will enjoy in the communion of saints and the treasures which he will receive from his celestial gift giver."[104] This knowledge would have been imparted to him, as a devout Christian who shared with his contemporaries an inspirational story about Christ.

After hearing the story of the Passion from the Cross, the dreamer wakes and once again reiterates that *þær ic ana wæs / mæte werede* ("there I was alone with little company"), highlighting how a worldly comitatus is no longer in his present experience.[105] However, throughout his vision the dreamer's self-schema was preserved while in communion with the Rood, which as we will see relates its experience almost entirely in terms of the heroic world. The dreamer therefore wakes to maintain his relationship with the symbol of Christianity, as a devotional thane, and expresses this wish while exhibiting both a public and private persona:

> Is me nu lifes hyht
> þæt ic þone sigebeam secan mote
> ana oftor þonne ealle men,
> well weorþian [126b–129].[106]

In this telling narration, the dreamer showcases the dichotomy of self that is often seen but overlooked in Old English poetry—the public and the private. The public sphere of identity may be gleaned from the dreamer's desire to honor and give fealty to the Cross—which is in line with heroic dictates of honor and duty—and the private by acknowledging that it is something that he must do alone. There is a striking similarity here to *Wan* and *Seaf*, but we must be prudent and recognize that in the latter poems, the narrators spend most of their journey in solitude and introspection, while the dreamer in *DrR* maintains connection with his cultural norms throughout. Indeed, although he has lost his friends in the physical world, the dreamer looks forward to the day where he can once again connect with his comrades in heaven:

> Nah ic ricra feala
> freonda on foldan, ac hie forð heonon
> gewiton of worulde dreamum, sohton him wuldres
> cyning,
> lifiaþ nu on heofenum mid heahfædere,
> wuniaþ on wuldre [131b-135a].[107]

Additionally, we should not overlook that the process of sharing his experience with his contemporaries gives the dreamer and the poem an air of a "community-strengthening" exercise that is created for "public discourse."[108] Herein we find positive examples of the earlier discussion of the semiotic exchange between the storyteller and the audience, as well as how the "I" functions in the pluralistic sense, both of which showcase communal notions of identity.[109] Ultimately, the dreamer's experience falls in line with images of group solidarity by his loyalty to the Cross and Christ, his sharing of this experience with a contemporary audience, his hopes of continuing his fealty in this world, and his desire for participation with his kin-group in the next.

As with the dreamer but less ambiguous, the narration of the Cross heavily propagates notions of communal identity within a heroic paradigm. As with the dreamer to the Cross, the Rood and its relationship to Christ also follows along similar lines of social identity and group functioning. The Cross begins the narration by describing its inception, from being cut down for the purpose of holding up the condemned Christ, and explaining how although reluctant, he dare not go against the will of God, lest his position as a loyal thane be in jeopardy:

> ic þa ne dorste ofer dryhtnes word
> bugan oððe berstan [35a-36a].[110]

Here we find the typical worry that a retainer may let down his lord by shunning his heroic duty. Interestingly, the Cross also confirms here that its identity is entirely entwined within a communal structure, since we are told that its creation and purpose rest solely on his ability to hold up Christ. The Rood is thus a victim of form and function, born into a world of social interchange, and hence its design is in fact a social one. A second self-identification occurs a few lines later, as the Cross reiterates its purpose in society, adding concern about remaining stoic over Christ's death:

1. The Paradigm of Identity in Old English Literature

> Rod wæs ic aræred. Ahof ic ricne cyning,
> heofona hlaford, hyldan me ne dorste [44a-45a].[111]

Many scholars have noted and questioned the purpose behind the Rood's supposed contradiction in his action (or inaction) to allow Christ, his lord, to be tortured and crucified, which is an "act counter to the service which is typically demanded of a Germanic retainer."[112] After all, the poet takes the time to detail how the Cross's identity is nearly one with Christ during the ordeal.[113] Magennis argues, and I feel is correct in saying, that "it is this horror of betrayal which gives the speech of the cross [...] a vital part of its emotional intensity and urgency."[114] However, if we look further into the heroic ideal, no duty has been eschewed, no obligation evaded. It is true that the Cross identifies strongly its social positioning with Christ, but we must also recognize the importance of God the Father's plan for His Son.[115] It is this higher authority that must hold precedence in the Cross's actions, and therefore the heroic code, and hence the Cross's communal identity, are preserved.

Additionally, while the Cross's persona maintains a communal identity with Christ via its status as a loyal retainer, further complexity is added when we consider its association with the audience as a whole. We should not view the Cross simply as an inanimate piece of wood, but as an active member of the dreamer's Anglo-Saxon contemporaries. Some scholars agree that the Rood is in fact a "complex form of prosopopeia," which transcends its ostensibly pedestrian function as a simple stake in the ground, and significantly, embodies "the presence of the common human being or humanity" during the time of composition. In fact, some scholars argue that the Cross "takes up the role of audience" as "the audience participates in the action through pity and fear and experiences a purging of those emotions."[116] Samuels too recognizes the debates surrounding the possible devotional uses for the Ruthwell Cross, citing as significant the potentially additional importance a contemporary audience may have given to the Cross in *DrR*. Similarly to the dreamer, then, the Cross is lamenting with the Christian audience, and hence is actually meant to represent them by "becom[ing] part of the communal audience."[117] Lines 70 and 73 are significant in this regard, as the use of "we" and "us" is precisely the kind of language we would associate with this type of identification. Indeed, the Cross itself mentions this connection with humanity in a simple yet haunting description, as Christ is put upon it:

A Life Both Public and Private

> Weop eal gesceaft,
> cwiðdon cyninges fyll. Crist wæs on rode [55b-56b].[118]

It is significant to observe that the Cross objectifies its own existence here, instead of using the first-person pronoun. Contrast this with earlier in the poem where we find the Cross describing how Christ *me wolde on gestigan* ("intended to climb on me").[119] And so it is clear at this stage that the Rood has begun to identify strongly with the audience, and indeed associates itself with that audience. More evidence of this form of communal association comes soon after the general lamentation of the crucifixion, and after Christ had been placed in the tomb:

> Hwæðere we ðær greotende [...]
> stodon on staðole [70a-71a].[120]

Here again the pronoun is significant, in that the Cross now identifies itself within the structure of the lamenting Christian community (in the form of the three crosses), in contrast to the earlier language of supposed isolation. We should take care also to note that the Cross refers to itself with the first-person singular again, when it reminds us that *On me bearn godes / þrowode hwile* ("On me God's son suffered for a time," ll. 83b-84a), and thus the Cross's identity is a complex amalgamation of its purpose to serve Christ and its identification with a Christian audience. And so however we may note the possibility of a change in the Cross's self-identification throughout the poem, its identity is even more complex. The poet masterfully creates a character that highlights two complementary identity schemas—both of which are thoroughly embedded within Anglo-Saxon consciousness—and because of this would have been recognized as familiar. The secular and the religious communal identities are the characterizations given to the Cross, and throughout the poem we have seen how neither dissolves and both are embraced.

The *DrR* is a fascinating example of the multifaceted communal self-identification that existed in the Anglo-Saxon period. Narration from the dreamer, interspersed with that of the Cross, work together to highlight secular and religious social identity construction in an engrossing web of heroic trope, shared history, and personal narrative. That the poem appears at first glance to highlight the individual, only to later show the complex social identity structure of the characters, is testament to this fact. Britt Mize captures this duality well in stating that for the narrator "the private mental life" is "directed towards the collective life and inter-

1. The Paradigm of Identity in Old English Literature

ests," and the reader "becomes a private mental participant in the enlightened veneration of the Cross and simultaneously a participant in the universal community of such veneration that the poem idealizes."[121] So we see that to ascribe real individuality with every use of the "I," or indeed every introspective narration, would be a flawed exercise. Undoubtedly, some commentators are quick to attach high individuality to any personal narration with an emotional element, which does a disservice to the intricate nature of Anglo-Saxon identity. Esther Berstein argues that "when written literacy is allowed for, the tribe splinters and its members become separate, individual entities."[122] This analysis stems from her idea that when a single individual reads a story (instead of it being sung), she would think uniquely about the narrative and thus be separate from her group. However, we have found that the opposite is in fact true in most examples, as individual "readers" are still perpetuating their communal notion of self as they read narration that solidifies their group's schema of identity. This is particularly true in *GenB*, *DrR*, and *Elene*. Therefore, *DrR* demonstrates how much more complex Anglo-Saxon identity was, and how that identity was concretized and propagated in the form of a poem and ultimately given voice by the audience as they identified themselves with the very characters in the verse.

My investigation of *GenB* and *DrR* has demonstrated how social constructionism worked in subtle ways to inform the social identity of Anglo-Saxons. Each of the characters in the verse, the poets themselves, and the audience at large had a function to play in this interchange, by their respective unconsciously-performed roles that permitted the continued propagation of heroic ideals and group coherence of the social self. Therefore, a personal identity that "involves seeing oneself as a unique and distinct individual, different from others," where personal desires take precedent over communal goals, does not feature as prominently as I will show moving forward.[123] Consequently, we are now better able to contrast the themes of this chapter (identity tropes that informed the vast majority of Anglo-Saxon identity) with those that do indeed prove that the individual was a real psychological reality—during the tenth century, at the least. This chapter has also uncovered how the self could be both a private and public affair, with expressions of individuality (particularly in Satan's character) evident but with significant qualifications and a scope of limited range. Ultimately, modern identity theory recognizes the need for interdisciplinary approaches and breadth of investigation, and so our conclusions

A Life Both Public and Private

about Anglo-Saxon identity should not be formed on pedestrian notions of simply "private *or* communal"; it is, of course, much more complex. If this chapter has shown anything, then, it is that Anglo-Saxon identity was just as composite as ours today, with a variety of influences and schemas that had an impact on characters both real and imagined. We cannot separate the group when looking at the individual person, and vice versa. Both inform the other, creating a dance of identity for each person. The fact remains that Anglo-Saxon communal identity also included notions of an autonomous individual, where the individual was simultaneously influenced by her community. In acknowledging the role of both the personal and communal in identity formation, perhaps Milton Singer said it best: "The search for and discovery of personal and social identities is not a hermetically sealed process of intuitive introspection inside individualized thinking substances, separate and distinct from bodily substance and isolated from one another. That the process depends on social interactions and associations with other minds and bodies, mediated by all available modalities of communication [...] is by now recognized as an implication of Peirce's conception of a semiotic self, and of the elaboration of that conception by the symbolic interactionists."[124]

= 2 =

Memory and Identity Formation

A Cognitive Construction of the Self in The Wanderer *and* The Seafarer

As I discussed in the introduction, introspection as a tool to understanding the self is one way theorists (of all disciplines) may approach the question of selfhood/identity, but unlike Hume's dilemma that introspection alone is insufficient in discovering a certain underlying, immutable self, the process of memory—that is, remembering one's past—is certainly an introspective process and can indeed be shown to aid in understanding the concept of self; this is especially true for the function of memory in *The Wanderer* (*Wan*) and *The Seafarer* (*Seaf*), respectively. It would seem that if Hume had subscribed to the idea of an unchanging self, it would have been more like what many would call the soul, higher self, etc. His aversion to perceptions is indeed understandable if one is to look for such an entity—and of course, Eastern philosophies are thronged with the idea that calming perceptions (thoughts and feelings) is a primary way in meditation to discover one's true essence (self, soul, God, etc.). However, my argument throughout this chapter regarding the definition of the self is quite different than Hume's.[1] Hence, in this chapter I focus on the use of memory in *Wan* and *Seaf* to highlight how the characters' identities change over time, arguing that each demonstrate a strong sense of individuality by the end of the poems.

It should also be noted that Hume's argument that inner contemplation cannot lead to recognition of the self is not a fallacy, however, but is predicated on his definition of the self, which, if we were to follow it, would yield a similar conclusion. Our understanding of the self must differ, then, if we are to use the memory process—which is almost entirely indebted to perceptions—in understanding and defining the particular type of self that we find in *Wan* and *Seaf*. Here, it is important to make a distinction between a self that is beyond our or society's control (soul) and that which is forged, influenced, and possibly a result of both memory and society (personal identity). For the purposes of this work, then, it is incumbent upon us that we formulate a definition of the self, that we may not confuse the various terms used throughout the discourse.

Memory and the Construction of a Personal Self/Identity

What constitutes, where resides, or whether or not human beings have an immutable self, such as a soul, residing somewhere is beside the point here—this is primarily because recognizing the actuality of a soul is something that we cannot broach using methodologies for understanding human individuals or societies as a whole; that is to say, the study of literature or history to prove the existence or non-existence of such a self (i.e., a self that many consider to be a kind of soul) is impossible.[2] Therefore, to benefit from a search for the self in poetry, we should recognize what it is that the literature can tell us about the deep recesses of the human mind. It is within this recess that I argue abides a certain kind of self that differs from what some would call the soul, and it is by seeing the layers of communal identity lose their grip on the person that I will argue a different kind of self can be seen. Thus, I have termed this sense of self colloquially here as "the personal-self," "self-concept" or more simply, "personal identity." These terms will be used synonymously and interchangeably throughout this work as a stand-in for the ubiquitous term "self." To be clear, the personal-self is akin to the human personality or individual identity—in that it is informed by experiences—but it is also more than that. The personal-self represents the deepest ideas of one's concept of person/selfhood, which may or may not be represented to the outside world, and in most cases it is not. The highly individualized being that a person believes she is when all of the layers of identity are removed is what I am referring to here. When a person thinks of her place in the world, considers her past, plans for her future, she is in a process of identity formation or personal self-amendment. And through concentrating on

2. Memory and Identity Formation

the application of memory, this is exactly the kind of self that we can discover and understand in Old English elegies like *Wan* and *Seaf*. This self is thus defined by both the depth and experience of the person involved. The "application of memory" refers to the process of *actively* considering one's own past, either internally or through another medium (like poetry). It is possible to process these elements passively, as well, and this is indeed most often the case. The latter is most common for human beings, as we are not normally hyper-aware/self-reflective of all of our experiences that, when taken together, combine to form who we are as a personality. So how does the application of memory help inform a self-concept? David Wiggins once described a person as a member of a species of "thinking intelligent beings, with reason and reflection," which are traits that "typically enable them to consider themselves as themselves the same thinking things, in different times and places"; thus, "memory is not then irrelevant to personal identity."[3] The idea here is quite simple: that memory, as a utility of the mind, allows us to see ourselves as the same person in the present as in the past, which sounds familiar when we recall the common adage "My past made me who I am today." Irrespective of the philosophical terminology, which is sometimes confusing, this is nearly how all of us experience our lives. Memory, then, requires "a strong conviction of the sameness of "a man's identity over time" in order to inform a personal self, and this identity extends "as far back as his memory reaches."[4] From these concepts we are then led into the memory-connected theory of personal identity (MCT), which states that "if x is a person at $t1$ and y is a person at $t2$, then y is the same person as x if x and y are memory-connected." There are, of course, debates on this theory within the literature. For one thing, there are some issues in the case of amnesiacs. That these individuals can have semantic memory without episodic recall poses a problem for MCT. For the purposes of our discussion, these arguments do not matter, because on a basic and intuitive level, if no exceptions are taken into consideration, it is an obvious statement that if x has a memory and can remember that memory, then he or she will naturally feel that both memories belong to the same person. This is how almost all human beings see themselves as having the same identity over time, so here I am taking into account how people actually work and not the deeper philosophical issues that cannot be criticized using the poetry.[5] A similar notion can be found in Carl Jung's work, although he terms it "individuation," which he says is a "process of *differentiation* [...]

having for its goal the development of the individual personality."[6] Additionally, Hume also spoke of individuation, claiming that it was "nothing but the *invariableness* and *uninterruptedness* of any object, thro' a suppos'd variation of time, by which the mind can trace it in the different periods of its existence, without any break of the view, and without being oblig'd to form the idea of multiplicity or number." Thus, memory allows for the idea of the personal-self to remain intact.[7] So, on its face value, the MCT works quite well for understanding how people see their current personal self as the same as a past personal-self, strictly based on memory. In *Wan* and *Seaf*, for instance, without this reflective attitude about the past, the first-person lament would hold no authority nor incite any sympathy in the audience, because we would not understand that the wanderer and the seafarer are referring back to a past personal-self, who is displaying a continuum of change throughout both poems (I argue). It is this idea of changing one's self-concept, through the application of memory, which is most important for us here.

Before moving into the literature, it is important to understand that memory as a driving force to incite personal change in modern people is well established. Memory helps to form the idea of individual consciousness and individual expression in our culture. For example, Butler says that "upon comparing the consciousness of one's self, or one's own existence in any two moments, there immediately arises to the mind the idea of personal identity," and that under certain conditions, the "I" twenty years ago and the "I" today are "but one and the same"; however, Butler is careful to point out that even though the general concept of personal identity may remain intact, the "personality is not a permanent, but a transient thing [... that] lives and dies, begins and ends continually"; Butler is also critical of the MCT of identity, saying that consciousness cannot be the same in any two moments. In this instance, the deep philosophical debate does more to hinder than develop our thesis that we may recognize our past identity with our current personal-self, *while* also changing our notion of self-concept through time. Taken to the extreme, one could argue that Butler's idea would allow one to claim no responsibility for one's past action, which obviously is not how laws in today's society, or that of the Anglo-Saxons, worked. What is important is how society functions, not how deeply we can take an argument, for this study.[8] Indeed, it is the idea of personality here that is highly important. I take "personality" as a part of the self-concept, and as Butler suggests, it is the personality

2. Memory and Identity Formation

that is under the influence of a variety of societal structures (which I discuss below) that help to precipitate individual change, thereby contributing to the overall modification of personal self that we know in our lives in the modern, as well as the Anglo-Saxon world. Wiggins similarly states that "the memory condition informs and regulates the continuity condition of personal identity, holds it apart from mere continuity of material body, and leaves its distinctive mark on judgments founded in it."[9] Therefore, memory is here seen as a prime cause for a person's identity over time; i.e., memory can help form and shape (change) a person's personal identity. A firm basis has hence been set up for understanding how, through the application of memory, modern concepts of the self are both simultaneously static and malleable over a period of time. We now must question if a sense of the personal-self in the Anglo-Saxon period could be changed by a similar process, or if the heroic-Christian world of, say, tenth-century England possessed a hold so strong on the individual, that a personal sense of self was discouraged from being expressed either outwardly or through internal monologue.

The Wanderer *and Omniscient Recall*

From the opening lines of *Wan*, we find an unnamed exile introduced by the narrator, who—even at this early stage—highlights the extreme solitude that will eventually aid in the wanderer's formation of a new self-concept:

> Oft him anhaga are gebideð,
> metudes miltse, þeah þe he modcearig
> geond lagulade longe sceolde
> hreran mid hondum hrimcealde sæ,
> wadan wræclastas: wyrd bið ful aræd [1a-5b].[10]

The emphasis on loneliness is a theme characteristic of this poem, and is a good indicator of the relationship between the individual and community in the Anglo-Saxon period. For instance, De Lacy has said that "from one point of view, the *anhaga* ("solitary one") can be characterized as the epitome of worldly philosophy—man without God," and this may be true[11]; however, Klinck has also pointed out that *anhaga* is glossed *passer solitarius* ("lone sparrow") in the eleventh-century Lambeth Psalter; additionally, she has remarked that *anhaga* may come from *haga* ("enclosure")

A Life Both Public and Private

or *hogian* ("to think").[12] The implication of *anhaga* here, then, is not only that the wanderer is alone, but that he is also one who "travels within or enclosed in his mind/thoughts." In either case, this exile exists deeply in the recesses of his mind (i.e., he is *completely* alone with his thoughts), and so at this stage he is a man without community, as well. The salience of this rests on the idea that community was one's main source—if not the only source—of identity/selfhood in this period, and this notion is what is precisely under scrutiny in this work.[13] Similar to De Lacy, Huppé has also suggested that at this point, "it is clear [...] that man is helpless in the grip of Fate, that he can find security only in the mercy of God."[14] From the opening, then, it seems that God is the only refuge for an exile in this period. However, as we move forward, we find that the process by which the exile comes to this realization is a highly personal, individual, self-changing exercise.

The next two lines represent an interesting shift in *Wan* and set the scene for a first-person lament that will help us to define who the wanderer is and how his self-concept will change:

> Swa cwæð eardstapa, earfeþa gemyndig,
> wraþra wælsleahta, winemæga hryre [6a-7b].[15]

It is unclear whether the wanderer *cwæð* ("said") lines 1a-5b, the following lines, or both. I feel that this construction introduces what is to come—i.e., the wanderer is about to relate his story to the audience—and that lines 1a-5b reflect the state-of-mind the wanderer eventually enters. Thus, the end goal is given first, and the process by which one arrives there comes after. The power of this is that the audience already knows the outcome before the final lines are read; therefore, the rest of the poem acts as a didactic, instructive device. However this is interpreted, the suggestion is clear that the wanderer is either analyzing the truth that God is one's only salvation (lines 10a-5b), or he is metaphorically about to take us into his mind and tell us his story (8a-29a). In either case, the wanderer's omniscient position as a first-person narrator suggests that he has already completed his journey and is hence relating, through memory, what has occurred. The *swa cwæð* construction occurs twice in the poem (lines 6 and 111), and it has been suggested that its purpose is to block off the first and last sections of *Wan* and not as a way to "analyse a subtle psychological continuity of thought" throughout this work.[16] I take issue with this last statement, as it will be made clear that a "continuity of thought" is

2. Memory and Identity Formation

absolutely what is established between lines 6 and 111, and that this construction reflects this purpose. The scene has thus been set, and for the next twenty-one lines, the psychology of the wanderer is explored and his early personal-self revealed via memory, before it is challenged and changed in the second half of the poem.

The First-Person Lament and a Communal Self-Concept

What follows in lines 8a-29a shows how a self-concept works through memory in *Wan*, and how recognizing this reflection of an earlier self is imperative to understanding the change of the personal-self that we will explore in later sections. We are told, in highly emotive speech, of the emptiness within the wanderer and his identification with his heroic world:

> Oft ic sceolde ana uhtna gehwylce
> mine ceare cwiþan; nis nu cwicra nan
> þe ic him modsefan minne durre
> sweotule asecgan. Ic to soþe wat
> þæt biþ in eorle indryhten þeaw
> þæt he his ferðlocan fæste binde,
> healde his hordcofan, hycge swa he wille [8a-14b].[17]

For a second time, we are reminded of the wanderer, alone (*ana*) and abandoned, introspecting his companionless lot (*mine ceare cwiþan*). The emphasis on the wanderer as being alone is telling, and states an obvious but rightly needed observation: that Anglo-Saxons (at least in the tenth century) could access and exercise an inner world that was distinctly separate from their communities, whether by choice or necessity.[18] And yet we find that the wanderer still tries to adhere to the cultural ethos of his time, its hold still a powerful force over him as it is the custom to *his ferðlocan fæste binde, healde his hordcofan*. Many scholars have noted the obvious contradiction of the wanderer to hold steady the custom of stoic reticence while inviting the audience into the deepest recesses of his heart. Indeed, the wanderer not only "keep[s] himself closed off in order to prevent what is outside from penetrating inside to the depths of his heart, but he is involved in an even more desperate struggle to keep what is already inside his heart (sorrow, weariness, doubt) from escaping or being

A Life Both Public and Private

expressed to the outside world, and thus contradicting the heroic exterior which he tries to maintain."[19]

Similarly, Bjork notes that "the wanderer thus once again abides by the dictates of his culture as he makes his actions conform to the demands of the situation."[20] But does the wanderer conform? Is he successful at holding back his feelings? The wanderer is absolutely unsuccessful at both, and that we the privileged few come to know his heart confirms this. Hill has likewise picked up on this failed attempt, and says that "the Wanderer is anything but stoic in his passionate lament for his lost lord and friends"; Hill is referring to lines 19–29, especially, and notes that in Icelandic family sagas, the poets enjoyed a freedom to express such thoughts and emotions with the audience, and thus, "we may therefore imagine that poetry itself is a kind of privileged medium in which warriors can lament openly without demeaning their masculine dignity."[21] While Hill's idea exhibits quite an interesting take on how a warrior could express himself emotionally without the fear of any loss of identity or communal associations, I feel that warriors in the Anglo-Saxon world would have seen this much differently. The wanderer, for instance, clearly states that he dare not tell what is in his mind from line eight, most likely because he felt such an acknowledgment went *against* the heroic code. Hence, that the wanderer reflects upon, and goes against the cultural milieu of his time suggests a tension between two realities for him. There is being established, even at this early stage in the poem, a kind of tension between an old and new self. On the one hand, the wanderer reflects upon how he is to act according to the heroic ideal, and on the other, he is beginning to learn that he can break free from this restriction and enter more deeply into an introspective state of reflection and change. While it is too early at this stage to assert this idea with any certainty, the next ten lines brings this argument closer to realization.

The next several lines continue the solitary and emotive themes in the first person that we saw in lines 8a-14a, but with the wanderer's reason for exile explained and his inner struggle further explored:

> Swa ic modsefan minne sceolde
> oft earmcearig, eðle bidæled,
> freomægum feor feterum sælan,
> siþþan geara iu goldwine minne
> hrusan heolstre biwrah ond ic hean þonan
> wod wintercearig ofer waþema gebind,
> sohte seledreorig sinces bryttan

2. Memory and Identity Formation

> hwær ic feor oþþe neah findan meahte
> þone þe in meoduhealle mine wisse,
> oþþe mec freondleasne frefran wolde,
> weman mid wynnum [19a-29a].[22]

Here we are told that the wanderer was thrown into a situation where he had to look for another lord, because his *goldwine* of days past is dead and buried. However, the use of *siþþan* presents us with a question that correlates with the discussion above on stoic reticence. It is initially unclear if the wanderer had to bind his anxieties *because* his lord has died (as a conjunction), or whether *siþþan* is being used adverbially to simply represent a moment in time. The answer presents itself when we refer to the previous discussion, for the wanderer has already mentioned the noble quality that is holding one's thoughts bound to their heart, and that the wanderer's attempt at this "is shown to be far from successful" is obvious[23]; hence, the wanderer is describing how his initial thoughts of loss and depression came about *because* his lord had died, and this naturally led to his attempt to suppress his feelings, as the "heroic code encourages such restraint as a counterbalance to the mind's frailty."[24] Although the wanderer believed he should remain rigid in this attempt, it is obvious that he has failed. Again, we should take note of this discrepancy between the old and the new, the wanderer's heroic value system circumvented by a nearly unrestrained emotional process that consumes his thoughts. Thus, while the wanderer reveals his past heroic ties with a lord and an abstemious mind, his dialogue showcases a new present, as the wanderer is at odds with himself while struggling to understand the changes that are occurring in his mind—all of which are contributing to the formation of a new identity, from a communal self-concept to something entirely different.

The Wanderer's Multiple Identities and Dream Recall

We find a dramatic shift in perspective in lines 29b-57b, where the first-person lament gives way to the introduction of a hypothetical wanderer/exile, who knows the pains of such a life and describes in detail the anxieties suffered by one who is separated from his community:

A Life Both Public and Private

> Wat se þe cunnað
> hu sliþen bið sorg to geferan
> þam þe him lyt hafað leofra geholena.
> Waraþ hine wræclast, nalæs wunden gold,
> ferðloca freorig, nalæs foldan blæd;
> gemon he selesecgas ond sincðþege,
> hu hine on geoguðe his goldwine
> wenede to wiste: wyn eal gedreas.
> Forþon wat se þe sceal his winedryhtnes
> leofes larcwidum longe forþolian [29b-38b].[25]

It would be an understandable argument to presume that this exile is different from the wanderer himself, but as we proceed with our thesis that the wanderer's past self-concept is changing as the poem continues, it becomes clear that the introduction of this exile represents the manifestation—via memory—of an earlier persona of the wanderer. As mentioned earlier, the position from which the wanderer is speaking is that of an omniscient platform, and hence the power of the numerous recollections throughout *Wan* is that they are born from a speaker who has already disassociated himself from his communal identity and embraced a new personal-self (which we are in the process of discovering). This disassociation with the old to make way for the new is suggested by Booth, as he speaks of "multiple selves over an individual's lifetime," depending on events that occur within that lifetime. Further, he explains that "time is dispersive [...] but memory collects: it gathers in a past that is mine/ours, and [...] maps out my/our persistence and distinctness across time. It also sets defining boundaries, distinguishing one person or community from another and [gives] individuals a part of the foundation of their embeddedness [sic] in communities"; thus, the past self—introduced in the third person here—is a self which has those communal memories, and functions as a self within that structure (i.e., it yearns for community, seeks out the comfort of kinsmen, and fears solitude). That the wanderer is shown to break free from this powerful force is extremely interesting for Anglo-Saxonists, who are typically introduced to individual personae via their role in a larger community.[26] Additionally, refer to Thomas Schelling's work on the battle between the multiple selves within us. He reminds us that "people behave sometimes as if they had two selves, one who wants clean lungs and a long life and another who adores tobacco."[27] The correlation here can be seen in the inner struggle the wanderer himself has, as he tried to hold on to an identity that can no longer

2. Memory and Identity Formation

exist because the communal elements that fostered that identity no longer exist.

This passage clearly illustrates the wanderer's disassociation, as there is a change in the concentration of the personal pronouns from the first (ll. 1–29b) to the third person. Indeed, some scholars have identified this retreat into the cerebral, as Clark and Wasserman suggest that the remembrance of a *goldwine* ("gold-lord") here "is tantamount to a retreat into the confines of his [the wanderer's] deeper self."[28] In fact, this "deeper self," or perhaps the imaginative faculty within the mind of the wanderer, is at once saddened by and separated from, the earlier memories of the communal identity. Here, the wanderer tells us that without companions, exile and a frozen heart take the place of the joys of community, thus detailing how his earlier self is tormented by this loss. The wanderer's refusal, at first, to put aside the emotions he feels for a communal identity speaks to the idea that an individual's "sense of action ultimately depends upon one's embeddedness within a particular sociocultural milieu," an idea cited by Rosaldo in her discussion on how communal identity is as complex as it is elusive.[29] This choice of memory is proven all the more important for us here when we realize that "memory is not just a self-contained cognitive task" but that "central knowledge structures relating to the self have been employed in representing the memory"; that is, a person's "growing sense of self and conception of how he or she fits into various relationships is an important factor in the way that events are remembered." Here, Gillett is referring to a child's sense of self-concept and how what she remembers is directly related to the ways in which her associations within her community are structured. I have included "person" here, because it is clear that no matter the age, one's memory still functions in this way.[30] What this means is that by remembering the importance of the hall, the lord-thane relationship, and the comforts of community, the wanderer is telling us that his identity was inextricably linked with these societal functions, a way-of-life that hitherto he has known nothing other. We may then quite reasonably not only associate Anglo-Saxon community here as the most important aspect of self-identity for the wanderer, but that it was "an analogue of inference—a state transition statistically favorable to the organism," which he was forced away from, but also had to adapt to, if he is to survive. This complex idea that Burge relates to "lesser" animals can also apply to humans and is simplified if we call the "analogue of inference" a "means of survival." For example, wolves must hunt in packs in order to

A Life Both Public and Private

survive—one cannot live alone for long. Similarly, human beings at early communal stages always depend on others for survival. This survival instinct naturally implies a dependence on the community, and thus, this dependence is the source of identity that one would know in this circumstance. In the wanderer's case, however, he has been forced out of this atmosphere, and this adaptation, I argue, will show a change in identity or personal self-concept.[31]

If the preceding section still leaves doubt regarding the power and application of the wanderer's memory to recall an earlier self-concept while simultaneously introducing a new and emerging personal identity in the form of the hypothetical exile remembering how community passes away, the dream and imagination sequences that follow will put those concerns to rest. In lines 39–48, emphasis is yet again put on the new via the old—but in a much more forceful and explicit way—and the application of memory in establishing this dichotomy the way by which it is revealed:

> Ðonne sorg ond slæp somod ætgædre
> earmne anhogan oft gebindað,
> þinceð him on mode þæt he his mondryhten
> clyppe ond cysse ond on cneo lecge
> honda ond heafod, swa he hwilum ær
> in geardagum giefstolas breac.
> Ðonne onwæcneð eft wineleas guma,
> gesihð him biforan fealwe wegas,
> baþian brimfuglas, brædan feþra,
> hreosan hrim ond snaw hagle gemenged [39a-48b].[32]

Herein lies the most explicit reference to memory in *Wan*, while continuing the themes set out above of recall and self-identification. Additionally, this memory is made all the more powerful in its specificity of an action that occurred in the past (*þæt he his mondryhten clyppe ond cysse ond on cneo lecge honda ond heafod*). In the whole of *Wan*, this is the only memory that could be considered episodic[33]—but we also must not discount the possibility that such an event was a common, and hence a well-known trope during this time. Regardless, it has been scientifically shown of memory recall, if not known intuitively by most of us, that "not all aspects of an experience are remembered equally well," and that "the memory of things that are central to the episode [...] appear to be remembered better than more peripheral or more subtle details."[34] Therefore, the generic quality of the memories in *Wan* may in fact not only inform our understanding of who the poet is, and whether or not he and the wanderer are

2. *Memory and Identity Formation*

one-and-the-same, but it may also show a disassociation from these memories by the wanderer himself, by his lack of specifics. The importance of this question is overshadowed in this discussion by the memories themselves. That is, whether or not the wanderer is the poet does not matter here, only that a progression of change within *an* individual is accounted for, and this change is recognizable in either persona, showing us how a self-concept functioned during this time.

Here again the wanderer is relating to an earlier self-concept by way of memory (*þinceð him on mode*), while juxtaposing an inchoate identity by its sudden thrusting upon us from the dream state. Here, the wanderer awakes only to sea-birds, dark waves, and hail-laden cold, all of which seemingly act as a metaphor for his new, forming identity. This dichotomy of old and new is striking, and that sea-birds immediately occupy his sight upon awaking from a dream where he had just enjoyed the company of his lord, suggests that the animals in the natural world are now surrogates for his kinsmen.[35] If this is true, then strengthening our theme of an old and new identity is the wanderer's memory of the lord-thane relationship (his early personal-self), while his awakening represents the emergence of a new self-concept, who still yearns for, but is beginning to realize is unable to ever again grasp, life in the mead-hall. It is important to note here that I do not believe this was a conscious process on the part of the poet, but instead an unconscious association with his understanding of how identity worked in his time, and hence it reflects in the literature. Indeed, Antonina Harbus has commented on this dream sequence, and says that "in the Christian tradition […] sleep is a metaphor for ignorance, death, or spiritual torpor."[36] In Old English, it can also mean "sin." Harbus says that "the dream is also significant at this point in the text, as it signals a major breech in the control of the mind by the self or the will." There is not an explanation here of the self, but Harbus is suggesting that the self has somehow lost control of a mind run amuck. Similarly, Godden has said that "it is the self, not the mind, which Anglo-Saxon writers considered responsible for 'conscious thought and understanding.'"[37] With a similar void in the definition of self, we are left wondering what it is if not the mind or its processes. My definition of the self has no such ambiguity, as it has been stated earlier that my definition does not refer to an immutable soul that is unrecognizable or so elusive as to cause semantic concerns. This definition sees the processes of the mind (in this case, memory) as a prime mechanism by which a self is formed—what that self is or where

A Life Both Public and Private

it is housed is a philosophical question not relevant to OE poetry. In any event, reading the dream as a metaphor for the death of the old self may be overzealous at this stage, but in the remaining lines leading up to the major shift in the second half of the poem, such a reading certainly seems possible, and perhaps even likely.

Following up with his feelings upon awaking, the wanderer reflects on how the memory of kinsfolk provides nothing but pain in his new reality:

> Þonne beoð þy hefigran heortan benne,
> sare æfter swæsne; sorg bið geniwad
> þonne maga gemynd mod geondhweorfeð
> greteð gliwstafum, georne geondsceawað—
> secga geseldan swimmað eft onweg,
> fleotendra ferð no þær fela bringeð
> cuðra cwidegiedda; cearo bið geniwad
> þam þe sendan sceal swiþe geneahhe
> ofer waþema gebind werigne sefan [49a-57b].[38]

In contrast to the joys that the memory of kinsmen brought the wanderer in earlier passages, the recollection of his lord and community are now only a source of pain, as he reminds us that *sorg bið geniwad* ("sorrow is renewed") when *maga gemynd mod geondhwearfeð* ("the memory of kinsmen passes through the mind"). In other words, the wanderer's mind is recalling the memory of his kinsmen. Cautious now, the wanderer watches these images, but does not overly engage with them in an emotional way as he did before, because his comrades *swimmað eft onweg* ("again swim away") from his memory. Theories abound as to what was intended by *secga geseldan* (here glossed *companions of men*). For instance, Owen says this is in reference to visiting sailors, who come only to leave again; Dunning and Bliss gloss "seagulls"; Leslie translates *geseldan* as a singular, meaning "companion" ("mind," in this case). However, it seems clear that this phrase is referring to the memories of his community, not a literal person or thing that he experiences outside of his mind (i.e., *gemon he selesecgas* ["he remembers the men of the hall"] in line 34, the *mondryhten* in line 41, and *the maga* in line 51).[39] Rosier calls the wanderer's memory here his "new *source* of sorrow," and with slight amendment (not the mind itself, but rather that which is brought to mind) this analysis is absolutely correct.[40] In a similar vein to Rosier, Irvine suggests that the mind is also the wanderer's root of grief in that the "inadequacy of memory would indeed contribute to the sadness of repeatedly sending a weary mind in loneliness across an expanse of ocean" and that "if the mind of

2. Memory and Identity Formation

the Wanderer does not bring back familiar utterances [...] then the fallibility of the mind is implied."[41] While I agree that the images of community brought to the mind via memory are certainly sources of sorrow for the wanderer, the mind is anything but fallible. In fact, the mind is doing its job, as the faculty of memory is indeed bringing back to the wanderer the source of sorrow for his earlier identity—i.e., community. Thus, it is clear in this first half of *Wan*, that through the application of memory, the "[wanderer's] identity presupposes an uninterrupted continuance of existence," a continuance that is itself implicit by the recollection of his earlier memories; these memories are thus a source by which the wanderer is changing his sense of personal-self, a process that culminates and resolves in the second half of the poem.[42]

The Wanderer's Questioning and a Redefinition of Self

In the preceding section, we explored the ways in which the first half of *Wan* emphasizes the dichotomy between the wanderer's past communal identity and emerging personal identity, with the more-or-less neutral concentration on both that was beginning to show signs of strain in favor of the new, much emptier, self-concept in lines 49–57; this process is developed further and fully realized beginning on line 58, as the wanderer—in the first person again—truly starts to question the purpose of grasping on to an identity that is no longer tenable:

> Forþon ic geþencan ne mæg geond þas woruld
> forhwan modsefa min ne gesweorce
> þonne ic earla lif eal geondþence,
> hu hi færlice flet ofgeafon,
> modge maguþegnas. Swa þes middangeard
> ealra dogra gehwam dreoseþ ond fealleþ [58a-63b].[43]

Here, *Forþon* (therefore) bridges all of the previous discussion, as a way to explain why the memory of the wanderer's community is now only a source of a dark mind, a misery that cannot bring solace to the exile. Thus, the act of remembering kinsmen has produced a freedom within the wanderer's mind, an introspection that has given him the tools necessary to incite a change in viewpoint. The comparison with men to the eventual destruction of the natural world (*Swa þes middangeard ... dreoseþ ond*

A Life Both Public and Private

fealleþ) displays the power of this introspection, as the wanderer is no longer associating his past communal identity with permanence or joy, but with a cold epiphany explains that the world of men cannot last, and by extension, the heroic identity he once enjoyed likewise cannot forever remain. In this way, a two-part structure in *Wan* is a well-founded reading, in that the "poem is a reflection of the Wanderer's mental states" over time, where "references to the past [...] illustrate the wanderer's progress in trying to reconcile himself to his present state as he moved from an attempt to recapture his past to an attempt to explain his loss."[44] Similarly, Selzer says: "It is clear, then, that the loss of the speaker's lord and the speaker's terrible wanderings both took place in the past and that he is recovering those experiences through memory [...] the speaker in his meditation is remembering an earlier self who wandered in search of his lord."[45] Not only is the wanderer remembering an earlier self in search for a new *goldwine* (generous lord), but he is also remembering the typology of a self who was attached to that life.[46] At this juncture, then, this "earlier self" has faded and given way to a new, more basic and less cluttered identity that—as we have read—associates the world and its inhabitants with impermanence and anxiety, themes that are continued for the next forty-seven lines with even more intensity and description.

Lines 64–88 highlight the wanderer's continuing reflection of worldly transience, while also implying the importance of memory through the recollection of heroic experience:

> Forþon ne mæg wearþan wis wer ær he age
> wintra dæl in woruldrice. Wita sceal geþyldig;
> ne sceal no to hatheort, ne to hrædwyrde,
> ne to wac wiga, ne to wanhydig,
> ne to forht, ne to fægen, ne to feohgifre,
> ne næfre gielpes to georn, ær he geare cunne.
> Beorn sceal gebidan þonne he beot spriceð
> oþþæt collenferð cunne gearwe
> hwider hreþra gehygd hweorfan wille.
> Ongietan sceal gleaw hæle hu gæstlic bið
> þonne ealle þisse worulde wela weste stondeð,
> swa nu missenlice geond þisne middangeard
> winde biwaune weallas stondað,
> hrime bihrorene. Hryðge þa ederas;
> woriað þa winsalo. Waldend licgað
> dreame bidrorene; duguð eal gecrong,
> wlonc bi wealle. Sume wig fornom,
> ferede in forðwege; sumne fugel oþbær

2. *Memory and Identity Formation*

> ofer heanne holm; sumne se hara wulf
> deaðe gedælde; sumne dreorighleor
> in eorðscræfe eorl gehydde.
> Yþde swa þisne eardgeard ælda scyppend,
> oþþæt burgwara breahtma lease
> eald enta geweorc idlu stodon [64a-88b].[47]

There is here an association with old age and wisdom (*wintra dæl/wis wer*), to be sure; however, we find a subtle reminder that it is through the application of memory—not simply old age—that one *becomes* wise. For instance, the wanderer tells us that one cannot attain wisdom *ær he age wintra dæl in woruldrice*, and that this *wis wer* must be moderate in all the categories of life until he *geare cunne* ("can know well/entirely/sufficiently"). What one is to know is answered in the line following, in which the wanderer states that a wise man must understand that the constructions of men are ultimately ruined by time, that kings will lie dead, and that warriors will often fall in battle. Thus, the theme of impermanence that we discussed for lines 58–63 continues here and contributes to what it is that the wise man should know, but now additionally we find an emphasis on the process of memory as a catalyst for understanding that attaching oneself to an old identity is futile in the face of inexorable change. In other words, the wise man here is represented by an old man who has had the wisdom to use his memory in order to realize the transience of the heroic world, and this has created a new sense of self that has far fewer associations attached to it. Indeed, if the wanderer were not able to use his memory in this way, then he would exist is a sort of limbo, where his former identity would remain, albeit un-nurtured by the community from which it was born. Pope also comments on how the second half of *Wan* highlights this dichotomy of past and present, with an emphasis on the present: "it becomes evident that the entire speech of the thinker is at one and the same time a lament and an antidote against the sort of misery that had long engulfed the wanderer."[48] The so-called "antidote" is revealed at the end of *Wan*, but part of that remedy is certainly the application of memory in the formation of a new self-identity. At this stage, then, it would be appropriate to suggest that solitude, introspection, and memory are all medicines that the wanderer uses to finally realize a new personal-self.

The application of memory as synonymous with a *wis wer* is continued, as the wanderer re-introduces the hypothetical exile who would contemplate these things:

A Life Both Public and Private

> Se þonne þisne wealsteal wise geþohte
> ond þis deorce life deope geondþenceð,
> frod in ferðe, feor oft gemon,
> wælsleahta worn, ond þas word acwið [89a-91b].[49]

Similar to the previous section, but now explicitly stated, the hypothetical exile refers to the thought process of remembering lost kinsmen as *wise geþohte*; that is, not only is he wise who thinks of the transience of the world, but the process of introspective memory is itself wise, as it is the mechanism by which one uses contemplation to change a certain viewpoint. Indeed, Woolf points out that "the description of the Wanderer's former life in his lord's hall make clear that he has to learn detachment from that life [...] because it is inevitable that everything that is loved on earth [...] must be lost."[50] Similarly, Hait states of the second half of *Wan*: "no longer does he [the wanderer] accumulate [emotions], but now he pours out his lament, empties himself of his thoughts"; thus the first and second half of the poem represent "fullness" and "emptiness," respectively, as "*The Wanderer* throughout the poem laments his involuntary exile and at the end of the poem focuses on the present moment with respect to his memories of the past."[51] Emptiness here should not create the belief that there is no self, but quite the contrary. This "more basic" self is a hyper-aware entity, that exists, that is conscious, that is unique, but that is not so cluttered in its creation now. Therefore, this reflection, combined with what we learned of wisdom from old age suggests that "the cognitive processes shaping self-concept during this period [middle age or later] are quite similar to those of young adulthood" in that some events may "trigger a major self-reassessment."[52] The salience of this study reveals that the Anglo-Saxons appear to have been able to "reassess" their identities into middle age (as we do today) based on life-changing events, or in this case, both the event of exile and the realizations via memory (the transience of life). Thus, the wanderer represents this reassessment here, as he asks rhetorical questions in the *ubi sunt* construction[53]:

> Hwær cwom mearg? Hwær cwom mago? Hwær cwom
>   maþþumgyfa?
> Hwær cwom symbla gesetu? Hwær sindon seledreamas?
> Eala beorht bune! Eala byrnwiga!
> Eala þeodnes þrym! [92a-95a].[54]

The realization of the transience of the world has now come full circle, as the wanderer concedes that under a fate uncontrollable by men, all

2. Memory and Identity Formation

relationships are bound to end, all treasure is an illusory pleasure, and the entirety of heroic society is but a small ship in the storm of destiny:

> Eall is earfoðlic eorþan rice;
> onwendeð wyrda gesceaft weoruld under heofonum.
> Her bið feoh læne, her bið freond læne.
> Her bið mon læne, her bið mæg læne.
> Eal þis eorþan gesteal idel weorþeð [106a-110b].[55]

The preceding lines have shown us that the wanderer's process of disassociating himself from his earlier identity has now nearly finalized, for he knows that he will never again find another lord to whom to pledge fealty, nor will he ever see heroic society as the only source of identity for him because of his new knowledge. It seems that at this stage, the wanderer is truly without a self or personal-identity, for his earlier self-concept has been destroyed by the act of introspection and memory, giving credence to the idea that "narrative is born out of such tension [referring to different "versions," or periods of the self] in that narrative activity seeks to bridge a self that felt and acted in the past, a self that acts in the present, and an anticipated or hypothetical self that is projected to feel and act in some as yet unrealized moment."[56] However, the wanderer has yet to discover a source of respite for his new understanding—he is, in effect, a man without a road forward or a "projected," "hypothetical self."

If the previous sections show a conspicuous lack of closure for how the wanderer can identify with his new self-concept, the final five lines offer this consolation:

> Swa cwæð snottor on mode; gesæt him sundor æt rune.
> Til bið se þe his treowe gehealdeþ; ne sceal næfre his torn to rycene
> beorn of his breostum acyþan, nemþe he ær þa bote cunne,
> eorl mid elne gefremman. Wel bið þam þe him are seceð,
> frofre to fæder on heofonum, þær us eal seo fæstnung stondeð [111a-115b].[57]

Here again we find the *swa cwæð* construction reintroducing us to the man who was at first an *eardstapa* ("wanderer"), but has now changed to a man *snottor on mode* ("wise in mind"). Based on this construction, I would argue that everything from lines 8–110 represents the inner dialogue in the mind of the wanderer, and that lines 1–8 and 111–115 are from a narrator, who has knowledge of this wanderer. From what we have discussed, such a reading is quite plausible. We have discovered that the body of the poem after line 8 shows a steady progression of thought, and that the wanderer was in the process of learning to uncover a new identity by necessity—that is, an identity that was once based on the communal, but has since moved on to the personal, the individual introspective self that exists without the multiple layers of communal influence and coloration. Pope has picked up on this and says that when the wanderer "sat apart [he was] communing with himself," and that this "suggests that he would normally have been expected to be communing with others."[58] Hence, that such an emphasis is placed on words like *anhaga* ("solitary one"), *ana* ("alone"), and *sundor* ("apart, separately") throughout *Wan*, we may conclude that a distinction is being made consciously between the communal and the individual. Why mention it, otherwise? De Lacy claims that by the end of the poem, the wanderer has not "gained anything by this insight [that is, sitting alone in thought]."[59] But has the wanderer not realized that the world is transitory, that mead-halls and companionship cannot bring everlasting joy, and that all worldly possessions cannot provide happiness? And has the wanderer not gained peace *to fæder on heofonum* ("from the father in heaven") as a solution to the happiness he once found in society? Even if the wanderer himself does not yet know of this consolation, the narrator does, and reminds us that when all elements of the social self collapse, there still remains something to which a person can hold on. Therefore, it is apparent that the wanderer has not only learned to sit alone, but has also found a permanent joy that cannot be taken away by time, wars, or the elements, and in this way has discovered a new self-concept that has moved away from the communal and into the personal. This self is defined as being unadorned by social influence, yet lucid, reflective, and conscious.

Concluding Remarks: Memory and the Defining of a New Self-Concept

Wan is a poem about personal change, a self-metamorphosis spearheaded by the application of the wanderer's memory. Saint Augustine famously said, "*Et est quidam imago trinitatis, ipsa mens* (and there is a certain image of the trinity—the mind itself), a mind that "is endowed

2. Memory and Identity Formation

with a natural capacity for remembering, understanding, and willing of itself; and when these powers are rightly directed, the self will be recognized in its true order of being in relation to God."[60] Indeed, it would seem that the wanderer has discovered this self—a self that is not only powerful in its own right, but is also deeply connected with its relationship with God as the wanderer's potentially new source of self-reference, which is antithetical to the sources of the wanderer's identity previously. Strengthening this idea, Doubleday suggests a three-part structure to *Wan* that highlights a progression of change in the mind of the wanderer, culminating in a new identity.[61] Doubleday asserts that this three-part structure correlates to the "three "faculties of the soul," memory, intellect, and will," citing lines 6–62 as *memoria*, 62b–110 *intelligentia*, and 111–115 as *voluntas*," respectively; via memory, the wanderer "reflects on the conditions of the world and on what the wise man must understand about it" by "recall[ing] his past hardships"; through the intellect, "he states as a directive for action what man must do to be saved from his grief" by understand[ing] fully that his lot is part of the general mutability of the world"; and with the will, "he perceives the remedy for that mutability in the grace of the unchanging Lord."[62] Following our discussion, then, it seems that individual change in *Wan* may be predicated on a reliance on God, and in order to realize it, the wanderer must come to terms with separation from his community. Similarly, Selzer has found an equivalent tripartite structure (originally defined by Lous Martz), which we can find in some religious lyrics of the seventeenth century, a structure that shows first, a "concrete, vivid, dramatic subject for meditation [which] is presented to the mind by the memory, while next, an understanding is applied to the remembered subject so that gradually the mediator's soul is lifted up to God," and finally, the "aroused will lifts [...] to address the divine."[63] Thus, the application of memory as a way of analyzing one's place in the world and redefining a self-concept that is highly aware, cognizant of its existence both past and present, and self-reflective of its current state in *Wan* is apparent. The wanderer has used his memory to present himself with the old, so that he could come to disregard it. Doubleday considers this idea "a consolation, for its pattern is from misery to hope," while I am inclined to say it is more akin to "community to individuality" or "past-identity to "new personal-self" that is utterly alone until the narrator reminds us that respite for an unadorned self may be found in God the Father instead of human community.[64]

A Life Both Public and Private

That *Wan* is a poem about the inner workings of the mind is well founded on past scholarship. Antonina Harbus has said that it "concentrates on the workings of the mind"; Godden claims that it "takes its meaning from a disjunction between the mind, the faculty of thought and emotion, and the self, the controlling seat of consciousness"; I would argue, however, that there is not a "disjunction" between the mind and the self, but that both work in tandem as complementary elements. In *Wan*, we cannot understand the mind or its faculties without understanding the self that existed before and the one that develops later. Also, Godden's definition of the self is a bit ambiguous, in that the "controlling seat of consciousness" is difficult to locate or identify.[65] Rosier argues that "it is intrinsically a mirror of a mind in its several states and faculties, of memory and revery [sic], of reason and imagination, of perception and conception"[66]; and Bjork remarks that "the poem has to do with the mind or processes of the mind."[67] Indeed, this we have seen throughout the poem, where lines 8–57b represent the application of memory to bring to mind the remembrance of a past self-concept that was entirely indebted to a communal personal identity[68]; lines 58–110b describe the process by which the wanderer further employs the faculty of memory to recognize truths about the impermanence of communal life, and finally, following line 110, we discover what the wanderer has understood from his introspection that one is able to redefine their identity, particularly if they are able to find something to replace the function that community once played in their lives—and in this instance, it is God. It is unclear at this stage whether or not losing one's primary sense of self is the only instance in which we find Anglo-Saxons changing their identities or showing a deep personal-self (this question is explored throughout the rest of the book), but as far as we are concerned here, it would seem that God could replace community as a determining identity marker in a person's self-concept.[69] It is also very important to note that a replacement need not be found in order for us to recognize the personal-self. Indeed, the unadorned self that I discussed earlier is the kind of self that I am most interested in discovering in this study. Thus, the wanderer's process of redefining his self-concept tells us that at least in some cases, Anglo-Saxons regarded themselves by a continuum of thought, a stream of consciousness that was strongly informed by past experiences, and that they could employ the very personal nature of memory to inspect, discover, and ultimately change their self-association by a cognitive reconstruction of the self.

2. Memory and Identity Formation

The Seafarer: *An Early Struggle Over the Self*

Seaf begins with a narration highlighting the dichotomy between solitude and communal security, but from the outset, the seafarer himself introduces these themes:

> Mæg ic be me sylfum soðgied wrecan,
> siþas secgan, hu ic geswincdagum
> earfoðhwile oft þrowade.
> Bitre breostceare gebiden hæbbe,
> gecunnad in ceole cearselda fela,
> atol yþa gewealc, þær mec oft bigeat
> nearo nihtwaco æt nacan stefnan
> þonne he be clifum cnossað. Calde geþrungen
> wæron mine fet, forste gebunden,
> caldum clommum, þær þa ceare seofedun,
> hat ymb heortan, hungor innan slat
> merewerges mod. Þæt se mon ne wat
> þe him on foldan fægrost limpeð,
> hu ic earmcearig iscealne sæ
> winter wunade wræccan lastum,
> winemægum bidroren,
> bihongen hrimgicelum; hægl scurum fleag [1a-17b].[70]

We should note here the early similarity between these two poems, in that since the seafarer is recounting his experiences, he is speaking from a position of seeming omniscience, and therefore has already experienced *bitre breostceare* ("bitter anxiety") caused by being *winemægum bidroren* ("deprived of kinsmen"), and is thus employing memory to relate to an earlier emotional state. The emphasis here is not on physical hardship, but the loss of kinsmen. Indeed, the reflexive pronoun *me sylfum* also emphasizes the seafarer's desolation and lamentation—since it signifies a deeply introspective and highly personal account of something that occurred in the past—as does the idea that *in ceole cearselda fela* ("much anxiety in a ship") could possibly be reference to "the ship of the soul," or something similar; Holton also suggests that the ship could be a reference to the church, but from what we have already seen in *Wan*—and what we will discover—I argue that the ship is a reference to the mind or some concept of the self; thus, the seafarer is suffering anxiety within his mind because of his thinking on these things. In any event, it is clear that the seafarer is alone on this journey.[71] Undoubtedly, then, that the seafarer is referring to himself in the past—as is the wanderer—and that this reflection is also a memory of his earlier personal self-identity. In fact, Grice tells us that "the self is a logical construction, and is to be defined in terms of memory," in that memory of particular events that are ascribed to the same person having the memory help to construct and mold the current identity.[72] Grice refers here to the Logical Construction Theory (LCT), which requires a person who has had an experience "to show a R [relation] to an experience which is belonging to the same self," and although specialist in terminology, it is important to note that memory is a critical component to the construction of a self-concept.[73] The distinction made between the seafarer and the man who *on foldan fægrost limpeð* ("is most fairly suited on land/fittingly exists on land") from line 12b aids in this interpretation, as the seafarer is not only making a general statement about all those who exist in a communal environment, but is reiterating that such a person is not he—at least, not anymore. Unlike the wanderer, the seafarer has yet to make a specific reference to himself being a part of community, although, that he refers to a hypothetical landdweller (and as I argue, a reference to an earlier self-concept) tells us that he has detailed knowledge of life on land—in addition, we are told that he has been at sea for a number of years, implying the time before was spent in society.[74] Thus, this section is quite similar to the introduction of the hypothetical exile in *Wan* (lines 29b-57b), since the distinction highlights the fact that the narrator is different but can identify with the mindset of one who lives on land.

Similarly, the seafarer's careful mention of the lonely reality of the natural world taking the place of a community on land—a similar trope we discussed in lines 39–48 of *Wan*—is indicative of his recollective state-of-mind:

> Þaer ic ne gehyrde butan hlimman sæ,
> iscaldne wæg. Hwilum ylfete song
> dyde ic me to gomene, ganetes hleoþor
> ond huilpan sweg fore hleahtor wera,
> mæw singende fore medodrince.
> Stormas þær stanclufu beotan, þær him stearn oncwæð
> isigfeþera, ful oft þæt earn bigeal
> urigfeþra. Nænig hleomæga
> feasceaftig ferð frefran meahte [18a-26b].[75]

It is important to note two things here: the first is that this section represents the only real personal identification with a past that could be considered a lament from the seafarer's perspective, but it is nowhere near as emotional or explicit as we see in *Wan*. It will become clear that *Seaf*

2. *Memory and Identity Formation*

focuses much more on the current state of the seafarer, in that there is a very conscious disconnect from him and the world on land. However, that he is able to speak of life on land from a third-person perspective tells us that he understands such feelings and simultaneously is wholly disassociated from them. Secondly, that the final clause appears to introduce the main theme of the poem even before line 58 seems to have been overlooked by scholars in the past. As with *Wan*, *Seaf* can be divided into two thematic sections: the first half discussing the world from the point-of-view of a narrator who has personal experience with that world, and a second half which concentrates on leaving that world behind by discussing impermanence, etc. This is clearly demarcated in *Wan*, but not as sharply defined here—although the division certainly exists. Additionally, the idea that no kinsman could support a lonely soul is very important to our understanding of the poem as a whole. It would seem that the seafarer is already conceding that associations from land-dwellers are either unable (because they are dead) or incapable (because they are only concerned with the comforts and security of community) of comforting the soul/mind/heart of the seafarer. I take the latter as the most probable definition, and translating *meahte* in the past tense does indeed support such a reading. Thus, my argument that the seafarer is, like the wanderer, taking us through a journey of understanding—from associating himself at one point with a communal identity, to a movement towards self-mastery or a new personal-identity—but is doing so from a much more impersonal position, is suggestive by his criticism of land-dwellers, while highlighting the fact that he has already changed his self-concept and is reporting to us from a position of omniscience because he already knows the outcome.

The distinction between the seafarer's past self-concept and his present are further highlighted, as he claims that life on land is easy in comparison to having to live separated from that security:

> Forþon him gelyfeð lyt, se þe ah lifes wyn
> gebiden in burgum, bealosiþa hwon,
> wlonc ond wingal, hu ic werig oft
> in brimlade bidan sceolde.
> Nap nihtscua, norþan sniwde,
> hrim hrusan bond, hægl feol on eorþan,
> corna caldast [27a-33a].[76]

That the seafarer is careful to make such a distinction between the self that is on his current journey and an earlier self-identity (i.e., those on land) makes it clear that he is "establish[ing] the duality of the singing self and the sung self," and by highlighting this duality, the seafarer is showing us how memory was used at once to associate and disassociate from one's past; Empric also posits that "perhaps it is too modern a viewpoint to assume too great a degree of self-consciousness in the Old English narrator/poet." But this type of self-consciousness is exactly what I am arguing both *Wan* and *Seaf* show us.[77] The seafarer's past, then, was one of dependence on his community—much like *Wan*—which is why community is mentioned in both of these poems with such regularity in the beginning. That is, the memory of the seafarer, like all of us, "is not like a series of recordings of autobiographical episodes but involves the retention in the extraconscious mind of a number of strategic clues and generic scripts that enable one to create a good-enough facsimile of a given autobiographical episode."[78] Here, I see "generic scripts" embodied in the mention of community in such general terms. That is to say, the seafarer is remembering the generality of what it was like to be identified with worldly things (e.g., flushed with wine, the mead drink) and not specific memories as we saw with the wanderer's recollection of kissing his lord's hand.[79] However, having pointed this out, the seafarer's recollection is no less important for our purposes, but indeed shows us that the seafarer is perhaps more disassociated from that existence at an even earlier stage than the wanderer. Thus, that memory allows the seafarer to refer to a past self while creating a new self-concept even at this early stage, gives credence to the idea that "all attempts to elucidate the notion of personal identity independently of and in isolation from the notions of narrative ... are bound to fail" because "identities are the names we give to the different ways we are positioned by, and position ourselves in, the narratives of the past."[80] Consequently, if the seafarer was positioned in a communal self-concept at an earlier stage, of what his identity consists now is unclear, but it is a question that we will be better able to answer in the passages to come.

In lines 33b-38, there is a return of the first-person narration that began the poem and here in earnest signifies the aspects of memory that are most salient to this study:

> Forþon cnyssað nu
> heortan geþohtes þæt ic hean streamas,
> sealtyþa gelac sylf cunnige;
> monað modes lust mæla gehwylce,

2. Memory and Identity Formation

> ferð to feran þæt ic feor heonan
> elþeodigra eard gesece [33b-38b].[81]

Reminiscent of line 58 in Wan, *forþon* acts as a bridge to the previous discussion, and works well if we remember that the audience is moving along this journey with the seafarer.[82] The ambiguity here as to what the seafarer means by *cunnige, ferð to feran*, and *elþeodigra eard gesece* may be approached if we see these ideas as metaphorical. For instance, let us read the seafarer's thought on whether or not to gain experience (*cunnige*) as an inner debate regarding if he should continue to think of life on land, the travelling spirit (*ferð to feran*) as the application of memory to recall worldly community, and the searching for a land of foreigners as a metaphor for the memory of community in worldly society. Even if this were not a conscious metaphor by the poet/scribe—and I do not believe it is—this interpretation still proves accurate. My argument here is that we can see the unconscious role of how memory applies to the idea of self in this period (tenth century). I believe that these concepts are metaphorical, but not—on the whole—used on purpose as a literary device in these poems. That is, we are witnessing an inner reality by looking at what is not explicitly stated. We have already been told that gaining experience of seafaring is a lonely exercise (*winemægum bidroren*), that moving over the waves is another way of implying the process of memory,[83] and that reference to a community beyond the waves applies to the thinking of a life on land, the searching for a new troop that would instill a sense of self, and a journey to find a group that would give the seafarer a feeling of belonging. Gordon tells us that "we are not told why the seafarer wishes to seek the land of strangers far hence," but it seems to me that he is trying to get back through memory what he has lost, so he does not lose that aspect of his identity. This is representative of an inner-struggle for the seafarer at this point.[84] Therefore, a paraphrase would read something like this: "For all of these reasons, emotions agitate my heart that I should seek out the experience of such a lonely life away from my community; the heart's desire always wants me to send out my thoughts to life on land, so that I may remember and continue to seek out such a life." Greenfield also questions the reason the seafarer would want to go on another journey "despite his previous discomforts," and we are now given the answer: he is *already* on a desolate, uncomfortable journey, so the prospective journey relates to the recollection of life on land—no doubt a difficult and lonely task—and not a physical trek.[85] Thus, through the application of memory, the seafarer experiences a division, an inner struggle that would see two personae fighting to exist. The evidence for this division comes from the fact that the seafarer is still actively thinking on his past self; it shows that it is still important to him. Empric drives home this point and tells us that "his stance, in contrast and later opposition to the non-seafarer, then, divorces him also from a former self: he knows, is deprived of, then willingly relinquishes the land-joys," and by using the term *sylf* (in ll. 1 and 35), the seafarer is "establishing a division of person."[86] A continuation of this theme follows, leading up to the second half of the poem, but with more emphasis on the reasoning behind the seafarer's ultimate decision to leave his earlier life.

Return of the Third-Person and Early Thoughts on Transience

As discussed in relation to line 27, the use of third-person narration works as a device to demarcate the earlier and current/future self-concept, but this time the first-person account does not appear adjoining, showing the beginnings of complete disassociation from a personal-identity indebted to life on land:

> forþon nis þæs modwlonc mon ofer eorþan,
> ne his gifena þæs god, ne in geoguþe to þæs hwæt,
> ne in his dædum to þæs deor, ne him his dryhten to þæs hold,
> þæt he a his sæfore sorge næbbe,
> to hwon hine dryhten gedon wille [39a-43b].[87]

The explicit mentions of certain aspects of the heroic ideal (i.e., bravery and loyalty) is also important to consider, as it seems that even the joys and security of land can not alleviate the fear inherent in seafaring. Another point here should be mentioned: what exactly the poet means by the sea voyage must be defined. As we have discovered, the concept of seafaring can be a metaphor for imagining kith and kin and/or the process of memory itself. Here, however, it appears that such a journey—however we understand it—is inevitable (the possessive pronoun as the modifier in the phrase *his sæfore*, instead of an indefinite article, suggests this inevitability). I do not believe that the seafarer is referring to all land-dwellers here, but instead read this section as a general observation relating to those on land who would take up a sea-journey. The power of this

2. Memory and Identity Formation

section, then, lies in its subtle comparison between those on land and those on the journey. Greenfield has also commented on this, reminding us that *dryhten* in lines 41 and 43 refers "to an earthly lord and to God," and that "it is a skillful accentuation of two different kinds of lord-thane relationship, the social and the religious."[88] I absolutely agree here but would add that the former is represented by the communal, while the latter by the personal experiences of the seafarer. The relationship with God should not be seen in the same communal light as the seafarer's past relationship with his earthly lord because like the wanderer, his past self has been completely stripped of worldly attachments and all that is left is the *possibility* of attaining a close relationship with God the Father, but at the present time the seafarer is still lacking a strong social self. So, whatever the purpose of the seafarer's journey, he is taking it *alone*; this process is one of complete solitude and introspection, and hence memory must play a key role in remembering a self that was concerned with society, while the contemplation of that identity aids in changing the self-concept.

The seafarer's further deviation from the norms of heroic society, and thus from his earlier identity, is additionally highlighted by the final lines of the first half of the poem, which not only clearly articulate general memories of communal life, but disregard the importance of such an identity by discussing its transience:

> Ne biþ him to hearpan hyge ne to hringþege—
> ne to wife wyn ne to worulde hyht—
> ne ymbe owiht elles nefne ymb yða gewealc,
> ac a hafað longunge se þe on lagu fundað.
> Bearwas blostmum nimað, byrig fægriað,
> wongas wlitigað, woruld onetteð;
> ealle þa gemoniað modes fusne,
> sefan to siþe, þam þe swa þenceð,
> on flodweges feor gewitað.
>   Swylce geac monað geomran reorde,
> singeð sumeres weard, sorge beodeð
> bitter in breosthord. Þæt se beorn ne wat,
> esteadig secg, hwæt þa sume dreogað
> þe þa wræclastas widost lecgað [44a-57b].[89]

Referring to the hypothetical exile in lines 39–43, the seafarer tells us that it is natural to disregard an identity that exists solely in the social realm, once one understands that, like the seasons, humanity changes and will move on at all times. The implication here reminds us of lines 64–88 in *Wan*, in that old age is a determiner of wisdom, and such wisdom

A Life Both Public and Private

is represented by the memory of the seasons changing, the buildings crumbling, lords dying, etc. Thus, the seafarer, like the wanderer, is beginning to cite the reasons for questioning an identity that he has held on to for so long, and the tension we have seen so far in the seafarer's self-concept is beginning to loosen in favor of a new personal-identity. That is, like the wanderer, the seafarer is using his memories of life on land in order to critically examine the import of continuing to hold on to an identity that has been removed from its source of development. We may better see this when referring to Demo's concept of a "moving baseline" for how a self-concept changes over time "across situations."[90] In other words, from line 1, this "baseline" has been the references to community for the seafarer. This is his norm and how he can relate to the audience—who no doubt also have a communal self-concept.[91] So, over time the seafarer is showing a movement away from the baseline and toward new psychological territory. This new identity is punctuated by loneliness and experienced by those who *wræclastas widost lecgað* ("travel the paths of exile most widely"). And as we have discovered, the paths of exile is really a path of introspection, a state-of-mind that forces one to recall and face their past personal-self in order to move on to something else, something more independent precisely because the vast majority of communal associations have been removed from the personal-self.

Earthly Impermanence and a New Self-Concept

As with lines 33 and 58 in *Wan*, here also do we have a coordinate (*forþon*) bridging what was previously stated with the rest of the poem. In this case, however, it seems more likely that the seafarer is specifically referring to lines 44–57—that is, the idea that the knowledge of transience will make one take the journey. Hence, the seafarer tells us:

> Forþon nu min hyge hweorfeð ofer hreþerlocan,
> min modsefa mid mereflode
> ofer hwæles eþel hweorfeð wide,
> eorþan sceatas; cymeð eft to me
> gifre ond grædig, gielleð anfloga,
> hweteð on hwælweg hreþer unwearnum,
> ofer holma gelagu; forþon me hatran sind
> dryhtnes dreamas þonne þis deade life,
> læne on londe [58a-66a].[92]

2. Memory and Identity Formation

A fascinating but subtle change occurs here in the way that the seafarer refers to the processes of the mind. For example, we explored in lines 33–38b how the travelling spirit seeking the land of foreigners can be read as the process of the remembering kinsmen. Similarly, the sea voyage in line 42 is representative of the path of exile in general. Bringing this all together, it seems that the seafarer's mind now moves *ofer hreþerlocan* ("beyond the breast"), *mid mereflode* ("over the deluge/flood of water"), and *ofer hwæles eþel* ("over the whale's domain"). There has been much discussion and debate regarding the precise meaning of this phrase. Some scholars translate "my heart is restless within my breast," others suggest "my thoughts are now roaming beyond the confines of my breast," and still another possibility is "my thoughts pass over the confines of my breast."[93] I agree with Salmon, in that "whatever their differences in detail [...] this passage [is] a figurative description of meditation on events (memory), presumably of the past."[94] It is also relevant to note that Holton suggests that *hwæles eþel* is a reference to the "wiles of Satan," and thus that the seafarer is starting to see his individuality through the process of memory and religion is beginning to take shape.[95] Additionally, Ambrose spoke of "the ability of the mind to transcend spatial and temporal limitations," in that "man's likeness to God lies in his soul, and not in his body, because of the soul's power to range throughout the world *in thought*."[96] Bede likewise spoke of Gregory the Great's ability to "pass in contemplation beyond the barriers of the flesh [...] even though still imprisoned in the body."[97] Taken together, then, we can say that the seafarer is no longer trapped by the memories of kinsmen and life on land; no longer will he experience the tossing of the horrible salt waves; he has finally let go of that desire, that identity, and is now above those things, beyond them—his mind thus moving in a new direction. Inquiring into what the seafarer is now setting his mind to reveals this new source of comfort—*dryhtnes dreamas* ("joys of the Lord"). As we have seen, then, the seafarer must put aside his former identity in order to understand how to embrace a new one. After all, Whitelock's argument about *Seaf* would see him as "an aspiring *peregrinus*, a voluntary exile who will relinquish earthly pleasures for the greater joys of Heaven," which is highlighted by a "continuity of thought between the halves of the poem" and punctuated by *forþon*.[98] Thus, for the seafarer, the mind "seems to be closely associated with mood and individual personality, a kind of mixture of id and ego in opposition to a superego," and not the representation of an immutable self, all of which is highlighted by

A Life Both Public and Private

this new change in outlook.[99] The seafarer's memory, therefore, is an application within the mind that aids in identity-development, not representative of a kind of soul or higher self.

This change of outlook is encouraged in the next forty lines by the seafarer's unyielding discussion on the transience of communal society, and by extension, identity that is based on such a society:

> Ic gelyfe no
> þæt him eorðwelan ece stondeð;
> simle þreora sum þinga gehwylce
> ær his tidege to tweon weorþeð:
> adl oþþe yldo oþþe ecghete
> fægum fromweardum feorh oðþringeð [66b-71b].[100]

The seafarer's differentiation here between himself and *him* is an important distinction. We have already discussed how his identity is changing, but now there is a conscious attempt to separate one from the other. The dative third-person personal pronoun in line 66b is probably referring to the unnamed person in lines 53–57, but even if the reference is not explicit, the division between the seafarer and those who identify with life on land is obvious. Similarly, continuing his rejection of worldly life, the seafarer tells us that as men will be taken away from the world, so too does heroic society itself fall away:

> Dagas sind gewitene,
> ealle onmedlan eorþan rices;
> næron nu cyningas ne caseras
> ne goldgiefan swylce iu wæron,
> þonne hi mæst mid him mærþa gefremedon,
> ond on dryhtlicestum dome lifdon.
> Gedroren is þeos duguð eal; dreamas sind gewitene.
> Wuniað þa wacran ond þas woruld healdaþ,
> brucað þurh bisgo. Blæd is gehnæged;
> eorþan indryhto ealdað ond searað;
> swa nu monna gehwylc geond middangeard [80b-90b].[101]

Reminiscent of the *Ubi sunt* construction in *Wan*, this passage describes the end of heroic society (e.g., no gold-givers or kinsmen), leaving us with a bleak image of those who still remain on land. Interesting here is the seafarer's discussion of the demise of nearly everything, yet *wacran* ("the weak") still dwell there. About whom is this reference? Considering everything we have discussed regarding the nature of the world and how it relates to not only a physical place, but also an identity within the minds

2. Memory and Identity Formation

of Anglo-Saxons, I suggest that this reference is a reminder that the weak are those who would still continue to see land-life as their self-concept. The implication of this is that the seafarer believes ignorance equates to a total self-concept based on heroic society, whilst freedom lies within each who would use introspection as a tool to realize that such a society is faulty, impermanent, fickle.

If the previous passage was ambiguous about who the *wacran* are, the narrator helps clear up this point with an analogy of old age—and unlike the wisdom of age we saw in line 64 of *Wan*, the seafarer implies here that it is not always synonymous with sapience, the latter emerging only after conscious introspection:

> Yldo him on fareð, onsyn blacað,
> gomelfeax gnornað; wat his iuwine,
> æþelinga bearn eorþan forgiefene.
> Ne mæg him þonne se flæschoma þonne him þæt feorg losað
> ne swete forswelgan, ne sar gefelan,
> ne hond onhreran, ne mid hyge þencan [91a-96b].[102]

Here we find a warning, however subtle, of what becomes a man who grows old in heroic society, yet has a life without thought/memory of the transience of the world. And although the body changes through his life (*onsyn blacað, gomelfeax*, etc.), his identity will remain the same. Thus, the bodily changes here are represented by time as a "stage of a thing's history," which does not necessarily define one's identity, for we have already discovered that through the application of memory, identity can remain static or change.[103] Hirsch believes that the body "can rightly be called a *criteria* of identity" [original emphasis], but by no means the *only* criteria.[104] A somewhat abstract example of this can be found when we recall how old age was indicative of wisdom in *Wan*, only because with old age comes the realization that the world and its pulls are transient. Thus, in some way, the appearance of old age in this circumstance could represent an outward display of an inner belief. However, in this example, the old man has not learned the lessons he should have learned in order to change his personal-self or self-concept, and in this way the body can at most be associated with this "criteria of identity" and not its determiner. Similar to Hirsch, but with more emphasis on memory, Locke has said that "the variation of great parcels of matter [bodily changes] alters not the identity," but that "the body goes to making the man," because the body may change "without a change of personal identity."[105] Let us also recall Locke's famous statement that a person is "a thinking intelligent being, that has reason and reflection, and can consider itself as itself, the same thinking thing, in different times and places."[106] Thus, the remembrance of experience as belonging to the same self is paramount to personal identity. Not only that, but by introspection on one's past, we may change our current and future outlook, thus changing our personal identity. This is precisely what we see here: a change in body without a change in self-concept. The seafarer is warning against this non-development, likening the deterioration and death of the body with the death of the self (*ne mid hyge þencan*) if precautions against a static mind are not taken. Finally, it appears that the seafarer relates the thinking mind to the self, and the non-thinking mind the antithesis to a personal self-concept.

Conclusions and the Final Lines of Seaf

The *Seaf* ends in a very similar fashion to *Wan*, in that it caps the discussion of worldly impermanence with a gnomic discussion of an immutable God. Thus, we are told,

> Micel biþ se meotudes egsa for þon hi seo molde oncyrreð;
> se gestaþelade stiþe grundas,
> eorþan sceatas ond uprodor [103a-105b].[107]

The remedy of a stagnant mind (one that does not reach out to anything other than the heroic world), then, is to think on God, because

> Dol biþ se þe him his dryhten ne ondrædeþ; cymeð
> him se dead unþinged.
> Eadig bið se þe eaþmod leofaþ; cymeð him seo ar of
> heofonum.
> Meotod him þæt mod gestaþelað forþon he in his
> meahte gelyfeð.
> Stieran mon sceal strongum mode, ond þaet on
> staþelum healdan,
> ond gewis werum, wisum clæne.
> Scyle monna gehwylc mid gemete healdan
> Wiþ leofne ond wið laþne ***bealo,
> Þeah þe he hine wille fyres fulne ***
> oþþe on bæle forbærnedne,
> his geworhtne wine. Wyrd biþ swiþre,
> meotud meahtigra þonne ænges monnes gehygd.
> Uton we hycan hwær we ham agen

2. Memory and Identity Formation

> ond þonne geþencan hu we þider cumen,
> ond we þonne eac tilien þæt we to moten,
> in þa ecan eadignesse
> þær is lif gelong in lufan dryhtnes,
> hyht in heofonum [106a-122a].[108]

Because of these final lines, there may be a tendency to interpret *Seaf* as a religiously didactic poem, interlaced with heroic idealism (or vice versa); Indeed, past discussions and scholarly debate often took this view, with a primary question being "What then is the answer to the riddle of the seafarer's identity?"[109] Donavin, for instance, has cited the possibility that the *Seaf* could represent a "journey of an individual soul towards heaven," while Whitelock has commented on the possibility that the poem is an allegory, as well, while also stating that we may find in *Seaf* a way in which Anglo-Saxons could change their association with their communities.[110] I also have tried to answer this question of identity and it is this question that has been under scrutiny throughout this section, and as we have discovered, it is not as important to the study of the seafarer's personal identity what his purpose has been throughout the work, but rather the *process* by which he gets to the end-goal. For example, Holton suggests that *Seaf* goes from "chaos to order," or the sea to the "fixity of the heavenly homeland."[111] Whatever the truth here, what we have to understand is that *Seaf* is not simply about a metaphorical (possibly) journey to Heaven, God, or a spiritual life, but it is an actual journey within the mind of the seafarer from a past thing to a present and future thing. That is, a past self-concept or identity (communal-self), with a present self-concept formulation (introspection and questioning of his past identity), to ultimately a future or eventual self-concept (an identity that is predicated on a belief in God). Likewise have other scholars picked up on this process, as Pope says that the literality of the journey is less important than the "voyage undertaken by the speaker as part of his effort to disengage himself from the grip of the phenomenal world."[112] This grip is represented by the early-lamented memories of community in *Seaf*, a tight fetter that keeps a spiritual aspirant away from the joys and peace of the heavenly kingdom. Communal identity, therefore, is seen as a hindrance in *Seaf*, part of an earlier heroic ideal that the seafarer sees as essentially ephemeral, temporary, and unable to provide permanent joy—a sentiment that is related to us in lines 80b-96.

Our conclusions, then, must match the clear message of past and present, the social and individual. The "unifying feature" of *Seaf* is the memory, or "'backward glances' in both halves of the poem," that act as signposts for the audience, offering glimpses of the mind of the seafarer over time.[113] Indeed, Klein has said that *Seaf* "rests poetically upon a recognition of the power of the individual mind."[114] The evidence presented in this study strengthens such a reading, and from what we have discovered, the Anglo-Saxons—in some cases—used their minds to question their idea of selfhood by organizing memories, developing an individual self-concept, and finally embracing a new personal identity quite different from the one that came before. In this way, *Seaf* is demonstrative of the very personal inner life/self-concept of Anglo-Saxons—what they thought about it, why they thought about it, and the very individual process they could embrace to redefine it.

Conclusion: Memory, Self-Concept and Individual Redefinition

An examination of *Wan* and *Seaf* highlights several tropes and themes that occur in much of the extant OE poetry (e.g., the lord/thane relationship, kinsmen, mead-hall revelry); however, it is in the content that lies beneath these highly emotive poems that we discover truly remarkable understandings of what the self, selfhood, personal identity, and self-concept could mean to Anglo-Saxons. Scholarly consensus views these poems as belonging to a small group of OE verse that showcases personal emotion and lamentable circumstances (i.e., elegies), and it is for this reason that *Wan* and *Seaf* are so important in helping to define the Anglo-Saxon self. Antonina Harbus has said that OE elegies have even been considered "the first genuine expression of the Germanic soul," as they all have a "personalised psychological focus," and a mental aspect that "emphasises a personal identity."[115] Indeed, much of what we have discussed throughout this chapter is based on the inner psychology of the wanderer and seafarer, thus revealing the idea of personal identity or self-concept.

For example, a theme permeating both *Wan* and *Seaf* is that of personal transition from one stage to another, related to the audience via the memory of the wanderer/seafarer/narrator. Pope says that both show a poet "who understood the ancient feelings and attitudes of his people and

2. Memory and Identity Formation

also the intellectual and spiritual claims of the new age."[116] Pope's assertion has been demonstrated by the early emotional investment when speaking of communal life in the first half of both works, and contrasted after line 58 in *Wan* where there remains a disassociation from that theme and a movement toward the contemplation of an immutable God. Doubleday is one of many scholars who has commented on this structure, as he notes the distinction "between past events and the present situation [...] correspondingly between joy and sorrow," and the tendency in the elegies for the poet to be "thinking in dichotomies."[117] Partly, this is true; however, it appears that neither *Wan* nor *Seaf* can so easily be split into good and bad, personified by community and exile. In fact, what was at first considered a lamentable situation soon becomes a source of individual power for both the wanderer and seafarer, as contemplation and introspection shed light on the inherent transience of the world and the futility of grasping on to a lord and kinsmen for security. This is evident, even though some have argued that "within the legal and social structure of Anglo-Saxon warrior society, the man without a lord seems to be virtually without an identity; he no longer signifies."[118] This research now invalidates the universality of such statements.

That both the wanderer and the seafarer have so successfully turned their emotional attention away from a community and its corresponding identity, and towards a personal relationship with God, is suggestive by their new identity formation, a *process* that would relinquish the old in favor of the new. Klein has astutely identified this aspect of *Wan* and *Seaf*, as he says these poems are "designed to illustrate the implications of [... and] the sources of human character, and their central concern may be seen as the process of human character itself."[119] Klein's "character" sounds a lot like "identity," and from what we have seen, identity and selfhood are nearly synonymous terms here, changed through a progression of thought within the minds of the wanderer and seafarer. For this reason, Irving has suggested that the "mind as separate from the self ... [is] characteristic of the poem [Wan] as a whole," while Harbus takes a similar stance, adding that the mind "emphasises a personal identity."[120] The mind *does* indeed emphasize identity but in itself cannot be shown to *be* one's identity. The mind simply informs how the self is created, and once it is formed—or indeed fractured from resulting exile or loss—the remaining thing could be considered "the self." We have seen this emphasis in action throughout both poems, as it is through the application of memory that the wanderer and seafarer analyze and emend their self-concept. For instance, the dream sequence in *Wan* is representative of the mental process by which the narrator contemplates his past personal identity, while also detailing the cultural pulse of the heroic world. Stockwell cites a similar and subtle cognitive process in *The Dream of the Rood*, where "the abstractions are not simply made concrete (such as through personification), but are presented with a sensitivity to individual consciousness: the poem directs the listener to listen and see and feel and call to mind familiar homely comforts [...] to map transcendental concepts into the schema of the individual's personal sense of life."[121] Here also do we have abstractions of personified ideas and "familiar homely comforts"—these represented by the sea-birds in *Wan*, gannets in line 20 of *Seaf*, and the early references to community in both, to name a few. Thus, the mind's potency to effect individual change in these works via memory is evident.

We may then conclude that the individual mind in this time functioned in diverse and unique ways. Patrick Geary suggests that the Carolingians used memory as a "political creation in the sense that individuals, groups, and leaders of secular and ecclesiastical institutions and parties sought to use memory as a tool of power," and this is particularly evident as the "tenth century [was] a period during which men and women struggled to impose the inherited order of the old system on a world that increasingly resisted such anachronisms."[122] We see this resistance throughout *Wan* and *Seaf*, as both narrators struggle early on to completely disidentify with an early heroic identity in favor of a new Christian self-concept, thus Geary's broadening of "the definition of memory to include textual transmission as well as oral memorization" is seen in the fact that both poems exist in a manuscript (Exeter Book) that would have been housed in a religious center. That is to say, the undeniable Christian theme of religious security juxtaposed with heroic/pagan turmoil is at once an attempt to supplant the "anachronisms" of the past as well as a blueprint for how social memory—via the wanderer and seafarer's memories of their pasts—could be used as a pedantic device to encourage Christian standards. In other words, it is possible that this was used as propaganda to strengthen the power of Church in the lives of ordinary Anglo-Saxons.

Modern studies into memory confirm this idea of communal influence and motive. LeDoux says that "explicit memories, regardless of their emotional implications, are not carbon copies of the experiences that cre-

2. Memory and Identity Formation

ated them," but they are "reconstructions at the time of recall, and the state of the brain at the time of recall can influence the way in which the withdrawn memory is remembered" since "memory [...] called a cognitive schema [...] includes the expectations and biases of the person doing the remembering."[123] Likewise, Damasio reminds us that "our memories are *prejudiced*, in the full sense of the term, by our past history and beliefs," while it is something within our "brains [that] holds a memory of what went on [...] and the interaction importantly includes our own past, and often the past of our biological species and of our culture."[124] I have already touched upon this idea that the memories of community in *Wan* and *Seaf* are often recalled generally by the narrators, suggesting the influence of these cultural pasts or cultural norms. That is, when speaking in generalities—not explicit memories—both narrators are attempting to reconstruct a social identity that is in line with a past history that nearly all of their contemporaries would have recognized. I am not suggesting that the wanderer or seafarer do not have actual memories of communal life. I still suggest that they, the poet, or both are reconstructing an earlier self-concept, via memory, to the audience. However, we should note how social memory was a force influencing these exiles. It is from the knowledge of this social identity that the narrators were able to describe the anxieties of the exilic life. In fact, our minds still work in this way, where we tend to "see things the way others see them [... to] learn what is normal from others, and [...] thereby partake in a common tradition which stretches back through a chain of generations into a dim past," which is one reason why some researchers "claim that any normal person is historical as a member of a historical community."[125] And it is precisely this idea of historical group membership in *Wan* and *Seaf* that aids in describing, through "storytelling, [and] cultural narratives," the earlier role this association had for the wanderer and seafarer—associations which act as "resources for self-construction."[126] In other words, these narratives are ways in which the self is defined, and in this case, redefined. Pierce puts this another way, saying that the "self is thus both a product and an agent" of communication via an "outreaching identity," meaning that our ideas and thoughts express themselves into the wider community, which is how a social consciousness of a society can remain stable over many generations.[127] A community keeps these general ideas about itself over many years, and this relays to new generations, cycle after cycle. Amazingly, in *Wan* and *Seaf* we find evidence of this process. Thus, *Wan* and *Seaf* benefit as much from a study about the personal self as it does a study on the communal influence on Anglo-Saxons.

We have seen how both the wanderer and seafarer change their sense of personal selfhood, from a communal self-concept, to an individual one predicated on faith and journey to God. However much these characters have changed, they have also retained elements of their earlier identities—this shown by their omniscient position and the use of memory throughout the poems. In this way, we can use the "loose and popular sense of identity" and say that no longer do the wanderer and seafarer emotionally identify with their past self-concepts, but have moved on from them.[128] And from what we have seen, this conceptual change in selfhood occurs over a period of time, aided by memory and introspection. Consequently, we may say with confidence that "the concept of a personal history is intimately associated with the concept of a person," in that "we can think of [...] *personal history* as a process."[129] This research has shown how this process works in *Wan* and *Seaf*, from initial reluctance to let go of a communal self-concept, to memory and introspective analysis of the vagaries of such an identity, to ultimately finding solace in a personal journey to God. In the end, we are left with a model for how the power of memory could aid in the construction of a new self-concept, and have shown that for the wanderer and seafarer, at least, the mind and its processes are ultimately subservient to a self which at once controls, but is also dependent, on it.

3

Living Vicariously and Identity Schema

The Multiple Selves of the Anglo-Saxon Scop

As my study of *Wan* and *Seaf* has shown, a revealing of the Anglo-Saxon personal-self does not occur within a vacuum, but rather is uncovered when viewed in tandem with the communal elements contrasting it; such is the case with identity no matter its guise, and this maxim holds equally true when we consider personal identity in Old English "*scop* poems"—namely, *Deor* and *Widsith*. These poems highlight significant "self-markers," or details in the narrative of the verse that betray and accent both the individual and communal sense-of-self of the poets and their audience. In a complex array of identity pointers, these poems speak to the intricate truths behind how both a communally-held self and individuality functioned in the Late Saxon period, with emphasis given to neither (unlike *Wan* and *Seaf*), but telling of each.[1] Hence, an understanding of the Anglo-Saxon personal-self in these examples requires a critical eye on the narrative of community and the collective schema of self, both of which will reveal not only the form of individuality assumed by the professional poet (oral performer and writer), but also the power these individuals had in their society, precisely because of their autonomy, their cognizance of their own society, and their ability to document their observations. Consequently, the idea of a societal self-schema (or how society as a whole viewed what made up a person) and how that schema is identified and used in the verse will show us how the *scop* was at once an intimate member of his community, but also an active observer, viewing reality from the outside and hence showcasing a strong personal-self. This

A Life Both Public and Private

analysis will show a personal self somewhat distinct from that investigated in the previous chapter, but still very much observable. This chapter therefore focuses on the unconscious group agreement of what a strong identity was in order to isolate the individual and conclude that the Anglo-Saxon *scop* had a strong sense of individuality.

The ubiquity of the *scop* in Anglo-Saxon society need not be questioned, and unfortunately we do not know as much about these people as we would like; nevertheless, scholars have made attempts at understanding the *scop*, and material still exists for us to make use of. Alcuin, for instance, confirms the prevalence of these early minstrels, while Bede's account of Cædmon in his *Ecclesiastical History* highlights the commonality of popular tales sung by both the professional poet and layman; both sources take care to criticize the singing of secular song.[2] For instance, Alcuin warned, "Let the words of God be read when the clergy dine together. It is fitting on such occasions to listen to a reader, not a harper; to the sermons of the Fathers, not the songs of the heathen." And of course, we recall Bede's differentiation between the devotional singing of Cædmon and that of the "frivolous or profane" taught by a "human teacher."[3] The salience for this study lies not in the latter, but the former, wherein we glean song's universality in society—and by extension singers—albeit via the admonition of learned men of the time. Thus, we know that secular storytelling must have been commonplace in the halls and courts of the Anglo-Saxons, and that those who held the title professional singer were probably comparatively few relative to general society; nevertheless, such an association most certainly would have fostered a certain identification with, if not pride in, the role of the poet.[4] To this I later return, but it is sufficient to note that although a regular fixture of secular Anglo-Saxon life, the professional *scop* was anything but an ordinary person, his sense-of-self anything but static. Recent commentary suggests that the *scop* in Anglo-Saxon society was at the very least quite various, owing his unique standing to the dual roles of "entertainer [... and] observer and recorder of important events."[5] Indeed, William Bascom looked at oral narrative and the poet and suggests that both "validate [...] a culture, justifying rituals and institutions to those who perform and observe them." Indeed, "it maintains social control by encouraging conformity to accepted patterns of behavior."[6] Both of these scholars recognize the power of the scop in society—a point that I focus on in more detail below.

3. Living Vicariously and Identity Schema

And while the sparse literary evidence of these professionals verifies these observations in poems like *Deor* and *Widsith* specifically because of their focus on the scop in first-person narration, it is when we more deeply consider the place of the *scop* in society, by looking at their presence and actions exemplified in these poems, that we will come to appreciate the dynamics of self in Anglo-Saxon England. A plethora of Germanic tales and analogues pepper the verse of these two poems, reinforced with first-person narration interacting with these old stories, both of which when combined form a coherent account of how the *scop's* sense of personal-self cohabited and fed off its association with this Germanic past. Roberta Frank has commented on this dynamic, astutely observing that both *Deor* and *Widsith* "introduce a fictive or new character into the known world of legend" and that each "meets and mingles with the heroes of past times."[7] For instance, the name of Heoden's first court poet, who lost his place to Heorrenda, is Deor—a fact that is only mentioned in the Old English elegy. Similarly, Widsith's many "encounters" with heroes of the Germanic past ostensibly place him in the presence of some of the most notable characters of Germanic history, situating him to potentially contribute to the layered history of those eras. Thus, what we find in these poems is an undeniable if subtle comparison between the *scop* as a representative of Anglo-Saxon culture at a particular time, his audience, and their shared communal history.[8] As it has been well established that the audience in an oral tradition contributes to the production of a work, an analysis of this interaction between *scop*, audience, and the societal consensus that follows is the method by which we uncover a personal-self that differs markedly from the individuality-by-denial that we discovered in *Wan* and *Seaf*, but nevertheless an individuality quite manifest in the literature.[9]

The Individual and the Role of Exile in Deor

Þæt ic bi me sylfum secgan wille,
þæt ic hwile wæs Heodeninga scop,
dryhtne dyre; me wæs Deor noma.
ahte ic fela wintra folgað tilne,
holdne hlaford, oþþæt Heorrenda nu,
leoðcræftig monn, londryht geþah
þæt me eorla hleo ær gesealde.
Þæs ofereode; þisses swa mæg! [35a-42b].[10]

A Life Both Public and Private

Thus ends the poem *Deor*, but for the reader this offers a good starting point for our understanding of how the narrator's reflection on those seemingly distanced from him aids in exposing how the concept of the individual—or personal-self—functioned and was constructed on multiple levels. Similarly to *Wan* and *Seaf*, the theme of exile in *Deor* gives us the tools to distinguish the individual from his communal surroundings, though with the motif less explicit in the latter. As we have seen, the exilic state for Anglo-Saxons was among the most unwanted, feared, and forlorn conditions one could experience. It was a state that lent itself to deep introspection and lament in the narrative, which in turn highlights the individuality, or personal-self, that I am interested in. Indeed, for many scholars, *Deor* is a poem that exemplifies this condition of exile, via its many historical references to popular Germanic tales and characters, as well as Deor's exile from his position as *scop* in his lord's court. The mention of Welund in the first stanza exemplifies this, as we learn from Deor that on account of Niðhad having *legde nede* ("laid constraints") on the smith:

> Welund him be wurman wræces cunnade,
> anhydig eorl, earfoþa dreag;
> hæfde him to gesiþþe sorge ond longaþ,
> wintercealde wræce.[11]

For Thomas Tuggle, in Deor's mentioning of Welund's suffering, the "spiritual [...] rather than [the] physical" aspects of the misery experienced are highlighted, and the language highlighting his sorrow and sadness bears this out.[12] Also, that Welund *wræces cunnade* ("suffered/knew exile") "stresses not only the loss of a warm Germanic hearth, but the more dreadful experience of knowing he is an exile."[13] Similarly, Mandel sees the collocation *sorge ond longaþ* as indicative of the "separation of a man from society characteristic of exile."[14] Thus, the situation of exile that Deor finds himself in at the end of the poem is comparative to the Welund episode at the beginning. That is, we are starting to see how Deor "artistically molds traditional examples to fit his own experience," instead of "thoughtlessly allud[ing] to examples of misfortune."[15] On this point, then, we may begin to conclude that Deor is vicariously living through the characters of his Germanic past, assimilating known Germanic tales that coincide with, and as I argue, solicit sympathy for, Deor's situation to which the refrain alludes. Put another way, *Deor* gives us the benefit of looking at the narrator's sense-of-self in addition to that of his characters, whereas

3. Living Vicariously and Identity Schema

in *Wan* and *Seaf*, the spotlight was on the characters' individuality exclusively.

As with the analogue of Welund, Beadohild's story accentuates the deep personal suffering of one who is estranged from her society, showing how Anglo-Saxons related their concept of individual selfhood through their association with the group. Unlike Welund, however, Beadohild's source of pain is less obvious and more internalized, acknowledging how dynamic emotionality was in this period. We are told in lines 8a-11a:

> Beadohilde ne wæs hyre broþra deaþ
> on sefan swa sar swa hyre sylfre þing,
> þæt heo gearolice ongieten hæfde
> þæt heo eacen wæs.[16]

The backstory behind Beadohild's pregnancy comes not in *Deor*, but in the Old Norse *Völundarkviða* centuries later, where we learn that she was in fact raped by Welund, as revenge for her father having imprisoned him, forcing Welund to use his skill to make precious jewels—a fact most certainly familiar to an Anglo-Saxon audience. While there is no certainty, there seems little controversy that a tenth-century audience—or earlier—would have been privy to more information than is presented in the Exeter Book. An Anglo-Saxon audience would not have appreciated the gravity of Beadohild's pregnancy if on the whole this information was not common knowledge. Considering that she was victimized by the man to whom Deor refers in the opening lines of the poem, it seems a near certainty that some semblance of the backstory supplied later in Old Norse was extant in oral tradition at the time of *Deor*'s composition, and perhaps earlier. Whether the audience is listening to an oral poet, or reading the poem in solitude, the audience is something of a co-creator for poetry in how they fill in the gaps of the story in order to find deeper meaning. Therefore, it is from this unsupplied information that we enter the mindset of an audience hearing a *scop* recite *Deor* in a meadhall, who would have immediately sympathized with Beadohild's plight of having been raped by her father's enemy, and effectively birthing a son without a traditional male influence. I should also say that I am not assuming that Deor specifically was recited orally by a *scop*, as there is no direct evidence to support this. It could be that *Deor* comes from an oral work that was once sung and eventually transmitted in the Exeter Book, or it could be that it as a creation of the Exeter Book scribe. This investigation into the personal self of the poet who is represented in this work can still be accomplished regardless, and therefore it is not necessary for this to be decided. Indeed, *Deor* need not have been orally transmitted for this process to work. Any audience, whether listening *or* reading, in groups or alone, would have responded similarly, by the very fact that they were being supplied information about a person to whom they could relate. So the poet tells us that Beadohild "presumably suffers the shame of being seduced and made pregnant by a man enslaved to her father."[17] Thus, as with Welund's story, an exilic situation is the key to uncovering the character's sense-of-self. It is also important to note that exile for the Anglo-Saxons could have been mental, as well as physical. I am here defining exile as *any* condition that sees a person's sense of communal identity weaken due to physical or mental isolation from that community. And for Beadohild, her shame seems to come from being in a mental exile, or indeed leads her to this exile, and is not a physical displacement.[18] Similar to Deor himself in this vein, who is the subject of the last seven lines, Beadohild's situation necessarily sets her at odds with her place in society, at least in her mind. And as with Deor's loss of power and prestige from losing such an honored place to Heorrenda, Beadhohild is forced into a situation of great degradation and mental strife, as her torment caused by an unwanted pregnancy overshadows that precipitated by the killing of her brother.

Regarding this, Condren has rightly pointed out that "her sorrow dates not from the ravishing but from the moment she *perceived* [my emphasis] she was pregnant," lending credence to the observation that Beadohild's sorrow lay not in the physical disrespect shown to her by Welund, but a deep mental anguish that forces her to reassess her place in society.[19] It is precisely her realization that she was pregnant that precipitates her suffering, and not the type of grief inflicted by the loss of a family member. From this we can conclude that the mental anguish caused by grief over loss, while immense, was not as strong as the type that could presumably cause disruption to one's sense of identity. Thus, Beadohild's sense-of-self is entrenched within her role in society—as well as Deor's, as we will see—and her suffering a consequence of that role being threatened. This is quite similar to what we find in *Wan* and *Seaf.* Mandel is right to note that the refrain after this section refers not to the misery caused by the rape or the eventual birth of her son, but "her subsequent unhappiness and specifically her suffering of spirit,"[20] stemming from the victimization, and while this may be an individualized feeling, it also translates to her role in society because she is fearing that this role will be lost

3. Living Vicariously and Identity Schema

or threatened. That is, the *þæs ofereode* in line 13a refers to Beadohild's mental anguish and the consequences of her victimhood, and not the physical actions taken by Welund—the latter, of course, are things that cannot be changed.

Further evidence for the personal-self in *Deor*, via vicarious identification, may be found in the mentioning of Theodric and Eormanric (lines 18a-27b), where exile is not as prominent as above, but the general suffering at the hands of a tyrant—commensurate with the suffering of Deor at the hands of his lord—highlights Deor's self-concept just the same. Not as much as we would like is said about Theodric, only that he *ahte þritig wintra / Mæringa burg. Þæt wæs monegum cuþ*.[21] Whether this section refers to the Ostrogoth or the Frank does not concern us here. Nevertheless, many scholars are in agreement that this division relates to some type of misfortune suffered by Theodric, noting that both he and Eormanric underwent a period of exile, strengthening the argument for communal separation.[22] My sense, however, is to agree with Frankis and Condren, who look upon this section and see "blame" to "tyrannical kings" for the suffering of man, as this would also fit in thematically with Deor's situation at the end of the poem.[23] No matter how we interpret it, in either case both the experience of exile and suffering at the hands of a king apply equally well to Deor's experience of losing his position at Heorrenda's court (exile), at the whim of his lord's decree. Less controversial is the information regarding Eormanric, which is clearly intended to incite an unfavorable opinion of the ruler. We learn of his *wylfenne geþoht* ("wolfish thoughts"), his reputation as a *grim cyning* ("savage king"), and those under his rule who

> Sæt [...] sorgum gebunden,
> wean on wenan, wyscte geneahhe
> þæt þæs cynerices ofercumen wære [24a-26b].[24]

Here we find an explicit mention of exile wholly lacking; however, we do find plenty of evidence for the theme of the victimization of men under a tyrannical lord. The description of Eormanric's rule and the suffering of those under him corresponds to Deor's lost position as honored *scop*, in that happiness of a people or individual is seemingly dependent on the actions of a ruler. Deor's allusion here is an implicit comparison to his own situation, which was artistically done so that his audience's shared sense of Germanic history would naturally come into play as they sympathized with his plight—a very strong example of self-consciousness and audience consideration. In this way, "he makes his own story worthy of a place beside [...] Germanic heroes of antiquity,"[25] providing us a view of how Anglo-Saxons considered their relationship to their forebears, and how Deor as an individual looked upon them to strengthen his sense of personal-identity. All of this leads us to consider Deor's sense-of-self, and how it was an existence strengthened by, if not dependent on, his audience's shared sense of identity.

The Personal-Self and the Reworking of History

While there are a variety of characters in *Deor*, many exhibiting a personal-self to be gleaned from their respective relationship with their community, it is to the fictionalized Deor himself that these identities harken back, revealing a self-concept that existed on multiple levels. For instance, as we look at the Germanic examples in the poem, "'happy' endings" seem to be elusive, although all evidently show "an exemplum of misery overcome."[26] This is equally true in the final few lines, where we are told of Deor's replacement in the court and given the brief refrain that promises relief on at least some emotional level. We can imagine, then, that in oral delivery, Deor's situation could quite possibly have been a current dilemma for a real *scop*, who cited past stories with negative associations to show how a silver lining always exists. This seems reasonable, as we can be relatively certain that an Anglo-Saxon audience would have known—as I have mentioned—the backstory of most if not all of the characters cited. And if this is true, then it would follow that by employing Germanic history with an audience of his peers, Deor is, in effect, relaying to us an almost mystical reality of the retelling of history, in that it had the power to incite sympathy and change minds (i.e., the minds of the audience).[27] Indeed, much has been written on the power and place of the poet in Anglo-Saxon England in this regard. Bloomfield and Dunn claim that stories were social functions, where "praise, blame, instruction, complaint, lamentation, or consolation, is usually expected," and the poet would often inject something new to increase his audience's pleasure.[28] The poet, whether of oral tradition or one who favored the quill, was a "creator [...] of public opinion," retainer of the status quo, and of great value to the community.[29] Perhaps John Niles refers to the poet's power

3. *Living Vicariously and Identity Schema*

and the role of narrative in society the best when he says that poets tended to "be known and honored by name in their communities" since they were the "makers of tradition, not its slaves" and that even though these individuals had a special talent, they should not be looked upon as "isolated geniuses" since they were all "active tradition bearers [who could] only flourish as members of a community of like-minded individuals."[30] Likewise, Bloomfield, Dunn, and Thornbury have all expressed the importance of the poet to the functioning of a healthy community, as it was poetry and the poet during this period that was able to express "the obligation of transmitting tribal wisdom" to the group, was "a way of being in society," and was the way in which "books and people thus join together in a single community."[31]

Deor's dependence on his audience's shared sense of history, in order to define an individual's sense-of-identity in the court, is most salient for this study. For example, many arguments for the referents of the refrain completing each stanza have been introduced, all of which are inconclusive. It seems reasonable, however, that we may safely associate *þæs ofereode* ("this passed away") with its preceding stanza, and *þisses swa mæg* ("so may this") to Deor's lament revealed in lines 35a-42b. If this analysis holds, we may also associate the first demonstrative of the refrain (*þæs*) with the miseries of Deor himself, as his suffering is mentioned through the guise of older heroic stories, while the second pronoun (*þisses*) applies to "any member of the audience" who is hearing/reading the poem.[32] Thus, the referent stories in *Deor* allow the *scop* to "console himself by giving vent to his feelings and hopes."[33] In other words, the confusion within the literature surrounding the ultimate meaning of the refrain is explained in one sense when we see that it works below the level of explicit language. That is, in one way, *Þæs ofereode* refers to the suffering of the specific individual or emotion mentioned in the stanza preceding it, while *þisses swa mæg* is giving a nod to Deor's anguish that he reveals at the end of the poem. However, simultaneously, the former also refers to Deor himself, because the characters cited are simply living analogues of an aspect of Deor's distress, while the latter is meant to appeal to whomever is hearing/reading the poem, as they would have appreciated the Germanic tales while they themselves saw the characters as suffering aspects of their own condition. The complexity of identity and how it works in the sharing of stories is thus made manifest and proves how complex in subtle meaning and profound in thematic colorations Old English literature is.

A Life Both Public and Private

This vicariousness of Deor's identification with his Germanic past has been an interpretation in the literature for some time, but of the interplay we have discussed with his audience, and the importance to his identity, nearly nothing has been said. For instance, referencing the first two strophes, Frankis notes that Deor's conscious use of the histories is not "inartistic," but that he "treats them [the characters] in personal terms, putting himself in the position of the characters of both sides," who are "comparable to [his] own troubles"; still, he does not mention the significance of these histories' ability to define the character of Deor himself.[34] Indeed, the mentioning of the many stories and characters is indicative of Deor's knowledge of his audience's consciousness, a sophistication to know how they would react below the simple level of listening to the story, and a sensitivity to include the audience in the tale if only to garner support for his own cause. This is just another way of saying that literature can affect the reader in ways that she is not consciously aware of. Subtle suggestion in contemporary marketing is a good example of how this works today. And indeed, poetry "effortlessly [has] a heavy cargo of meaning," and "it would be a hardy scholar these days who would claim that all the effects of a given work of art are the product of the conscious intentions of its maker."[35] Thus, and as I discuss below, Deor's (and in many respects, Widsith's) inclusion of a common Germanic past represents an intimate knowledge of a specific self-paradigm, or group schema of identity that is crucial to realizing his personal-identity and that of his audience generally, and the very mentioning of these episodes is evidence of Deor's conscious endeavor to affect his audience. This is absolutely crucial in our discussion of the interplay between the narrator and audience, the personal- and communal-self, and its inclusion by the poet is revealing of an individuality on the part of the *scop*, as his actions assume a division between himself and his contemporaries at large. This division is also addressed below, but at this stage it is enough to note the sensitivity to multiple levels of identity at work in this poem (e.g., Deor's individuality, Deor's recognition of his audience's social consciousness, and Deor's own sense of communal self falling apart), particularly those relating to Deor's individuality and his audience's identification with characters from their past—all of which is revealed via the lens of a shared Germanic history. Thus, if we are to learn about Deor's self-concept, his first-person narration must be seen in tandem with the various references that appear throughout the poem. Indeed, we are reminded that *Deor* is based on "the thoughts of an individual, not

3. Living Vicariously and Identity Schema

a type, [as] it mentions specific names," and just as with *Widsith*, the poet created a fictitious character "only in the imagination."[36] At first glance, these statements seem disparate, but they need not be in competition, since the importance lies not in the truth beyond a particular person called Deor at some point in Anglo-Saxon history, but that the poet had a particular person in mind when he created him and a paradigm for such a person as he composed the complaint. This indicates that an individual such as Deor was present in the consciousness of Anglo-Saxons, and hence we may confidently agree that a person of that model had existed at some point in early English history. Any number of complementary accounts exist in modern fiction, where a character is created of a particular type (police officer, wife, son, teacher, etc.) that reflects the reality of such a person in actual life. This is no different in the writings in the Anglo-Saxon period, generally. An exception could be argued for historical or biblical writings, where no known referent exists that is contemporary with the composition—but in such a case, those characters are undoubtedly colored by the culture that tries to understand them. This final point was especially important in Chapter 1. In these ways, an interplay between scribe/poet, fictionalized character, and audience therefore all come together to reveal the communal and the individual.

Hence, reading *Deor* as an exposition of a specific individual's suffering analogously referred to by known Germanic examples of such suffering, naturally leads us to look at some possible interpretations of the poem and how they reflect Deor's sense-of-self. The two most prominent views in the last hundred years describe *Deor* as either a complaint or consolation, with slight variation.[37] However we see it, though, an analysis of Deor's individuality works just the same. For instance, as a complaint, Deor's account of losing his honored position to Heorrenda can be correspondingly seen in the exilic conditions of Welund and Beadohild, as well as the mention of general suffering at the hands of a tyrannical lord (i.e., the subjects under Eormanric). Correspondingly as a consolatory pattern, *Deor* depicts the strength of the individual mind to overcome suffering in times of strife (e.g., Welund's imprisonment, Beadohild's rape, Theodric's exile or iron-fisted rule, and Deor's own account of suffering). In each instance, no matter how we interpret the general theme of the poem, the refrain can be seen in terms of personal acceptance of the things that one cannot change. This is clearly indicated in lines 28a-35b, which explains the inexorable nature of events out of the control of man:

A Life Both Public and Private

> Siteð sorgcearig sælum bidæled,
> on sefan sweorceð, sylfum þinceð
> þæt sy endeleas earfoða dæl.
> Mæg þonne geþencan þat geond þas woruld
> witig dryhten wendeð geneahhe,
> eorle monegum are gesceawað,
> wislicne blæd, sumum weana dæl [28a-34b].[38]

This is the only mention of God in *Deor*, and unlike *Wan* and *Seaf*, he is seen not as a new focus to attach one's identity to, but this may be seen as a cursory nod describing God's general watch over the events on Earth. In other words, here the emphasis is not on seeking God after calamity, but looking to one's own power for respite (in the form of the refrain), with the simple act of acknowledging that one cannot affect events, but only weather them to the best of their ability. Some scholars think the fatalistic formula of the refrain may be counterbalanced by the "pious acceptance of the divine will," while others see the introduction of the Christian element as the final hope for "happiness altogether away from the material world and toward a blessedness that could only have been reached" at the end of one's life.[39] However God may or may not be invoked in Deor, it is clear that for Deor to approach acceptance of his loss of position, the process was deeply personal and individual. Deor and the characters in the poem all had to come to terms with their loss of self. Thus, contrary to the opinion of some scholars, it is to the individual, not God, to whom we should look in order to find the central power in this poem, an individual who becomes clearer to us when we read the stories mentioned as but elements of Deor's emotional pain, a dialogue between him and his audience. Tuggle, for instance, sees the mention of God here as an acknowledgment of God's better judgment in the lives of men, and Mandel similarly gives a greater role to God, noting that the refrain is used to suggest that it is God alone who allows all hardship to pass away.[40] And while God may be an element of respite for these individuals who have lost some sense of their past selves, the journey of introspection itself is what presents us with their individuality. It is the reflection that is important here, as well as the fact that in the end, there may still be hope that the person may find some semblance of normality within themselves, as they strive to recreate their sense of self. I would also say that the weakness with these readings is that there is no other mention of God in the poem, and what *is* supplied about God only says that he ordains the circumstances of men of the world. That is, God causes events to happen,

3. Living Vicariously and Identity Schema

but it is for man alone to realize that eventually the troubles will pass, since their occurrence is dictated by a force inconceivable by him.

As we have seen, the disparate stories in *Deor* were not intended to form a "continuous or systematic allegory"; instead, each section represents "an isolated aspect of human relationships and misfortune, and tells of a situation parallel to one part of Deor's story."[41] In this way, thematic emotional elements in certain episodes (such as Welund and Beadohild's exile, and the general suffering at the hands of a tyrannical lord, such as Eormanric) not only apply to Deor himself, but also tell us of his feelings toward these situations, and thus shed light on his self-concept. For instance, Deor's relating to a shared past with his audience speaks to the sense of group consciousness that existed between the professional singer and his contemporaries, as the incorporation of this "scop's so-called sampler of random allusions to some of the great moments in the Germanic past" showcases an intimacy between the speaker and hearer, requiring the participation of both parties for any meaningful exchange to take place.[42] Both *Deor* and *Widsith* highlight the "singing of poetry by far-off, fictive Germanic scops," and this should diminish the sense that "an extraordinary solidarity [developed] between narrator and audience" since the audience is deeply involved in the creation and popular reception of the content.[43] Other scholars have commented on this interplay, citing the allusive nature of the stories presented as evidence that they were "still current and presumably well known."[44] In fact, this argument strengthens what we have already mentioned and what Roberta Frank has noted peripherally: that is, that Germanic stories in *Deor* are not simply idle tales, detailed without cause, but that these stories "belong to both the poet and his public," as both "shar[e] in an erudite game of understanding"; Frank also believes that "Germanic legend was something people had to know [...] if they wanted to be thought cultured."[45] I would not only agree, but also suggest that in order for this poem to work, the poet was absolutely depending on his audience's knowledge and their emotional connection to such stories. As with any good writer in the modern world, sensitivity to the audience's sensibilities by delicately employing certain wording has the power to sway opinion in favor of the writer. As I argued earlier, the author's inclusion in this kind of reciprocity demonstrates a very independent talent, a person who could not only share, but also incorporate societal belief in how the self functioned. This sharing, then, signifies what Deor considered salient for his self-concept: mainly that position in society was a force that aided in the perception of one's sense-of-self because this self was strictly a communal one, and therefore to highlight the destruction of such a self, the author is demonstrating his objectifying of what was important for the self-concept in his culture. And while the general thematic momentum of these stories reveals the significance of the group in establishing and maintaining one's identity, we cannot discount the power of the individual, which although subtle, is expressed by the *scop*'s cognizance of his society and his ability to reflect and mold to his will the shared sense of history that contributed to his society's self schema, which is a self that was based on communal values and associations.

The Scop's *Role and the Schema of Self*

As there are no living Anglo-Saxons, and hence we cannot benefit from their reader response to Old English poetry, our understanding of what their paradigm—or schema—of personal identity was must be partly conjecture. However, as the surviving texts act as living witnesses to the period because of their reflection of a culture at a certain time and place, we look to the words, collocations, themes, and tropes to supply what we lack in a living participant. Consequently, any discussion concerning the Anglo-Saxon schema of personal identity and the *scop*'s role in its preservation/dissemination will benefit from at least acknowledging the transmission and composition of Old English poetry. The two main schools of thought regarding oral poetry revolve around a memorial or improvisational oral poetic tradition.[46] Stated briefly, the memorial school argues that orally recited literature depended on the poet's use of paradigms in the form of phrases, syntax, stories, collocations, etc., to provide the "body" for his/her text, while he added material *ad hoc* during a particular delivery. The improvisational hypothesis, on the other hand, would see poetry that does not exhibit "word-for-word or phrase-by-phrase transmission" as indicative of a creation of each subsequent retelling that relies little if at all on an exemplar.[47] In practice, however, most oral poetry consists of a combination of both, and hence Jabbour's terms of "primarily" memorial/improvisational more aptly apply to such poetry.[48]

Thus, and seen as a combination of memorial and improvisational elements, Old English poetry that highlights the *scop* reveals significant

3. Living Vicariously and Identity Schema

details regarding how the poetic artist viewed the world, how he believed his audience related to society, and their comparative similarities. For instance, in *Deor* and *Widsith*, we find a "'primarily memorial'" tradition, which we may deduce from the various formulae, or stock language, that punctuate its lines.[49] In *Deor*, the mentioning of various past heroic peoples (Welund, Beadohild, Eormanric, etc.), irrespective of the particulars of their story, is demonstrative of a such a memorial tradition, in that the poet reciting these stories worked with his knowledgeable audience, who would have had a cultural knowledge of these episodes. Similarly, *Widsith's* exotic account of the itinerant *scop* relating to various ancient rulers like Alexander, Atilla, Caesar, Eormanric and Theodric likewise represents a shared memorial transmission of key themes and ideas that would have allowed for the "filler" information in any redaction subsequently.[50] Magoun also referred to these formulae as significant in that "in the presence of a live audience by means of ready-made phrases," the Anglo-Saxon poet was able to add additional information that, perhaps, applied to that particular time and place.[51] Thus, the formulae of language and themes—such as the mentioning of Germanic heroes, the itinerant *scop*, and the gift-giving ceremonies between Widsith and his patrons—represent an expression of how society actually functioned, or at least how tenth-century Anglo-Saxons imagined the world to function for their ancestors. In other words, discussion of memorial and improvisational verse not only supplies a general theory for how poetry was mentally organized and disseminated, but also how society as a whole related to a particular story over time (memorial) and how both the very poet and his specific audience thought about the details of that story (in the case of the improvisational elements), which would have changed over time, revealing the state of consciousness of Anglo-Saxons at a certain moment.[52] Hence, we need not look far to find examples of this in the literature.

The three *thulas* in *Widsith*, for instance, are representative of such a process. Kemp Malone has argued that the *Widsith* poet did not compose these elements, but that they were part of an older Germanic formula, whose genesis would have emerged in a time prior to the Anglo-Saxon migration to Britain.[53] This hypothesis points to a memorial transmission that acts as a reflection of Anglo-Saxon historical consciousness over time, and hence, Germanic group life in contemporary (tenth-century) Anglo-Saxon society.[54] Put another way, the *thula*, as a representation of the poet's and his audience's understanding of their shared historical legacy, contrasts quite subtly with the individual represented by the character Widsith in the poem. That is, the stock elements of the poem (e.g., the thulas) represent the group-think of communal identity during the time of recording in the Exeter Book, while the specific elements that refer to the individual Widsith tell us of a specific person's relationship to that history, and thus reveal his sense of personal self. For example, in the first thula, Widsith begins by telling us,

> Ic wæs mid Hunum ond mid Hreðgotum,
> mid Sweom ond mid Geatum ond mid Suþdenum.
> Mid Wenlum ic wæs ond mid Wærnum ond mid wicingum.
> Mid Gefþum ic wæs ond mid Winedum ond mid Gefflegum.
> Mid Englum ic wæs ond mid Swæfum ond mid Ænenum.
> Mid Seaxum ic wæs ond [mid] Sycgum ond mid Sweordwerum.
> Mid Hronum ic wæs ond Deanum ond mid
>   Heaþoreamum [57–63b].[55]

The veracity of these statements is not what interests me here, but rather that the poet seems to be "adopting a literary pose for the amusement of his public."[56] For example, modifying language describing any emotional tie to these events is conspicuously absent. The thula is thus a cold description, its purpose unaided by the poet, and its effect on the audience uninfluenced by any artistic flourish provided by the *scop*. Accordingly, the audience's interpretation is hindered in no way, and ostensibly because of the commonality of these themes, it did not have to be. Thus, *Widsith*, similarly to *Wan* and *Sea*, but unlike *Deor*, represents a persona type, and is not intended to reflect a specific individual.[57] However, this is not to say that we cannot look upon Widsith as giving us evidence of a strong sense of personal-self in the Anglo-Saxon period. Both Deor and Widsith, when seen as individuals alongside their communal tropes and apparent audience, reveal a fascinating display of individuality synchronically with their society's self-schema, regardless of whether or not they are representative of a specific person. The character-poets in these two poems need not have been real people. However, it is important to note that these characters acted as tropes of what tenth-century Anglo-Saxons, at the very least, thought their ancestors could have been like, and this representation in the tenth century reflects what an audience at this time felt as important to a person's sense of self. In other words, the Anglo-Saxons at the time of the composition of the Exeter Book held a notion of their society's self-schema, and this schema is represented in

3. Living Vicariously and Identity Schema

the characters in both *Deor* and *Widsith*, as is what these fictional poets thought, and what the other characters in the poems also considered salient to their identities.

An understanding of the self-schema in *Deor* and *Widsith*, then, relies on our understanding of their society's self-script, which was their "socioculturally defined mental protocol" for conceptualizing how their personal identity functioned in their culture.[58] That is, a self-script represents a baseline for how one relates one's sense of identity with one's world. In *Deor* and *Widsith*, for instance, this script is represented by the common elements of communal associations, which not only inhabit these two stories, but also can be found in any number of poems in Old English. Obvious examples include Deor's lament on his current, jobless situation, and the numerous descriptions of how a proper ruler acts in *Widsith*. In the former, Deor's account reveals the importance of station in Anglo-Saxon life as an integral part of one's societal self-concept, while simultaneously providing us with a glimpse of how his very individuality is expressed in the loss of such a position. Similarly in the latter, Widsith details the proper warrior/ruler trope (as in the example of Offa—*geslog / ærest monna, cnihtwesende, cynerica mæst*)[59]—alongside his individual thoughts of his world's exaltation of such qualities:

> Swa ic geondferde fela fremdra londa
> geond ginne grund. Godes ond yfles
> þær ic cunnade cnosle bidæled,
> freomægum feor folgade wide.
> Forþon ic mæg singan ond secgan spell,
> mænan fore mengo in meoduhealle
> hu me cynegode cystum dohten [50a-56b].[60]

In both of these examples, the communal self-script is evident in the various descriptions of communal elements that can be said to house one's sense-of-self, while additionally providing us the benefit of showcasing a specific individual's understanding of those elements. That is, the self-concept of both Deor and Widsith is found by looking at the descriptions of their culture's values of group identity and shared historical knowledge base that ostensibly hides any sense of individualism. Thus, both *Deor* and *Widsith* showcase an interplay on multiple levels that gives us a vision of Anglo-Saxons' general concept of identity, as well as a more intimate look at specific individuals' self-concepts. Furthermore, that these poems may have once been delivered orally only solidifies my theory that the

A Life Both Public and Private

interaction between poet, audience, and content all work in tandem to help us identify a unique self-concept on the part of the *scop* via the use of his society's schema in the texts. In other words, the very fact that the scop is conscious of his society's communal self-schema means that he is objectifying it; he is outside of it.

The possible oral nature of *Deor* and *Widsith*, then, necessarily describes the *scop's* responding to, and awareness of, his audience's shared sense of identity and what they considered salient to that identity. And even if there was no oral tradition attached to these poems, the fictive characters reflect this importance on a tenth-century audience at the least. Hence, to say that "literature is a heteronomous object, existing only when activated and engaged by the animating consciousness of the reader"—or listener, in this case—offers us a fascinating glimpse into the inner world of everyday Anglo-Saxons while also providing insight into the individuality of the verse-performers themselves.[61] Consequently, to look at the content of *Deor* and *Widsith* is to learn of the most general concepts of self to the majority of Anglo-Saxons (shown by schema reinforcing language) and the individualized outlook on that society (by reading how fictional characters like Deor and Widsith emotionalized and/or described that reality). Thus, the schema preserving and schema reinforcing language in these poems is not only contrasted by the mentioning of specific people who have a view of their society's self-schema—in the instance of the *scop*—but also by our knowledge that these poems were quite possibly performed by people who identified themselves as professional singers, and who would have identified with the character poets in the verse.[62] Indeed, schema preserving language confirms existing schemas in society that have been encountered before (a general theme of exile from one's community as a lamentable situation would be an example), while schema reinforcement "strengthen[s] and confirm[s] schematic knowledge" by adding new knowledge or information to a schema (any improvisational poetic information added to a memorial tradition).[63] Thus, that "schemas belong to people not texts" shows the ability of Old English literature—and indeed all literature—to provide the mirror by which society is reflected.[64] And in this case, the mirror reflects tenth-century Anglo-Saxons' schema of their sense of self, that of their forebears, or both.

This function of poetry to reflect the sense of personal self in society, then, is never exercised in a vacuum, but only by acknowledging its opposite is it highlighted. As Guy Cook states succinctly: "'the essence of

3. Living Vicariously and Identity Schema

schema theory is that discourse proceeds and achieves coherence by successfully locating the unexpected within the framework of expectations."[65] In this way, the *scop's* very expression of individuality works as a schema disrupting device to some extent, challenging the communal identity schema by contrasting those elements throughout *Deor* and *Widsith* with the background of social identity constituents.[66] That is, when we read of the loss of identity for Deor, for instance, we are simultaneously witnessing the contrastive elements of the social self within the characters. Hence, the power of the written word and oral tradition in the Anglo-Saxon period should not be understated, as schema disruption is necessary in discourse in order for "schema refreshment and "cognitive change" in a society to take place.[67] In other words, language—whether it be oral or written—has the power to induce a change and also demonstrate contemporary thoughts on societal beliefs over time, in a culture that sees the written word as primarily communicative; and in this present analysis, we are witnessing how this works in action.[68] We have already seen the change of self-concept in *Wan* and *Sea*, but there are plenty of other examples in the corpus—much of which I explored in Chapter 1 and will further look at in Chapter 4. For instance, Antonina Harbus agrees that there appears to be "the existence of a culturally specific self schema in Anglo-Saxon England which acknowledged an individualistic inner self rather than a more "collective" self," exemplified in ll. 70a-78a of *Resignation B*:

> hwæþre ic me ealles þæs ellen wylle
> habban ond hlyhhan ond me hyhtan to,
> frætwian mec on ferðweg ond fundian
> sylf to þam siþe þe ic asettan sceal,
> gæst gearwian, ond me þæt eal for gode þolian
> bliþe mode, nu ic gebunden eom
> fæste in minum ferþe. Huru me frea witeð
> sume þara synna þe ic me sylf ne conn
> ongietan gleawlice [70a-78a].[69]

This section of the poem does indeed show a clear distinction between the soul and some form of an inner self that is distinct from its role in society. The personal-self here displays the same strong personal will that we witness in *Wan* that leads one on the path toward God. However, Harbus' use of the word "rather" implies a one-or-the-other segregated outlook that would exclude one in favor of another. In *Deor* and *Widsith*, at least, this personal-self exists precisely *because* of its obvious disassociation with this more "collective self"—indeed, as "characters are figures against the ground of their settings"; in fact, this "ground" is the schema of self that is communal, and is the foreground against which the personal-self can be found, not vice versa.⁷⁰ Both the individual and communal aspects of self work in tandem here, representing the figure and ground, respectively, allowing us to identify the schema of the collective self, the *scop's* role in describing it, and the individualism he expressed because of his loss, and highlighting, of it.

The Power of the Scop *in Society as an Expression of a Personal Self*

As I have shown, one of the roles of the *scop*—highlighted particularly in *Deor* and *Widsith*—was to express the group consciousness of their society's schema of self; however, this very expression also provides us with a way of understanding and witnessing the *scop's* personal self or individual self-concept. On the surface of things, it would appear that for the *scop*, "[the] most immediate goal" was to "acquire and keep a generous patron."⁷¹ Read thus, and as I have already explored, the personal self of Deor and Widsith would appear to be dependent on their station and place within society, and so conforms to the general themes of the communal self-schema set out in both poems. In *Deor*, for instance, this is explicitly stated in the final stanza, as the *scop's* identity is weakened nearly to non-existence via the whims of his lord (e.g., *me wæs Deor noma*). Likewise, in *Widsith*, the various descriptions of gift-giving pervade the poem and act as a function of the *scop's* association with his world.⁷² However, these descriptions of the communal aspects of the Anglo-Saxon self by a *scop* whose self-concept is ostensibly entwined within these images reveals the power and hence the individualism of the professional poet. For instance, the *scopas* in these poems express much more than general themes of community, artistically rendered within the backdrop of a fictional character. The highlighting of his society's concept of self displays a sensitivity that concretely presents the *scop* as one who "preserves the culture and personalities of his society," and is a "vocal conscience of the community," a "guardian of community," and was a "moral rudder" for his society; thus, the poet's influence and power in society was "substantial," and we are beginning to get a clearer picture of the *scop's* sense of individuality from this clarity.⁷³

3. Living Vicariously and Identity Schema

This power of the professional singer is clearly expressed in what Stephen Evans views as the primary role of the *scop*: to promote the "status of his lord."[74] Numerous occasions in *Widsith*, for instance, would support this idea, but perhaps the most explicit reference lies in the final nine lines:

> Swa scriþende gesceapum hweorfað
> gleomen gumena geond grunda fela,
> þearfe secgað, þoncword sprecaþ,
> simle suð oþþe norð sumne gemetað
> gydda gleawne, geofum unhneawne,
> se þe fore duguþe wile dom aræran,
> eorlscipe æfnan, oþþæt eal scæceð,
> leoht ond lif somod; lof se gewyrceð,
> hafað under heofonum heahfæstne dom [135a-144b].[75]

Here clearly we find reference to the *scop's* ability to mold public opinion. For example, of this historical era, it is said that both "honour and shame were of essence public" and the "publicizing of reputations was thus essential [...] and the preeminent mode of publication was praise and satire in poetry."[76] The *scop's* business then, was in the "entertaining [of the] chief and his warrior-band with song and story" of common themes of community and group identity; this reveals the poet's sovereignty over how he shared the subject with his audience, since, as "the only historian among the early Anglo-Saxons," he "embodied their history."[77] We are reminded that the poets' power in their society came also from their roles "as the discoverers, preservers, and transmitters of wisdom," who have the ability to "hold the bonds of society together."[78] Thus, the *scop* was potentially a threat in as much as he could secure public opinion through the alchemy of both story and his audience's consciousness.[79] The poet often modeled morality, which took the "function of social control," while having the power to "emulate the positive" while "scorn[ing] the negative" values in his society."[80] Because of this, the *scop* was uniquely able to highlight the "quiet objectivity which rules people's lives" by "boasting," and using "comparisons of merit" that were "demanded by a sense of public honor."[81] That is to say, Widsith's highlighting a story which he knew his audience would share a response to solidifies his place as simultaneously part of, and distant from, the very self-identifiers detailed in the poetry. Additionally, in that the *scop* was arguably the most accessible source of history to the laymen, he was, in essence, telling his audience what to believe, molding in their minds the material which he felt significant, and ultimately, influencing their very identities with these stories—not unlike modern newspapers/news broadcasts.

The *scop's* exalted position in the various courts (e.g., moving about without any "loss of prestige") as described in *Widsith*, was "probably due in part to the fact that the singer exerted a powerful influence upon public opinion."[82] Hence, that special consideration was given to this vocation details the importance of the written and spoken word in this period, and during the time of documentation. We are finding in *Deor* and *Widsith*—and in Old English literature more generally—that its "creation, as well as its ceremonial declamation (e.g., recitation in the meadhall) were functions of the communal life, and contributed to the consciousness of tribal cohesion and identity."[83] Additional evidence of this is manifested in *Maxims I*, where we read

> Muþa gehwylc mete þearf; mæl sceolon tidum gongan.
> Gold geriseþ on guman sweorde,
> sellic sigesceorp, sinc on cwene,
> god scop gumum.[84]

Here we are shown standard associations of daily life; that is, the need to eat is as natural as associating swords with warriors, ornaments with the nobility, and a learned poet for the benefit of all men. Consequently, the *scop*, both in fictive form and his presence in history, highlights the imperative function these professionals discharged in order to preserve in their society a shared historical sense of identity that was defined, molded, and disseminated by the very actors who were both members of, but more importantly individually distinct from, their respective communities. This is evident in their consciousness of their communities' self-schema in both poems, and by the removal of the narrator's identity in *Deor*. There is some uncertainty, and Roberta Frank makes an interesting comparison when she says that "the search for the Anglo-Saxon oral poet is at least as frustrating as looking for traces of Anglo-Saxon domestic architecture: of course they had houses, and possibly these structures were among the most perfect achievements of the age; but almost all were built of wood and, unlike stone churches, have vanished."[85]

We have seen that *Deor* and *Widsith*, and indeed the characters that are associated with them, existed in a complex world of selfhood multiplicity, where the interplay between communal identity and a shared historical past shines light on an individuality expressed by the *scopas* that is often subtle but becomes manifest through analysis. That the vast majority of Old English poetry must have been orally transmitted in the first

3. *Living Vicariously and Identity Schema*

instance is the scholarly consensus and should add credence, if not certainty, to the notion that the *scop*'s presence in the poetry and implied presence outside of it, highlights his own self-concept as distinct from that of his community. This is because an oral poet reveals an introspective state that necessarily placed him outside of his society as an observer, providing us with a deep insight regarding how professional singers may have associated with and viewed their world, culture, and their communities' self-schema. Indeed, even if neither of these poems were not orally performed, this analysis still holds as an example of how a particular person felt about the schema of self at a certain place and time. If *Deor* and *Widsith* exist only as a creation of a tenth-century poet, then his characters reflect what he considered salient to his contemporary culture; if these poems were recreated stories from an older oral tradition—and I believe they were—then the same conclusions are valid. A firm stance in this matter is therefore not needed for this analysis. And indeed, both the fictional poets in these poems, and certainly the scribes/poets that recorded them must have viewed their society under the lens of communalism, the person's sense of self interlocked with their roles in society, and as we see in *Deor*, their happiness was dependent on that identity. In *Widsith*, for instance, "the main narrative seems to be of two kinds, the details of personal experience, and the enumeration of peoples and rulers."[86] A duality thus pervades this study, and can be associated with memorial vs. improvisational elements of oral delivery or the schema reinforcing/schema disrupting associations that I looked at earlier. In both cases, we find clear divisions between the communal and subjective sense-of-self—revealed as the communal and personal aspects of self in the former, and the intimate sensitivity with those concepts on the part of the *scop* in the latter. Hence, the *scop* exercised a mental dominion and exerted a tremendous power over his society, and displayed an individuality that was distinct from that of his peers, reflected in the ways he related to his world, described his culture, and identified his fellow men and women with strong communal identities. His stories were manifestations of his own self-concept and his beliefs about his culture. In this way, *Deor* and *Widsith* are an invaluable resource for the understanding of both an individual sense of identity and the communal schema of self in the Anglo-Saxon period, and the preeminent position of the *scop* in society is testament to the relatively scarce—but nevertheless, present—nature of the personal-self in the literature.

⸺ 4 ⸺

A Case for Female Individuality in *The Wife's Lament* and *Wulf and Eadwacer*

> A single individual, especially a woman, could not in Anglo-Saxon society live one's life as if the person were an autonomous being. Indeed, autonomy was then, as for the English opinion through the time of Shakespeare, an ideal only for the ambitiously demonic. No creature could thus declare his or her independence from kin and society or from their social forms and ritual: the individual must subordinate himself to the societal role.[1]

This quote is representative of the past scholarly consensus concerning Anglo-Saxon female individuality. I do not believe such an argument can be sustained, and hence it is precisely this supposition that I have been arguing against in the last three chapters—focusing primarily on men as yet; however, any treatment of the Anglo-Saxon inner world must also include a thorough comparative analysis of women, so that we may in the literature uncover exemplars of the personal-self, discover gender differences, and discover the autonomous mental human being in a sea of communal identities and societal roles. These paradigms of the personal self in Anglo-Saxon poetry are not confined to conjecture—an academic amusement sans evidence—but can be found in all of the poetry investigated until now, manifesting in diverse variety. Indeed, *Wan*, *Seaf*, *Widsith*, and *Deor* are ideal examples of poetry that betray the individual cognitive outlook of Anglo-Saxon men, in tropes both grandly outrageous—as with saw in *Widsith*—and relatively banal. Still, there is work to be done to discover if and how high individuality functioned for Anglo-Saxon women, with the final goal a comparison between the genders, which will detail a kind of roadmap of self in the Anglo-Saxon period more generally.²

Questioning past adages in the discourse of the Anglo-Saxon female self, while simultaneously bringing in new investigations, is necessary. Former appraisal of the female self in Old English poetry has often concluded with a position that touts a binary gender division of the weak woman/strong man, leaving no room for "alternative constructions of female (or male) identity."³ There is no doubt that such a limited stance not only denies an autonomous inner life for women (and men, for that matter), bolstering antiquated research that the heroic world and an individualistic self-concept were incompatible, but also suggests a kind of personal-self-fatalism that would see any autonomy exclusively through the lens of the heroic code and thus destroy the notion of individuality for women before it ever gains a foothold in the analysis. So, to expand our understanding of the Anglo-Saxon woman, I will look toward a feminist approach to the literature, which seeks to uncover "self-identity and psychological autonomy for women," while simultaneously appreciating their communal associations and the social strata of the heroic world.⁴

Recent years have been witness to growing scholarship that gives prospect to a highly individual voice for Anglo-Saxon women. Edith Williams' comment that an Anglo-Saxon woman was "a psychological entity" and a "spirited individual"⁵ generalizes nicely this scholarship that highlights the independent nature of these women, questioning past years and the painting of the pre–Conquest woman as a "passive, peaceful, and colorless addition to society."⁶ Just a cursory look at women in Old English poetry (e.g., Juliana, Judith, Elene, and Hildeburh, for instance) attests to the falsity of the supposedly exclusive passivity, peacefulness, and colorlessness identity markers of the female character trope. In fact, it is by means of the deviation from an identity schema based entirely on community that we come closer to a true Anglo-Saxon female identity.⁷ It has thus been said that "on a very general level, identity is the idea of a self separated from individuals surrounding us"; Dr. Astrom also claims that a cultural identity is something to which "an individual either belongs, or does not," and I am in agreement, generally, but the normal self-reference in society (certainly in cultures that are more tribal than post-industrial ones) is nearly always based on one's culture, her position in society, and the general communal paradigms of identity (schema).⁸

4. A Case for Female Individuality

Hence, my argument is that once we cease to belong to a community that harbored most of our sense-of-self, there is a fundamental shift in identity and a chance for the researcher to "see" this very personal and intimate change of the psychological self via the narrative descriptions of emotion. The way this is portrayed in Old English literature tells us two things: how important communal identity was to Anglo-Saxons, and whether or not individuals had the ability to psychologically "survive" this loss of self and display their inherent autonomy. So far we have seen that this was certainly possible.[9] However, more often than not, identity (especially in the Anglo-Saxon period) most often reflects communal associations, to which one belongs or contributes. This "baseline" identity, once it is in flux by the whims of circumstance (as it is in the exilic state, for example) crushes one's center of reference, resulting in an existential identity crisis. This is clearly evidenced in *Wan* and *Seaf*, for example, where the narrators' sense-of-self changes from the communal baseline to the very personal, autonomous self that emerges *from necessity*. The extent to which we may identify a similar process in the female psyche, and thus discover if an autonomous personal-self similar to her male contemporaries existed in Anglo-Saxon culture, is precisely my goal in this chapter.

The current chapter will approach this question systematically, in order that we may first partition personal and/or communal identity for Anglo-Saxon women, then analyze the data to conclude if, how, and when a type of personal-self existed for Anglo-Saxon women in the literature. Thus, my investigation will begin with a brief overview of the general perception of Anglo-Saxon women in the scholarship, so that the commonly held academic view is given its proper consideration. Next, I will move on to a more pointed and focused discussion of how the female voice in Old English elegies has been considered by scholars and what this means for our study into the concept of the personal-self and individual autonomy. These overviews will then be compared with textual criticism of *The Wife's Lament* and *Wulf and Eadwacer*, which are the only two gendered Old English poems in the female voice—and thus the reason I chose them for this analysis—in order that we may find disagreement or affinity with what has been noted previously by scholars. Finally, I will consider a few of the expressions of the female voice, in order to analyze how the self is expressed (or not expressed).

A Life Both Public and Private

The Status of Anglo-Saxon Women in Scholarly Discourse on the Self

The scope that has been given to the female personal-self in Anglo-Saxon studies varies considerably, with emphasis ranging from the perfunctorily superficial to the wholly neglected, with the question of self often avoided in favor of the more accessible discussion of the general status of women in society. For instance, scholars are in a general agreement that the status of women in the Anglo-Saxon period appears to have been on the whole in a type of stasis. Elizabeth Judd even goes so far as to argue that "a rough equality between the sexes seems to have prevailed" over the majority of centuries, and that the potential for "the improving status of women joins such factors as secularism, individualism, and scientism."[10] If it is true that a stasis existed, at the least, then we must ask why that would be the case—and individualism is the key. If Anglo-Saxon women were unable to express any form of individualism, or identify with a personal self-concept even if only slightly removed from communal associations, then a centuries-long statis of identity would not have been possible, since it is when there is no outlet for individuality that we see conflict with the status quo in societies, often in the form of political movements and uprisings. Indeed, rather than a negative, a stasis in identity in fact equates to having a positive sense of individualism, a psychologically powerful motivator that allows for freedom of mind even in the midst of confined subjugation (at the extreme) or existing in relative social obscurity (as with "rough equality"). For example, this would help explain the assertion of some scholars, for instance, that the rise of the Christian bureaucracy in Anglo-Saxon England, and for centuries afterward, hindered women's self-expression, and thus contributed to a decline in women's status in society more generally; that is, a possibility is that individual self-expression was not given the freedom that it had previously, and this emotional constraint manifested in an overt experience of inequality. The notion of the rise of Christianity and its influence on the psyche of Anglo-Saxon women is a significant study on its own, and can only be hinted at here. I have introduced it only to advance the possibility that it might have been a causative factor in limiting female self-expression over time.[11]

It would seem logical, then, that we would look to poems composed contemporaneously to prove a test for how status, and by extension, selfhood, manifested in society. Indeed, with the use of formulaic words,

4. A Case for Female Individuality

phrases, situations, etc., Old English poetry "encoded [...] cultural data" that "existed within the shared cultural knowledge of composer and audience and did not need full description to become present to both"; in fact, Belanoff also argues that "we read individual Old English poems and understand their characters [...] best against the background of all Old English poetry since this background enables us to approximate [...] the requisite cultural and poetic knowledge embedded in the traditional language."[12] These data represent the schema of identity in a particular group (see Chapter 3) and inform us of societal norms at a certain time and place. Apropos of *The Wife's Lament* and *Wulf and Eadwacer* (hereafter *Wife* and *Wulf*), some scholars have even argued that cultural anxieties about women may have been at the fore as embedded "cultural knowledge" during composition. Shari Horner and Helene Scheck propose complementary arguments, claiming that as a "movement toward strict active enclosure [for female religious] may well have prompted the composition of these poems" (*Wife* and *Wulf*) and perhaps they "express[ed] male anxiety about the need for female enclosure [... or] female anxiety about enclosure."[13] Enclosure was a "masculine attempt to regulate and silence the feminine articulation of self."[14] Whether or not the specifics of the argument are true is irrelevant to the discussion at hand, which is to say that these poems, regardless of exactly *what* anxieties they represent, are at least symbolic in some fashion of real situations in the lives of women. Belanoff's position is thus a contraposition regarding Cynewulf's Juliana, where one argument suggests a rejecting of "the values of a heroic society, setting [Juliana] outside secular structures of power."[15] It has also been suggested that as monasteries lost their high status over time (where women could play quite important roles), this "impinged on the role of women in the church," and hence society at large. In this way, the rise of a state bureaucracy is a causative factor in the loss of human individuality—or at least mutes its ambitions; this notion can be found in political rhetoric in the early-modern and contemporary era (Locke, Rousseau, Hobbes, etc.).[16] One may then argue that this hypothesis would *ipso facto* see the heroic style and secular language as a hindrance in the representation of an Anglo-Saxon woman's sense of individuality, since it would naturally show a patriarchal worldview in poetry: Juliana's individualism was possible precisely *because* of this lack of heroic language. This argument is not entirely convincing, however, as we will see below: more heroic language does not necessarily equate to less individuality, or its opposite

A Life Both Public and Private

does not necessarily mean more female power in society; literature was and is a written representation of how a society thinks and feels about many things that are important in its culture.

Situations in which women find themselves in Old English poetry provide insight into how their sense-of-self was created and/or sustained. Scheck posits that "the woman bereft of her husband is just as lost as the warrior without his lord—a parallel that implies the impossibility or unacceptability of female autonomy."[17] And while the first part of this analysis juxtaposes men and women, and a major situational source of anxiety for both in the Anglo-Saxon period, to claim that a woman anxious over the loss of a husband necessarily implies that she can have no sense of autonomy—and presumably a man without his lord similarly prohibited from a sense of individuality—must be seen as false.[18] On the contrary, a study of *Wan* and *Seaf* has already shown the complete opposite to be true (at least with men), as when the loss of one's center of self-reference is taken away, one must adapt to form a new center, and the wanderer and seafarer formed their new self-paradigms based on a strong sense of autonomy that arguably never would have formed without the agitating catalyst of exile (the schema-disrupting device I mentioned earlier). Another analysis suggests that the voicing of female suffering in the elegies emphasizes "human pain and weakness," since "women were never part of the system."[19] This posits that to lament equates to playing a subordinate or peripheral role in society, whereas we already know that Old English elegies are rife with male exemplars of lamentation over the loss of community—and no Anglo-Saxon scholar would suggest that men played a limited role in their society. I suggest, then, that we may benefit not only by looking at the differences in thematic lamentation by men and women, but also by looking to the similarities which would accentuate any common denominator, that we may begin to compare the personal-self and individualism between the genders. For instance, it is not only that the women in *Wife* and *Wulf* "represent their exile by defining their situation within their marriages," but also that they feel a "cultural 'exile' [...] from the center of power and the central sources of identity in [their] culture."[20] Just as the wanderer, seafarer, and the *scop* Deor lament the loss of their centers of identity (the lord-thane relationship), so do the female characters bemoan their corresponding central self-markers. One is not better or superior than the other—they are simply different. Indeed, the female voice has been said to be inherently powerful, albeit in a different way

4. A Case for Female Individuality

than overt physical actions, as women seem to have had the duty to "'remember and remind' their respective societies of the obligation to live the heroic code of taking up arms and revenge."[21] Such a function is quite similar to the role and power inherent in the male *scopas*, where the duty to report societal norms in a primarily oral society fundamentally displays the importance of such a person in that society. Hence, the puissance of the female voice is not to be underestimated, but appreciated and understood in order to discover its function in the corpus and what is says about the female personal-self.

The Female Voice in the Elegies

Of chief concern as it applies to the female voice is the degree to which the subject matter either retains schema-reinforcing female stereotypes, or, alternatively, schema-disrupting literary devices/themes that would facilitate an inquiry into the female self. In other words, does female narration in Old English poetry always preserve the typical of "men of action" and "women of emotion" characterization, or do we find at times this is perhaps falsely attributed?[22] The remainder of this chapter seeks to answer these questions and to investigate a female sense of individuality, personal autonomy, and self. But to associate emotion with weakness or a lower status than action is untenable, since there are more examples of male emotional lament in Old English poetry than those from women. As we have seen, also, emotion in narration allows us to investigate the self more fully, as well as to discover any deviations from communal self-schema of identity. By their very nature as texts from an age that cannot be seen as socially progressive, Anglo-Saxon historical sources do not often question gender stereotypes, but primarily reinforce those that are most salient and conspicuous, buttressing the general status of subordinate gender positioning and dichotomous social standing that is ostensibly based on the heroic code of Early Medieval Germanic society. The view that would see the *geomuru ides* ("sad woman") as "the dominant female stereotype in Old English heroic poetry" is not uncommonly held, or even entirely unfounded.[23] The Anglo-Saxon feminine self could be said to be almost entirely indebted to its communal associations—if representations of women in the corpus were exclusively of this sort. But of course they are not, since the mournful woman juxtaposed with heroic language is only one example of female characterization in the literature. Strong women of action and/or women who are not weeping emotional stereotypes appear throughout Old English literature, including heroic poetry; for example, Wealhtheow, Judith, and Juliana. However, those who would argue for a stereotype of the Anglo-Saxon woman as a *geomuru ides* with support from the elegies would be mistaken, for the elegies can tell us something quite different.

We have already discussed how the elegies showcase emotion just as much for men as they do for women, and therefore to exclude men and somehow see them as "above" the vagaries of a doleful mood in Anglo-Saxon society would be erroneous. For both genders, emotional narration furnishes us with deep insight into the most intimate beliefs about society and self. The female lament is rich with important commentary about a woman's role in society, and also her self-concept as it corresponds (or not) to that role. It is therefore of considerable significance to realize that elegies "are backward looking [... from a] favourable past [... to an] unhappy present."[24] Thus, nostalgic lament thrives when the present is "deficient" in some way; "For human existence and experience, then, nostalgia is a familiar, collective, and prominent state [... that is] culturally, ethnically, chronologically, and geographically specific."[25] The implications of this astute observation are that cultures esteem nostalgic sentiments based on their own value system. Hence, nostalgia over a lost past that is based within a communal structure (e.g., a marriage or a lord-thane relationship) exposes the value that society places on that paradigm as a form of self-identification.[26] We should also take care to note that we are being told what was *not* important in society. Physical beauty, for example, "is not explicitly relevant to their [women's] place in society or to the themes of the literature," it was actions that designated status in the literature and revealed a portrait of self in a certain group.[27] Accordingly, a loss of this type of communal identification would be unappealing, since it is antiparadigmatic and challenges general notions of normality and selfhood. Put another way: "nostalgia involves both the individual, and the larger societal group/s (variously defined) within which the nostalgic individual participates. This duality primarily stems from societies' determinations and prescriptions regarding the socially acceptable individual expression of nostalgic sentiments [... while] societal expectations and interests propagate nostalgia, since societies dictate what appropriate and approved subjects of nostalgia are."[28] A typified female characterization in the elegies

4. A Case for Female Individuality

that centers on "psychological realism" with "an interest in persons as individuals apart from their functions as members of a group" is of high interest because of its contiguity with the very contrary notions of group identification and communal conventionality.[29]

In the elegies, this kind of structure is expressed and "denotes [the narrator's] identity in the social framework of Anglo-Saxon culture," since a past sense of communal identity is differentiated from the "new present" of individuality in its expression of the pain of being outside one's center of self-reference.[30] Thus, this communal center appears in the literature as the predominant, but not exclusive, image of the female exile, since Old English poetry "encoded" Anglo-Saxon "cultural data" by using formulaic words, specific phrases and situations, etc., which shows that these "images existed within the shared cultural knowledge of composer and audience and did not need full description to become present to both."[31] And so it is that both the communal *and* individual are expressed in the female-voiced elegies, precisely because both were salient to Anglo-Saxon society and known to the audience as illustrative models of life in Saxon England. I would argue that this is also what we find when we read about men. It would seem that the "heroic ethos" works in tandem with emotional language to "comprise the world view" in its totality.[32] An understanding of the personal-self of women in the Anglo-Saxon period then benefits from an inquiry into the gender of the speaker(s), so that a comparison of the salient themes of identity may be made between a female narration that is ostensibly—if not actually—from a woman (gendered), or a female voice that is inarguably from a man (genderized), the former recognized when we read a female narrator speaking for herself, while the latter is identified when the narrator is telling about what a woman said or did, even if the woman is speaking in the first person.

Gendered vs. Genderized Female Narration

There is still often and has been in the scholarly discourse of Anglo-Saxon studies a tendency to relegate a discussion of narration to the banal paradigmatic notion of an entirely male-authored, and thus male-centric, view of the world; this assumption has in recent decades begun to be questioned. Gone are the days where scholars must blindly accept that "all female words expressing grief are filtered through the undeniably male voice of a narrator," or whose "'lyric cries' are 'put in the mouths of women.'"[33] The issue is not purely academic, but it has to be addressed if we are to make a distinction between the gendered and genderized voices of women in the corpus. Indeed, it has been said that the gender of the author is unimportant in anonymous texts, but the "gender of the speaker becomes all-important."[34] Similarly, a question asked by some scholars is whether or not we need to "prove or assume female authorship in order to read these poems as expressions of women's interests."[35] The value of the former is in its suggestion that determining a narration to be either male or female contributes to its overall picture of gender differences in Anglo-Saxon society, while in the latter it is assumed that even if entirely created by a man, a genderized female voice still tells us something about women's interests in ages past. However, these statements are incomplete and only of partial value, since both assume either a nil, or imperceptible difference in tone and theme whether the narration be gendered or genderized. A modern example would be that of a male novelist who creates a female character from his own knowledge and experience, compared with a female novelist who writes a woman's narration from personal experience. We will perhaps never know if the female narrations in the elegies were composed by women themselves, by men who had heard a woman tell the story, or entirely created by a man. I am questioning whether or not there is a difference in the conceptualization of self in those that are genderized (e.g., *Judith*, *Juliana*, and *Elene*—some of which were discussed in Chapter 1), compared to gendered narration (*Wife* and *Wulf*). Part of this investigation, therefore, seeks to uncover whether or not female narration ostensibly "authored" in some way by a woman (which I will refer to as "gendered") reveals more or less individualism, autonomy, and a personal-self—at least partially removed from communal associations—than one which makes no pretense of female authorship ("genderized" here). Chaucer's *Wife of Bath*, it has been said, "however complex and alluring, is still *his* creation and therefore demonstrates a man's view of how a woman *might* act in any given situation"; and thus, if the elegies were similarly "male authored and imagined, [they would] pose problems of representation and appropriation of the female voice," and therefore self-concept.[36] In other words, our understanding of women and their emotions in the lyrics would be imperfect, but not without value.

However scholars choose to debate the notion of female authorship in *Wife* and *Wulf*, most are of the opinion that the narrators themselves

4. *A Case for Female Individuality*

are meant to represent a woman, irrespective of whether or not the *scop* reciting/creating it was female.[37] Again, this should not give cause for concern, since even if an argument for a female *scop* proved inaccurate, we would still benefit from having the view of an Anglo-Saxon woman, given us by a contemporary. The minority of scholars that deny the female narrator often use statements like "The female narrator is a practical impossibility since this would entail a sympathetic rendering of a woman's troubles in a warrior's world and it would speak of experience from a woman's point of view."[38] This notion is without supporting evidence from the Anglo-Saxon era, but posited on the basis of modern notions of the warrior code and concept of fealty. Furthermore, even a cursory examination of women in the poetry shows us ready instances of so-called "woman's troubles" not circumvented, but instead often highlighted with regularity.[39] Additionally, that a female narrator would lament the loss of her husband or lover parallels a male narrator's anxiety over the loss of his lord and community, since both correspond to the same kind of grief: the separation of oneself from his/her communal associations. Hence, while the female voice represented in both elegies displays a dichotomy between self and community, it is still a voice "firmly constrained within social and spatial boundaries."[40] That is, to extract any sense of individuality that these women may have harbored, we must be able to make a distinction between a communal self-concept and its opposite. For example, the women in *Wife* and *Wulf* both "feel [their] own self strongly [...] situated in a particular situation with a particular connection (or lack of connection) to others."[41] It is her inner self that is felt, an intimate emotional presence distinct from her communal identity, still within group constraints, that we see in these poems. Some scholars have noted this and posited that *Wife* and *Wulf* "exceed the male-voiced elegies in their emotional depth and egocentrism, thereby heightening the sense of an interior selfhood," while "offer[ing] [...] insight into the Anglo-Saxon female psyche."[42] In this way, we may come to "understand the 'self' or 'subject' of these elegies as the individual identity produced through a given set of linguistic, discursive, and gendered properties or behaviors."[43]

Therefore, this study skirts the oft-cited heroic representations of women—i.e., great women or those who achieved greatness—who share life in the hall, in favor of women whose individuality is highlighted precisely because of their disassociation from their immediate communities.[44]

A Life Both Public and Private

It is this individualism that contrasts with an image of woman-as-peace-weaver prevalent in the scholarship. Indeed, the narrators in *Wife* and *Wulf* may be said to have "involuntarily" failed as peace-weavers, allowing for a new "image and role" that is set apart from her communal identity.[45] And while traditional heroic imagery of women is conspicuously absent as a primary focus in both poems, this dearth provides an avenue for these women to express their emotions openly, even while physically constrained.[46] It is of specific importance to note that only in these two poems in the corpus are the speakers restricted in this way (i.e., physical enclosure). Indeed, the wanderer, "though exiled [...] is not imprisoned," and while the imagery of fetters in *Deor* appears similar, the refrain following the passage gives us an expectation of hope, promising all will be fine.[47] One may then inquire the reason for such imagery. Is physical constraint perhaps a metaphor for the stifling of self, a visual representation of one's selfhood confined, without an outlet for expression; and is the emotional narration an open attack against this position, an individuality being expressed as a way for the self to survive in this new world? I am not arguing for a conscious decision by the poet to create such a complex metaphor, but suggesting that it might represent the loss of communal associations in a time when such a loss equaled a substantial, if not entire, loss of one's identity. Whatever the truth, it is this dichotomy between emotional freedom and physical constraint that gives particular power to what these women are saying. We are thus tasked with unweaving a complex web of personal identity to uncover what it meant to be an individual for these women and the extent to which that individuality was imbued with communal associations and obligations. For much of its history—and indeed still today for some—it has been said that *Beowulf* holds the best material relating to the women of the Anglo-Saxon period.[48] However, we will find that this is anything but true. Richard Burton's statement is now antiquated, and speaks to his contemporary conceptions of what a woman was supposed to embody in the Anglo-Saxon period. Giving advice, fealty to one's husband and lord, and hall-participation are now seen as aspects of women's experiences during this time, but not the totality of that experience. We must look to the emotional narration of unwelcome circumstance, that we may broaden our understanding of female life in this period—taking into account both the communal and the private. And as it has been said that *Wife* and *Wulf* have the greatest emotional range of all Old English poetry, so it is to them that we now turn.[49]

4. *A Case for Female Individuality*

The Personal-Self in The Wife's Lament

As a poem true to the elegiac form, *Wife* presents to us some of the richest language of personal tragedy and individual self-reference in all of Old English literature—a fact that shows its character as both a study in Anglo-Saxon communal norms and interior lament in response to those norms. Scholars are afforded little in the way of contextual aids or a vision of any "circumstantial narrative."[50] However, a general consensus may be found regarding some key elements. These include (1) that the narrator is an unhappy woman, (2) this unhappiness is the result of being separated from a man, and (3) a three-part structure can be readily interpreted from the context.[51] The first five lines set the stage for a narrative of suffering and self-reference:

> Ic þis giedd wrece bi me ful geomorre,
> minre sylfre sið. Ic þæt secgan mæg,
> hwæt ic yrmþa gebad, siþþan ic up aweox,
> niwes oþþe ealdes, no ma þonne nu—
> a ic wite wonn minra wræcsiþa [1a-5b].[52]

The intensity of emotional language in this passage is arresting, and we are at first struck by the immediate "assertion of the self" by the concentrated use of personal pronouns, which when coupled with the emotions of sadness and misery, creates an immediate sense of suffering and loneliness.[53] Straus argues that the tone of the language suggests that the narrator's speech acts as a possible "form of action" in what was a male-dominated culture.[54] In a passage of five lines, that the poet chose to include five personal pronouns in the nominative (*Ic*), two intensive emphatics (*minre sylfre, me*), and a possessive (*minra*), is indicative of a conscious effort to ensure that the opening section of *Wife* highlights a theme of the deeply personal throughout. There are fifteen occurrences of *Ic* in the poem, comfortably exceeding other elegiac laments with an equivalently mournful theme.[55] Thus, and if read as the first section of the poem, this opening introduces the two most important themes of *Wife*: the concentration on an introspective state, and—supplied at the end for emphasis—the precise reason for that state (i.e., *minra wræcsiþa*)—both of which will provide insight into the personal-self. Adding some ambiguity to the poem is the collocation *minre sylfre sið*, which I have translated as a description of the narrator's "journey of myself." Interestingly, only three times elsewhere does a similar collocation appear in the corpus—

A Life Both Public and Private

and only in religious poetry, where the self is almost certainly referred to as the soul or some other supernatural spirit.[56] Here we have a divergence in the sentiment of self from the eternal soul in the religious verse to something more tangible in *Wife*. It is the inner emotional self here that is being described—the personal-self that has been the focus of this investigation—and as the narrator continues her story, a well-defined individual who will find a new identity beginning to emerge.

As the first section introduces the theme of the introspective personal self by way of communal separation, the midway point sees this separation turn to isolation—a theme in both *Wan* and *Seaf* as well.[57] We are told not only of the narrator's exile, but of her total lack of companionship (*ahte ic leofra lyt on þissum londstede, / holdra freonda*) and physical isolation from society.[58] Thus, the narrator is at once removed both from her lord (husband) and the wider community, causing a lacuna in her social experience that translates into losing her "'center of existence'" on the whole.[59] This is an important point, since to lose one's center is to essentially lose one's sense of identity; consequently, the loss of identity necessitates the filling of the vacuum of selfhood, as is clearly the case in both *Wan* and *Seaf*, for example. How a person refills this center is what ultimately provides us with details of their inner world and expressions of their sense of individual identity. Two identities have been lost for her, the communal and the intimate, and the loss of the latter is the primary cause for her pain. It is her husband's trickery, deception, and disloyalty that confounds her more than her banishment from kith and kin:

> Forþon is min hyge geomor,
> ða ic me ful gemæcne monnan funde,
> heardsæligne, hygegeomorne,
> mod miþendne, morþor hycgendne [17b-20b].[60]

To the emotional exclusion and torment we can of course also add the narrator's physical exclusion from her society, which only exacerbates her sorrow.

> Heht mec mon wunian on wuda bearwe,
> under actreo in þam earðscræfe.
> Eald is þes eorðsele, eal ic eom oflongad.
> Sindon dena dimme, duna uphea,
> bitre burgtunas, brerum beweaxne,
> wic wynna leas. Ful oft mec her wraþe begeat
> fromsiþ frean. Frynd sind on eorþan,
> leofe lifgende, leger weardiað,

4. A Case for Female Individuality

> þonne ic on uhtan ana gonge
> under actreo geond þas eorðscrafu.
> Þær ic sittan mot sumorlangne dæg,
> þær ic wepan mæg mine wræcsiþas,
> earfoþa fela. Forþon ic æfre ne mæg
> þære modceare minre gerestan,
> ne ealles þæs longaþes þe mec on þissum life begeat [27a-41b].[61]

Scholars' frustrations with the attempts to locate the oak tree and cave in the phenomenal world stem from the fact that "the poet is describing a mental landscape [and] in its loneliness and desolation it is a visible embodiment of the narrator's invisible grief," not a physical location from the Anglo-Saxon period.[62] We see this pathetic fallacy in both *Wan* and *Seaf* as well, where stormy seas and bitter cold approximate, in descriptive form, Anglo-Saxon emotions with precise and vivid metaphor. It is the meaning behind these images, then, that reveals how the narrator's sense of identity has been uprooted by the removal of both her personal relationship with her lord and her wider social group. Specific attention given to the former has inspired some commentators to suggest that *Wife* hence "conveys the female's social identity only in relation to that of the male persona."[63] This conclusion somewhat misses the mark with its uninspired analysis of the complexities of human identity development and how it is sustained. More complex is the transference of this concept into the Anglo-Saxon period, where social identity is the primary source of identity outlined in nearly all the historical sources.[64] However, if the narrator has any ostensible dependence on her husband, it is only because of the position of her husband in her identity matrix (that is to say, the communal role). For example, her lord—just as with the wanderer and seafarer—symbolizes the center of her social identity. Hence, any argument that would see this social network pejoratively would fail to recognize that *both* men and women were dependent on a strong central figure that would reinforce the communal structure of the heroic world, and thus their position within it. That an Anglo-Saxon woman's primary source of identity could be her lover need not dishonor her place and is no different socially than a thane and his lord. Therefore, if we are to "indisputably" acknowledge suggestions that the narrator's misery is "contingent upon the forcible sundering of a relationship," we not only need to concede that it is a relationship rooted in emotional attachment to a lover, but that it is also one based on social positioning, reinforcing the narrator's communal self-concept.[65] Indeed, Davidson touches upon this when he says that

A Life Both Public and Private

Wife "is [...] about incompleteness and social and psychological displacement" due to her separation from the narrator's husband, which implies incompleteness and the yearning to "become one whole being."[66] A piecemeal self continues to appear until the last section of the poem, where opinions are split concerning its resolution.

The fourth and final section of *Wife* (ll. 42a-53b) is markedly different from the preceding three (ll. 1a-5b, 6a-26b, and 27a-41b), having a theme that when untangled reveals how and to what extent a personal-self is expressed in the character of the female narrator:

> A scyle geong mon wesan geomormod,
> heard heortan geþoht, swylce habban sceal
> bliþe gebæro, eac þon breostceare,
> sinsorgna gedreag, sy æt him sylfum gelong
> eal his worulde wyn, sy ful wide fah
> feorres folclondes, þæt min freond siteð
> under stanhliþe storme behrimed,
> wine werigmod, wætre beflowen
> on dreorsele. Dreogeþ se min wine
> micle modceare; he gemon to oft
> wynlicran wic. Wa bið þam þe sceal
> of longoþe leofes abidan [42a-53b].[67]

Concerning this section, the two schools of thought dominating the discourse are the so-called "genteel" and "vindictive" interpretations; while the former argues for a gnomic desire to "express philosophical resignation concerning the lot of unhappy lovers of either gender who are forced to endure the absence of their beloved," the latter asserts the narrator's desire to curse a lover who wronged her.[68] The distinction is not insignificant, either, since they differ considerably in how they would represent the female narrator's sense of autonomy. As a gnomic narration, the ending would simply be reinforcing the narrator's communal identification with her lord and all he signified. On the other hand, an argument for a curse would display an autonomy on the narrator's part that would eschew her association with the heroic world and hence considerably weaken her communal self-concept. Some commentators see as a theme the narrator's gradual disassociation, or "a reversal of [...] subservience" to her husband, as the poem progresses; that is, from a strong attachment to the communal, in favor of the individual.[69] Indeed, epithets for her husband do in fact change over time, which correspond with a narrative change in tone of the narrator's feelings toward her lover over time; so the early terms

4. A Case for Female Individuality

Hlaford ("lord") and *leodfruma* ("prince"), change to *freond* ("friend") and *wine werigmod* ("miserable friend") later on. Of course, these terms do not entirely carry pejorative meanings, but when taken in context with an obvious change in narrative tone, they become all the more significant. Niles, for instance, claims that the narrator is indeed cursing her lover while still referring to him with "endearing terms."[70] However, I would not go so far as to say these terms are positive, considering the context in which they are present.

A curse—or a revenge theme at the very least—is strongly supported by both the change in epithet and clear evolution of tone. This is not to say, however, that a "genteel" reading is wholly excluded from discussion. In fact, the evidence suggests that both a gnomic *and* revenge scenario are playing out simultaneously. Consider the first and final lines of the last section, for example, where the narrator's reference to an everyman neatly sandwiches a more personal discussion of her lord. The subject in 44a is a *geong mon* ("young man"), while 52b-53b ("Woe it is to him who must, out of longing, wait for a loved one") considers how anyone in that particular circumstance is to be sympathized with. And yet, neatly contained within these clauses we find discussion centering on *min freond* ("my friend") and *min wine* ("my lord/friend") in bleak emotional circumstance. Thus, the narrator in *Wife* is at once outlining a revenge theme against her lord, while passive-aggressively associating him with any man who would be in such a position. This "authoritative speech" and revenge theme is not a fantastic idea, as it is well-attested in the literature and scholarship.[71]

In a society where kin groups most commonly outlined and defined one's sense of identity the concept of revenge was not only necessary to solidify and sustain group ties, but it could also contribute to the survival of one's sense of self, as well. Anglo-Saxon society therefore relied on a sense of "collective responsibility," where "a wrong done to an individual was a wrong done to the kin group," simply because the personal and communal were in many way inseparable.[72] This latter concept is clearly seen in *Wife*, since neither physical nor emotional distance from her lord and kin entirely removes the narrator from this "nexus of social relationships."[73] That is, until the end, she continues to lament the fact that she is in exile and removed from her communal associations. Hence, we could either argue for a revenge that was imbued with a sense of communal obligation, or one that is entirely personal, based on a need to cause suffering for its own sake. As it applies to the former, I see no textual evidence suggesting that the narrator's vengeance was based on anything but her own personal prerogative, a sort of "coming into her own," an individual attempting to remedy the destruction of a former self by adopting a personal will disassociated from the wider group. This is reinforced in the final 11 lines, where we read that happiness depends on one's own self, where a once important person in her life is now the narrator's "miserable friend" who might be "flung far into hostile nations," and where the man that caused her grief might "suffer great anxiety." In some ways, this challenges prevailing ideas; Robert Albano, for example, suggests that "revenge [was] part of the lives and culture of the Anglo-Saxon people, both male and female," and that Norse and Anglo-Saxon women "were willing to put all else aside, including human emotion, to accomplish their vengeance"; indeed, he argues that one's "commitment to vengeance outweighs any and all such personal concerns" as a way of solidifying group conformity.[74] In *Wife*, however, it appears as though the narrator's revenge is *precisely* a personal matter, in direct contrast with the goals of sustaining a strong sense of communal identity—this, of course, not by choice. Here is an example where an individual could assert her own autonomy in order to exercise action available to an Anglo-Saxon woman in her situation. That is, she has lost her sense of self because of her exile from lord and community, and she directs her anger at him who once acted as her central identity marker. Therefore, as the narrator has lost her identity with communal ties, she asserts her sense of personal autonomy by her curse, effectively shedding any link to community she once had. This curse essentially acts as a "source of solace" for the narrator, a "consolation for the speaker," by way of her own agency.[75] The narrator is thus expressing a strong sense of a personal-self by cursing a husband for his cruelty to her, positively "accomplish[ing] the superimposition of her experience upon the man" who is the cause of her suffering.[76] Additionally, Belanoff has noted the conspicuous lack of dual pronouns in the final section of *Wife*, arguing for a "finality of the narrator's separation from the man she describes" (e.g., separation from her former identity). Before section III, there are four dual pronouns to describe the narrator's exile from her husband, and none from line 26b onward.[77]

While highlighted here is individual action removed from societal obligations, there is still a clear relationship between the personal and communal in *Wife*. Unlike *Wan* and *Seaf*, for example, the narrator here

4. A Case for Female Individuality

does not find any clear consolation with some gnomic utterance that could be interpreted as succor in an unwanted situation. The narrator "scarcely seems capable of breaking beyond the bounds of her own tormented experience," since neither remedial future hope nor embrace of her current situation are expressed.[78] Indeed, unlike *Wan* and *Seaf*, the narrator in *Wife* does not develop a new center or sense of self over time, but in one cursing action at the end asserts her individuality, while still ostensibly attached (emotionally) to her lord and community, and herein lies a prime example of both the public and private.[79] This continuing attachment is made clear by the lack of consolatory language and a seemingly innocuous statement in lines 46b and 47a, where the narrator suggests, *sy æt him sylfum gelong / eal his worulde wyn* ("let all his worldly joy depend on his own self"). This is not an idle comment, but is substantially relevant and I believe expresses the deepest feelings about the role of the individual and community in the Anglo-Saxon period. Indeed, inherent in nearly every piece of poetry during this time is the truism that "a joy reliant on the self is no joy at all, since the isolated individual lacks those joys of the hall so essential to a social identity."[80] Even more important is this statement when we understand that this "social identity" was not some peripheral, subsidiary, or simply one of many identities for Anglo-Saxons, but was most in fact the predominant center of identity for the vast majority of people, which when threatened, presaged the very real danger of losing oneself entirely. However, when this happens, we have seen how a new center, a more personal individual, by necessity comes to the fore—almost as a survival mechanism—and exerts itself as a new center of identity. This new center is a rawer type of self than that which was encased in community, and therefore is a type of personal-self that we can identify in the literature. In the case of *Wan* and *Seaf*, this center becomes strong and reinforced with hopes of attaching to something higher than worldly affairs, while here less so.

What can we say then about the personal-self of the narrator in *Wife*? Has an essential shift in identity occurred? Is the display of individuality of the same character and strength as we see in *Wan* and *Seaf*? What revelations does *Wife* give us into the female personal-self in the Anglo-Saxon period? While elements of a strong personal-self are certainly evident in *Wife*, we do not find any shift in identity in the psyche of the narrator. Unlike *Wan* and *Seaf*, where consolation comes from a new center of self being formed through devotion, here we find the narrator with no new center in which she can rest, no final refrain as in *Deor* that all will be put right in the end. Thus, no new identity marker presents itself for the narrator to find solace. However, to recognize this is not to deny the presence of an individual, personal-self, which is non-dependent on communal associations. Indeed, the autonomy expressed via the narrator's curse reflects an individual will that does not rely on a communal conception of revenge—since there would have been no kith or kin to witness or buttress her actions—but in fact on her own notion of it. This strong, independent voice cursing her husband and damning other men who would with similar predisposition wrong a woman, foretells an extremely resilient personal-self that would reject communal norms and presumably future communal ties in favor of the satisfaction personal revenge would bring. Therefore, although a new self-center has not been formulated for her, the narrator has gained something through authoritative action that would have otherwise gone unnoticed and un-manifested in her life. Unlike *Deor*, then, where the refrain readies the audience to believe in a respite for the *scop*, *Wife* provides us with no such hope. The lack of discussion on the frailty of communal life, the inexorable destruction of its citadels, and the joys of the meadhall clearly reveals that the narrator is still under the spell of community, while paradoxically expressing an individuality that is wholly her own. Thus, *Wife* is demonstrative of the dual nature of identity in the Anglo-Saxon period. And so, while a consolatory framework is lacking in *Wife*, we nevertheless find that the expression of a personal-self need not rely on the embodiment of a new source of self-identity for its articulation, but indeed could be individually expressed without any hope that one would eventually find respite in another lord, new community, or a new center of self that is dependent on those structures.

Wulf and Eadwacer

While admittedly a much more difficult text to come to terms with than *Wife*, *Wulf* does still lend itself to discussion in regard to the female personal-self. As one of the most ambiguous texts in the Old English poetic corpus, *Wulf* has a scholarly history filled with interpretations and reinterpretations, ranging from the simplistic to the highly metaphorical. With a text as enigmatic as this, some liberties must be allowed in interpretation,

4. A Case for Female Individuality

and conjecture naturally plays a role; however, this analysis will primarily work to uncover the self from the poetic elements that are less debated in the literature. For instance, as with *Wife*, an almost unanimous scholarly consensus sees the speaker as a female, who is enduring an extreme state of emotional discord, with her present pain coming "from some grief-giving love relationship in the past with someone named Wulf."[81] Also touched on are the "universal thematic components of hostility, suffering, union, and separation that inform the poem."[82] As we have seen, these themes are well suited as an avenue into the study of the female personal-self.

As with *Wife*, the narrator in *Wulf* is separated from her husband at an early stage in the poem, and this informs the tone for the rest of the narration. Added to the lament of separation from her lover we also again find geographical descriptions as proxies for her inner state. For instance, we are told:

> Wulfes ic mines widlastum wenum hogode;
> þonne hit wæs renig weder ond ic reotugu sæt [9a-10b].[83]

Just as with many other elegies, a pejorative topographical description often follows a description of the inner state on which it rests. So not only with descriptive language, but also with visual aids are we told of what mattered most to the narrator: separation from her husband, first and foremost. Thus in *Wulf*, as in *Wife*, the narrator's "social identity [...] is made problematic by her geographical and emotional separation from her lover."[84] We may, of course, take this further and say that not only social identity, but also the narrator's entire sense of self is uprooted by her separation. Isolation from one's social networks was akin to dissolution of the communal self—i.e., the predominant self. In the case of *Wulf*, the narrator's identity was solidified by her attachment to her lover, who was the symbol of society that formed the major part of her identity. Indeed, debates on the identity of *Wulf* are rampant in the discourse. For instance, Frese claims that the "utterance of grief, separation, anxiety, and consummate anguish derives from the predicament of a mother lamenting a lost son," while Peter Baker argues that Wulf is most likely the narrator's husband, if the narrator be married at all.[85] Whether a lover or a son, however, the same conclusions apply as to the role this person plays in the narrator's self-concept (i.e., both perform a communal function, tying her to the heroic world and her place in Anglo-Saxon society). That the narrator's husband—as I associate him—symbolically represents her identity is made clear in lines 13a-15b, when the narrator exclaims:

> Wulf, min Wulf, wena me þine
> seoce gedydon, þine seldcymas,
> murnende mod, nales meteliste.[86]

So, while the poem is full of examples of how communal separation leads to grief and anxiety, we must now ask how, if at all, the narration reveals individuality on the part of the narrator.

Unlike *Wife*, *Wulf* scarcely exhibits the same level of lucidity in revealing a description of personal-self; and although it is not overtly highlighted—similar to *Deor* and *Widsith*—we may still uncover by its contrary theme of community a sense of it. Indeed, the first two lines not only exemplify the motif of community, but in fact provide us deep insight into *how* the narrator viewed community:

> Leodum is minum swylce him mon lac gife;
> willað hy hine aþecgan, gif he on þreat cymeð.
> Ungelic is us [1a-3a].[87]

Frese sees this opening as "the beginning of the elegiac utterance which articulates the communal sense of loss before moving to more private and personal configurations of grief."[88] However, this passage continues to be one of the most vague and unclear sections of all the Old English elegies, and hence its meaning is not easily rendered. Some scholars translate a part of this section as welcoming Wulf "as they would a gift," while still others suggest that Wulf could just as easily be a sacrifice.[89] Nevertheless, an attempt at understanding must be made, and so I submit that the obscure meaning comes from its subtle comparison (perhaps a direct metaphor) between the relationship of a heroic man and a potential new community on the one hand, with the intimate relationship between these two lovers on the other. For instance, it seems clear that this community (*leodum [...] minum*) is typical of what we know of the heroic world, in that a strong thane (*mon*) would be welcomed into a community (*willað hy hine aþecgan*) if he had something to offer (*gif he on þreat cymeð*). Emily Jensen reads this in a similar fashion, arguing that Wulf is "introduced as someone who is welcomed graciously by the narrator's community."[90] Indeed, the idea of a man being welcomed into different communities is not unheard of in the literature. Beowulf, for instance, is welcomed into the court of Hrothgar, while Widsith is received well in the various courts

4. A Case for Female Individuality

that he visited—each had something to offer to their respective courts. No matter the particulars, though, the refrain, *Ungelic is us* (it is different for us), is clearly meant to differentiate their relationship in some way and the two opposing situations (one communal, and one more personal—although still not disassociated from society).

From this, I propose that the narrator is making a distinction between acceptance of a person based on what he can offer to others, and that of an unconditional acceptance to each other. That is, the narrator is lucidly defining how community functioned in her society and makes it a point to show that the situation between her and her lover is not based on that same kind of reciprocity. Their relationship is different in some way, as we are told. Consequently, if we can accept this interpretation, what we find here is an early description of romantic love that proves it could differ from that of a typical lord/thane relationship. That is, marriage or an intimate relationship did not need to be based solely on what each partner could bring to the table. The importance of this interpretation is simply to highlight the significance of the lover to the narrator, a relationship that, however unique, still hinges on communal identity.

If any sense of a personal-self is to be found in *Wulf*, it is to the situational elements of the poem that we must turn. Horner, for instance, sees the narrator's enclosure as "the force that shapes her identity."[91] However, this does not shape her identity as much as define it, since shaping implies that her sense of self is created or remolded because of her enclosure, and throughout *Wulf* there cannot be said to be any new identity formation through time. Indeed, her enclosure characterizes her continuous attachment to things of the communal (i.e., her lover), as her thoughts do not deviate from Wulf during the entire episode. She may indeed be alone (*Wulf is on iege, ic on operre*), but she finds no reason to discontinue thinking on or yearning for him. She in fact discovers no new consolation (as with *Wan* and *Seaf*) or new identity marker. Still, some scholars claim that less overt expressions in *Wulf* highlight a type of personal-self. That the narrator is weaving her own story, for instance, may show self-agency and thus declare a kind of "feminine self-hood," in one example.[92] Of this argument, though, I am not entirely convinced, since this line of thought could then apply to any female first-person narration, even if that narration concretizes communal themes and group conformity. This is precisely what I am questioning here, and situationally at least, *Wulf* is not an exemplar for this kind of communal refusal.

A Life Both Public and Private

That there is no corresponding situational element (explicit) that develops findings from implicit assertions in defense of a personal-self, however, does not necessarily imply the negation of it, and this is an important point about understanding the narrator's sense of self in this poem. Chance asserts that the narrator "fears the ephemerality of her earlier happiness with Wulf, therefore seeking a permanence through song (and the song *is* all that remains of that union)."[93] In this way, one could argue, the narrator seeks "self-expression, through creating a text, and thereby a textual self"—a self that would be in opposition to her communal identity.[94] This argument powerfully contributes to the notion of the expression of a strong personal-self in *Wulf*; however, it relies on the assumption that it is a gendered poem (either originally composed by a woman or a real story about a woman).[95] Still, though, *Wulf* is more complex than this. Her song may certainly be indicative of an autonomous action that expresses an individualistic self (as with *Wife*), but we must remember that a woven tale looks backward—it is a function of memory, and memory is a key factor in identity construction. That is, while the narrator is expressing her autonomy by telling her story, she is simultaneously linking her identity with her past. In this way, then, *Wulf* is demonstrative of how two identities could function at the same time (i.e., the public and private). Scholars have hence chosen to argue in favor of one identity or the other, when in fact both are expressed in equal measure. Emily Jensen, for example claims that the final two lines show the narrator "divorc[ing] herself from any dependence on him [Wulf]," that she is "independent of him," and therefore achieves "self-awareness" and "an independent self."[96] Conversely, and on these lines, others have argued that its hypermetrical nature "emphasiz[es] through its length how she has been conquered by longing," and hence still attached to a communal identity.[97]

It may be that *Wulf* proves too ambiguous to definitively argue a case for absolute meaning or theme, but of the prospect of a female personal-self we may come to some conclusions. Firstly, the narrator identifies herself by means of her relationships to other people, namely Wulf.[98] This is clear from the outset, with her initial concern over their separation and later her worry of his infrequent visits. Baker likewise notes the narrator's early concern and worry and suggests that she "expresses herself through an opposition: her illness is not physical [and] it is brought on by her endless waiting, her anxious mind."[99] Hence, and as with *Wan, Seaf, Deor,* and *Wife*, a preoccupation with communal structure and identity is evident

4. A Case for Female Individuality

from the start. Second, *Wulf* is at the same time an expression of the female personal-self with its "highly autonomous dramatic monologue," representative of an individual "textual self," as Horner suggests, and which is not too dissimilar from the function of the curse in *Wife* in that it designates a personal will, motive, and function. But of the ending what can we conclude? Does the narrator find consolation and embody a new kind of personal identity divorced from community? Admittedly, the narrator does at first appear to remove herself from the longing over her husband in the final lines, and some critics have argued that over the course of the poem, where at first the narrator sits "tearful" and waiting for Wulf's seldom visits, but at the end of the poem she removes herself from any dependence on" Wulf.[100] However, I read the final lines as a concession on the part of the narrator; she is giving up her hopes and yet still attached to the desired outcome. All of her anxieties about her relationship, together with her hopes about it, are still there. Therefore, unlike *Wan, Seaf,* and *Wife*, the answer must be a qualified no, since the narrator never "cut[s] herself free from all connections with the human order."[101] Indeed, the dual pronoun at the end still confirms a desire for her Wulf:

> Þæt mon eaþe tosliteð þætte næfre gesomnad wæs
> uncer giedd geador [18a-19b].[102]

There are many difficulties with coming to terms with *Wulf*, and scholars have debated the meaning of the poem for many years. However, of the overall themes, we can make some conclusions. A majority of scholars consider *Wulf* to be a "highly autonomous dramatic monologue," "spoken by a woman," who is separated from her spouse/lover, Wulf.[103] There are also considerable "thematic components of hostility, suffering, union, and separation that inform the poem and contribute to the narrator's anxieties.[104] These "agreed" themes in the academy are enough to make an inquiry into the self of the narrator if we are to assume that the poem is namely about a relationship, a separation, and a lament caused by the separation. Unlike *Wan* and *Seaf* for instance, we do not find the narrator finding consolation or a new sense of identity, but what we do witness is an emotive monologue that displays a speaker who is "virtually real," telling her story of separation and longing.[105] No consolation is therefore necessary, and no positive refrain is needed for the narrator to demonstrate her individuality—her story is enough. And still, though she finds no respite for her lament, or new center of identity in which to develop a new sense of self, the female narrator in *Wulf* expresses her individuality as she tells her tale, while entreating us to listen.

Genderized Female Representations and the Personal-Self

We have seen how the expression of a personal-self in gendered first-person female narration is articulated in the literature; however, when we look to genderized representations of women, something entirely different emerges.[106] The suffering of Beadohild, as we have seen, and genderized by the narrator Deor, is predicated on the fact that she is with a bastard child, which would have considerably threatened her status in society as part of a kin group. Recall that

>   hyre broþra deaþ
> on sefan swa sar swa hyre sylfre þing,
> þæt heo gearolice ongieten hæfde
> þæt heo eacen wæs [8b-11a].[107]

No sense of inner monologue or introspection is even hinted at here, but that her character was created in a man's imagination shows deep contrast in the way her mental state is represented from the gendered (and ostensibly female creation/inspired) language in *Wife* and *Wulf*. More examples of female characterization aimed at the communal can be found in *Beowulf*. Representations of Wealhtheow, Freawaru, Hildeburh, and Hygd, for instance, demonstrate how they were "guided by their identification with the communal good of their patriarchal society" and were "supportive of men and also dependent on men."[108] One caveat should be made here: "men" could easily be changed to "community," since the men in each of these women's lives were representative of the women's communal self structure. That is to say, a pejorative interpretation of Magennis' comment that would suggest it implies female emotional weakness would be out of place. As with men, women in the Anglo-Saxon period relied on their immediate communities to make sense of their identity and concretize their sense of self. To be reliant on community was to be in the status quo of interpersonal relationships and the designation of one's self-concept. It is in fact the exilic condition that deviates from this norm, which is why it gives us insight into a part of the self that was largely independent of

4. A Case for Female Individuality

community. However, this condition is not evident in *Beowulf*, or any other poem in the corpus outside of the elegies.

The character of Hildeburh, for instance, is a good example of how genderized female representation conforms to the communal schema of self in the Anglo-Saxon period. The Finn episode is a fascinating example of elements that only appears to provide insight into the personal-self; however, when we look more deeply, we discover the story does not, owing to the fact that a man almost certainly created her character. High emotion and a woman all but exiled from her community because of the death of primary members (son, brother, and husband) of her immediate kingroup punctuate nearly ninety lines of verse. Elaine Hansen likens Hildeburh's circumstances to "the women in the Exeter book laments, [in that] she is the helpless and innocent victim of human passion and fate."[109] However, unlike the women in *Wife* and *Wulf*, Hildeburh displays no high individuality over her situation, neither refrain in hope of better days, nor introspective lament in any form. She does indeed grieve (*gnornode*, l. 1117b) and mourn (*geomrode*, l. 1118a) the loss of the place where she *ær mæste heold / worolde wynne* ("before held the greatest joy in the world," ll. 1079b-1080a)—namely her son and brother, and by extension their respective peoples—but she demonstrates no outward action or emotional expression that is inherently hers, no introspective autonomy that can be said to be her voice and hers alone. This lack is even more surprising, since Hildeburh essentially suffers from a "double grief"—that is, the death of her son coupled with her inability to keep the peace-pledge.[110] Coupled with this grief, we find the additional loss of her brother and husband, both of whom represented potent structures in her communal identity (i.e., her sibling and husband, and her relationship with their respective kingroups). Hence, any relief that Hildeburh may have found in a revenge scenario would have only further caused a disintegration of self, since siding with either her brother's or husband's family would have divorced her even more from that group, compounding her already-dissolving identity.[111] But this is precisely the point: she has open to her this availability of revenge as action commensurate with her identity as part of being a woman during the Anglo-Saxon period (as we have seen with *Wife*, and as Glover discusses). No action is taken, however. No revenge scenario is acted out as part of a group, or to satisfy any personal gratification after a destruction of self. Dorothy Porter suggests that Hildeburh displays a conspicuous lack of grief over the death of Finn, and never expresses a desire that revenge *not* be taken for her son and brother's deaths, which indicates a "continuing close relationship to her birth people."[112] Even so, I am not convinced that the so-called lack of instruction to seek blood implies license for armed requital. Albano likewise agrees with Porter, suggesting that "Hildeburh clearly considers her brother to be much more important to her life than Finn."[113] In either event, the text shows that Hildeburh's identity, whichever end of the patriarchal spectrum it favors, still *clearly* favors some form of communal association and completely lacks any display of autonomy. All of this indeed suggests that the *scop* "knew that in Hildeburh he was presenting and defining a stereotype" and "signaled this fact by the curiously approving assessment *þæt wæs geomuru ides*" in line 1075b.[114] That Hildeburh was stereotyped is highly significant here, as it suggests that as a male creation, Hildeburh does not display any characteristic that would threaten the schema of self in society. That is, her sense of identity is couched in the social positions she holds in her culture—an admittedly patriarchal order—whether she be a queen/wife, sister, or mother.

Finally, we may make yet another comparison in *Beowulf*. Much has been written on the female mourner at Beowulf's funeral, and while extremely brief and full of textual conjecture due to manuscript lacunae, it still acts on the reader's emotions due to her violent, outward lament.[115] Indeed, it has been said that she is "empowered" by her speech, and that "excluded from the world of action, woman becomes the reader of its text, author of its record."[116] The significance of this statement is two-fold for my purposes. On the one hand, we may conclude that the representation of emotion does not ipso facto denote high individuality, and on the other, that the mourner's position in society is in fact akin to what we saw in the characters of the *scopas* Widsith and Deor, who were essentially the voice of their communities, the propagators of the schema of self and identity of their time. To this I suggest yet another element of import given to this woman and others like her: she is giving voice to the collective emotions of others around her, articulating the grief of both men and women at the funeral pyre. The mourner's position is thus wholly attributed to communal activity, even though her speech is highly emotional, and unlike the *scop*, we do not find any disassociation from a communal role or identity. Scholars have even noted this lack of personal will with other female characters in *Beowulf*. In Wealtheow, for instance, we still only read a speech that "is constructed through lexical differences that code gender at the

4. A Case for Female Individuality

same time as they express her kinship focus."[117] Again, we may now conclude that genderized representations of women in the poetic corpus we have examined lack expression of an individual identity or personal-self, but this does not imply that descriptions of women's communal function in society was subservient or less meaningful then men's.

Concluding Remarks

We have seen how female characterization of identity in gendered first-person narrations reveal layers of identity, with expressions of an autonomous personal-self removed from communal associations, while genderized representations highlight an identity immersed in society. Hence, past assumptions that "good women in Old English poetry simply do not exist outside this role of wife," and if this "social contract is for some reason broken [...] the female becomes a poetic voice for all lonely and innocent victims of fate" no longer holds up to scrutiny.[118] We could just as easily apply this logic to "good" men, who do not exist outside of their role of thane/*scop* (e.g., *Wan*, *Seaf*, *Deor*, etc.). Both exist outside of these communal functions, and exist completely as individuals that have in some ways been reduced to the bare essentials of identity. And so it is clear to say that identity then, as it is today, was highly flexible and determined by a number of factors. The narrators in both *Wife* and *Wulf*, for instance, have been said to "do" gender by showing us how the "performance of gender [is] enacted by the speakers" based on cultural norms and values.[119] Descriptive identity based on cultural norms is simply another way of saying that the way one's sense of self is portrayed in the poetry is based on the schema of self at the time. As we have seen, though, the elegies by their nature often divorce the narrators from this schema, and from that position we are able to uncover any personal identity that is left. It just happens that the only two poems in the corpus that give us insight into the female personal-self from this angle are *Wife* and *Wulf*. It is also critical to note that not all first-person female narration that has an emotional element in Old English poetry establishes a clear line to the personal self. Eve's speech in *GenB* and Wealtheow in *Beowulf*, for example, each demonstrate the social actor, and therefore have strong communal self-concepts. In *Wife* and *Wulf*, however, we are able to find an autonomous self behind the voice.

A Life Both Public and Private

It has also been shown how female identity associated with its communal structure need not be considered pejorative, either. Heyworth and Desmond agree, saying that these women "occupied a meaningful position within the social framework of the community."[120] Indeed, we see this with the mourner at Beowulf's funeral and Hildeburh, both of whom perform important functions in heroic society. The elegies are unique in that they define the lamenting individual, showing us how "Suffering is most often caused by separation resultant from death or some form of exile."[121] This suffering, accompanied by exile, psychologically and physically removes one from their group, allowing for the expression of intense grief. Such grief is "not the prerogative" of women, either, as *Wan, Seaf,* and *Deor* all demonstrate that men and women are "equally subject to the blows of fortune" and hence the expression of emotional lamentation.[122] Consequently, the sharing of this grief arises from the inner self and gives voice to one's deeper identity, irrespective of whether or not consolation is found. In *Wan* and *Seaf,* for instance, ultimate consolation for their lament allows for the formation of a new sense of self, while in *Wife* and *Wulf,* there is "no philosophical basis for hope."[123] However, although no ultimate consolation is found for either woman in these poems, both still give us insight into a personal-self distinct from their communal identities—one via a curse, the other by virtue of her song. Ultimately, unless another elegy in the female voice is brought to light, we are forced to rely on the exemplars of *Wife* and *Wulf.* And while some scholars claim that two poems "are not enough to generalize much of anything, let alone identify a characteristic female voice or experience," I submit that the unique character of these two poems and how they differ in tone from other speeches of women in the corpus allows us to do just that—uncover a unique personal-self in gendered female narration that may just bring us one step closer to concluding that *Wife* and *Wulf* were either composed, or inspired by real Anglo-Saxon women, and that women did indeed harbor a unique personal-self outside of their position in society.[124]

Conclusion

Moving through the diverse and complex identity markers in a representative sample of Old English poetry, this investigation has challenged the long-held notion that the Anglo-Saxons exclusively harbored simplistic social identities that displayed little evidence of what we would call "individuality." Simultaneously, the analysis has questioned any idea that the individual was a construction from no earlier than the twelfth century. For this investigation I have submitted a variety of modern methodological approaches in self-studies, as well as an analysis of the literature that strove to be objective. That is to say, where I could, I intentionally shied away from debates in the verse that either did not contribute to the question of the personal-self or are quite simply too peripheral to my study to warrant consideration. Indeed the poetry could have been looked at from many angles, and space would not allow me to look at all of them. As with any research that discusses identity, subtlety and conjecture necessarily play a role; however, progress has been made in this research, and I believe that we may hence offer strong solutions to the question of the Anglo-Saxon self that has often been neglected, circumvented, or antiquated in its treatment.

This research identifies some strata of Anglo-Saxon identity and argues for the existence of a personal-self that was as far removed from its communal ties as we can discover by reading literature. My aim was to find a way to get to the heart of the self by looking at circumstances in the poetry that would occasion its discovery. Often times, this self is identified best during times of deep introspection and/or exile, or some other form of separation from communal structure. Significantly then, a reading "between the lines" at the unconscious inclusions from the poet/scribe has given this study an objectivity that is often lacking in traditional literary analysis. To this statement I may add that no historical study can

Conclusion

ever be entirely objective—likewise not all inclusions are unconscious—and yet even without this certainty I can say that we are now in a position to argue that the inner world for Anglo-Saxons was at least similar in complexity to ours in modern society.

Chapter 1 for instance stands alone as a study that showcases the "standard" themes of the Anglo-Saxon, highlighting the most common kind of self for Anglo-Saxons—the communal kind. This chapter articulates the commonality of the social schema of identity in most Old English narration, and thus demonstrates its demarcation from the three chapters that follow. My argument for a personal-self in the literature was thus strengthened and reinforced from this study, as it demonstrates the majority, but in no way exclusive, kind of self that Anglo-Saxons experienced. This analysis also discussed how and why the group aspects of Anglo-Saxon identity were so salient and commonplace, by looking at Christian identity markers and the concept of fealty within a warrior society.

In Chapter 2, I demonstrated how the sense of self for both the wanderer and seafarer altered over a period of time—demonstrated by their own will and introspective "use" of memory. The function of memory in the poems as a signpost to the agitations of the self within the protagonists was certainly not a conscious effect by the poet. What I showed in this instance was a positive example for how the self is often "realigned over time as social circumstances are altered."[1] In the modern world, this alteration contributes to individualism, and that it is found in Old English poetry is of importance toward a positive argument for the Anglo-Saxon personal-self. This research, then, offered an analysis of the self by way of contrasts (the personal and communal), which is a well-known method for uncovering personal identity within an individual.[2]

In Chapters 3 and 4 I also looked at contrast to uncover what Anglo-Saxons considered the trope of identity to be. By looking at the character of the *scop* in Chapter 3 for example, I was able to identify hidden identity markers within Anglo-Saxon society in a variety of circumstances. For instance, the scribe copying *Deor* and *Widsith* was by his very existence a representative of Anglo-Saxon society at the time of composition of the Exeter Book, and whether or not he may have been copying from an exemplar, his beliefs and experiences with the introspective mind show how in touch he was with his society's values and norms, which gives us insight into how a *scop* was both within and without his community. Secondly,

Conclusion

the characters within the poems idealized this notion of the roles that the *scop* played in society. Furthermore, the dialogue and activities of the *scopas* themselves highlight the inner world of a person who had a very unique and special position in their culture. This position occasions an understanding of what the audience would have thought relevant, and therefore by unpacking what is specifically addressed in the poetry, we may uncover the schema of self in a certain context. In this case, it was a communally-based self (e.g., Deor's lament over the loss of his position demonstrates that this was something seen in a negative light) that both identified the communal schema, and *also* a very personal identity within the narrator because of the examples of the destruction of self in the poem. The result was a subtle, but perhaps the most interesting example of the self out of all the chapters. That is to say, the scribe, the characters in the poems, the perceived audience of the poetry, and even the audience of the fictional *scopas* in their respective worlds, all displayed notions of identity that contributed to my conclusion for a positive finding of individuality.

Chapter 4 similarly revealed examples of the individual apart from her communal role. My concentration and comparison between gendered versus genderized female narration allowed me to differentiate how identity functioned in the female constructed voice. The goal of this chapter was to determine whether *Wife* and *Wulf,* for being recognized as the only two poems in the corpus that are entirely voiced by women, show any meaningful difference when looking at the notion of self compared with other female narration. I concluded that these two poems display a sharp contrast to the other female narration investigated in the chapter, and that *Wife* and *Wulf* show how the personal-self was present for these two female characters. The differences in how identity is highlighted in the gendered and genderized female narration reveal such a contrast that, if anything, we can now cite yet another reason why *Wife* and *Wulf* are such incredible examples of the richness of Old English literature and of Anglo-Saxon emotion.

By looking at Old English verse, it has been my aim to isolate the unconsciously included elements below the explicit references in the text that lead us to uncovering the Anglo-Saxon self. This concentration is an exciting way of examining medieval culture, and includes a variety of disciplines and subjects. Indeed, Culler suggests that "the critic can interpret the work not by pulling out what the poet was aware of putting in but by

Conclusion

extracting the elements of the various modes, genres, symbols, and myths which may have been put in without the author's explicit knowledge."[3] Such sentiments have proved an inspiration for this research and have produced positive results for our understanding of Anglo-Saxon identity. To be sure, that "the Anglo-Saxons would undoubtedly understand the value we place today on the individual" is no longer in question.[4] Ultimately, the Anglo-Saxons lived in a complicated and diverse world of societal tropes and identity markers that informed their sense of self and motivated their understanding of their inner worlds. As with identity for the majority of the world today, the outer and the inner conspired to instantiate one's personal identity, an identity that often included very personal and individual elements of the self-construct. John Searle thus said it succinctly, when he wrote that "the individual apprehends himself as being both inside *and* outside of society."[5] This of course has been demonstrated to be accurate, not only in today's world, but also in the world of Anglo-Saxon England, where its inhabitants lived a life both public and private, showing that the latter was a manifest reality in the inner lives of those living in Anglo-Saxon England.

Chapter Notes

Introduction

1. Descartes' *Meditations* was first published in 1641.
2. Often, a distinction is made between the idea of "self" and "individual"; here, however, I have used them interchangeably to account for a popular view that they can be associated with one another.
3. By this, I mean the peculiar situation in time and place that the idea is had, i.e., a subjective idea of the self is not universal but a fluid construct that is dependent on culture, time period, and situation. This is made clearer in chapter 1, where I discuss the social construction of the self in religious narrative.
4. Toon Van Meijl, "Culture and Identity in Anthropology: Reflections on 'Unity' and 'Uncertainty' in the Dialogical Self," *International Journal for Dialogical Science*, 3.1 (2008), 165–190 (p. 177).
5. Lewis P. Hinchman, "The Idea of Individuality: Origins, Meaning, and Political Significance," *The Journal of Politics*, 52.3 (1990), 759–781 (p. 762). Similarly, Burkitt tries to understand how "we come to identify ourselves among others as having specific characteristics." See Ian Burkitt, *Social Selves: Theories of Self and Society*, 2nd ed. (Los Angeles: SAGE, 2009), p. 23.
6. Yi-Fu Tuan, "Community, Society, and the Individual," *Geographical Review*, 92.3 (2002), 307–318 (p. 308). An extensive discourse is set around the idea of the "I-self" and the "me-self," in one form or another. William James has identified characteristics of the two, where the "I-self" includes self-awareness (emotions and other mental states), self-agency (authorship and responsibility over one"s actions), self-continuity (the same self over time), and self-coherence (the idea that a self is coherent and one, contained into one entity). For an overview of the discussion, see Susan Harter, *The Construction of the Self: A Developmental Perspective* (New York: Guilford, 1999), p. 6.
7. For example, in chapter 2 I argue that good reason exists to believe the Wanderer and Seafarer's self-identity has changed over a period of time, suggesting that identity was not only a malleable expression of oneself during this time, but that this malleability often coincided with life circumstances outside of one's control. See Harter, p. 8.
8. Charles Lindholm, "Does the Sociocentric Self Exist? Reflections on Markus and Kitayama"s 'Culture and the Self,'" *Journal of Anthropological Research*, 53.4 (1997), 405–422 (p. 407). Here, Lindholm is considering Markus and Kitayama's view.
9. For a concise bibliography on the self, see Charles Taylor, *Sources of the Self: The Making of the Modern Identity* (Cambridge: Cambridge University Press, 1992).
10. Jerome A. Shaffer, *Philosophy of Mind* (Englewood Cliffs: Prentice-Hall, 1968), p. 57.
11. There exists much criticism to the theory of dualism, which cannot be broached here. Generally speaking, then, I will not comment on the various physicalist theories of the self (however, some ideas, such as the short section below on how neuroscience is finding new ways to "search for the self" inside the brain, are necessarily physicalist theories of the mind). However, in truth, the reality of whether or not the mind (self, perhaps) and its processes are physical things entirely, or if they are distinct, as Descartes suggested—one existing in the realm of tangible experience, and the other in the abstract idea of the ether—is not critical for my discussion, because our concern is how the Anglo-Saxons described their selfhood. And so whether or not it derives from this a more physicalist or dualistic ideology will naturally

Chapter Notes—Introduction

become clearer as we move on. See Rene Descartes, *Meditations on First Philosophy: With Selections from the Objections and Replies*, trans. by Michael Moriarty (Oxford: Oxford University Press, 2008), pp. 19–20.

12. Shaffer, p. 35.

13. Galen Strawson, "The Sense of the Self," in *From Soul to Self*, ed. by M. James C. Crabbe (London: Routledge, 1999), 126–152 (p. 131).

14. In psychoanalytic theory, cognitive behavioral therapy (CBT) acts in just this way.

15. H.P. Grice, "Personal Identity," in *Personal Identity*, ed. by John Perry (Berkeley: University of California Press, 1975), 73–95 (p. 79).

16. David Hume, "Of Personal Identity," in *Personal Identity*, ed. by John Perry (Berkeley: University of California Press, 1975), 161–172 (p. 162).

17. My purpose here is to provide an understanding of how we may come to believe that the self is a construct of society, in a very general way. An in-depth analysis of this idea and offshoots of it are investigated in chapter 1.

18. Here, Gertler is referring to Russell's affirmation that the self may be perceived during introspection, after perceptions are quieted. This idea has many parallels with Eastern philosophies that suggest a true self exists behind the seemingly endless framework of runaway perceptions (e.g., Advaita Vedanta, Zen Buddhism). See Brie Gertler, *Self-Knowledge* (New York: Routledge, 2011), p. 210.

19. Jaegwon Kim, *Philosophy of Mind*, 3rd ed. (Boulder: Westview Press, 2011), p. 32.

20. Jean Decety and Jessica A. Sommervile, "Shared Representations Between Self and Other: A Social Cognitive Neuroscience View," *Trends in Cognitive Sciences*, 7.12 (2003), 527–533 (p. 527).

21. *Ibid.*, p. 528.

22. *Ibid.*

23. Burkitt, p. 38.

24. W.M. Kelly, et al., "Finding the Self? An Event–Related fMRI Study," *Journal of Cognitive Neuroscience*, 14.5 (2002), 785–794 (p. 785).

25. *Ibid.*, p. 786.

26. *Ibid.*, p. 789.

27. The conclusion in this study revealed that the "self-referential thought seems to be mediated by a specific, anatomically distinct region" or "neural substrate" in the brain, *ibid.*, p. 790.

28. See chapter 3 for an in-depth analysis of this type of self-formation.

29. Stanley B. Klein, Keith Rozendal, and Leda Cosmides, "A Social-Cognitive Neuroscience Analysis of the Self," *Social Cognition*, 20.2 (2002), 105–135 (p. 112).

30. *Ibid.*

31. *Ibid.*, pp. 113, 126, and 124.

32. How this argument is developed is complex and too lengthy to approach here; however, I provide a discussion on the general ways in which this development occurred when exploring whether or not we see a discernable shift in the emphasis of self-identity in the Anglo-Saxon period over time in chapter 2. See Hinobu Kitayama and Jiyoung Park, "Cultural Neuroscience of the Self: Understanding the Social Grounding of the Brain," *SCAN*, 5 (2010), 111–129 (p. 112).

33. *Ibid.*

34. D.W. Murray, "What is the Western Concept of the Self? On Forgetting David Hume," *Ethos*, 21 (1993), 3–23 (p. 7).

35. *Ibid.*

36. Kitayama, p. 118.

37. This idea is broadly Confucian. See *ibid.*

38. Kitayama, p. 120.

39. Communal identity is discussed with specific emphasis in chapter 3 and is the key discussion point in chapter 1. See Lisa Zunshine, "Lying Bodies of the Enlightenment: Theory of Mind and Cultural Historicism," in *Introduction to Cognitive Cultural Studies*, ed. by Lisa Zunshine (Baltimore: Johns Hopkins University Press, 2010), 115–133 (p. 118).

40. John R. Searle, "Social Ontology and the Philosophy of Society," *Analyse & Kritik*, 20 (1998), p. 153.

41. It is not possible to review the many volumes on this subject here. Provided herein is a short background with different ideas of how we may use this critical approach. See the chapters below for a larger, but by no means extensive, bibliography.

42. Tony E. Jackson, "'Literary Interpretation' and Cognitive Literary Studies," *Poetics Today*, 24.2 (2003), 191–205 (pp. 191 and 199).

43. Alan Richardson, "Literature and the Cognitive Revolution: An Introduction," *Poetics Today*, 23.1 (2002), 1–20 (p. 3).

44. Elizabeth F. Hart, "The Epistemology of Cognitive Literary Studies," *Philosophy and Literature*, 25.2 (2001), 314–334 (p. 316).

45. The point is that the use of science in literary interpretation only *strengthens* traditional methods, not hinders it. It is not the

Chapter Notes—Introduction

theories throughout this work that are under scrutiny, after all, but it is my analysis of the material through its lens that may be questioned; and if we can critique the former in the process (which I certainly do), it may be a bonus for my purpose. See Jackson, p. 200.

46. This is key to the arguments in each chapter below, but particularly chapters 1, 3, and 4. Refer to those chapters specifically for discussion. See Alan Palmer, "Storyworlds and Groups," in *Introduction to Cognitive Cultural Studies*, ed. by Lisa Zunshine (Baltimore: Johns Hopkins University Press, 2010), 176–192 (p. 176).

47. Although somewhat arbitrarily apportioned to the topic, these terms will help us locate this discussion under a particular framework and tradition of inquiry.

48. It should be noted that if any article or longer monograph exists that details individuality in the Anglo-Saxon period, I am unaware of it. Slightly more scholarship can be found, however, that discusses "the self" in one form or another, with an emphasis on its location and/or quality likened to a soul, spirit, etc. (abstract thesis), and it is the extraction of personal-identity from this discourse that I am most interested in.

49. Antonina Harbus, *Cognitive Approaches to Old English Poetry* (Cambridge: D.S. Brewer, 2012), p. 137.

50. *Ibid*.

51. Leslie Lockett, "Corporeality in the Psychology of the Anglo-Saxons" (Unpublished PhD Thesis, University of Notre Dame, Medieval Institute), 2004, p. 22.

52. This is the kind of discourse that we often find in self-studies, especially of the Anglo-Saxon kind. Because of the ambiguity of the terms, and the difficulty in establishing clear subject definitions, there is often a disconnect between how we discuss the self and how we investigate it. *Ibid.*, p. 60.

53. Lockett is here referring to line 544 in *Guthlac A: ne him gnornunga gæste scodun* ("neither did sadness injure his soul"). She has attributed this finding to Malcolm Godden in "Anglo-Saxons on the Mind," *Learning and Literature in Anglo-Saxon England: Studies Presented to Peter Clemoes on the Occasion of His Sixty-Fifth Birthday*, ed. by Michael Lapidge and Helmut Gneuss (Cambridge: Cambridge University Press, 2009), 271–295 (p. 289); however, Godden did not specify the line number for his reference. For more discussion, see Lockett, *Corporeality*, pp. 54–55. Refer also to Leslie Lockett, *Anglo-Saxon Psychologies in the Vernacular and Latin Traditions* (Toronto: University of Toronto Press, 2011), pp. 34–35. Additionally, Alexandra Ramsden has commented on the soul''s sideline participation, that "although the *sawul* is frequently depicted as being joyful or sad in its afterlife, it is hardly ever associated with emotions or with thought during human life." See Alexandra Ramsden, "Anglo-Saxon Conceptions of the Inner Self: An Exploration of Traditions and Innovation in Selected Cynewulfian and Alfredian Texts" (Unpublished PhD Thesis, University of York, Centre for Medieval Studies), 2008, p. 51.

54. Lockett, *Psychologies*, pp. 34–35.

55. The references here refer to lines 312–313 in *Maldon* and 36–38 in *Wand. Ibid.*, pp. 34–5 and 41. See also chapter 2 on how memory is instrumental in the dissolving of the wanderer and seafarer's old self and the creation of a new one.

56. Ramsden, p. 51.

57. *Ibid.*, p. 52. Also, as one of the very few articles of its kind that explicitly and directly discusses the notion of the Anglo-Saxon self, a must-read is also Antonina Harbus, "The Medieval Concept of the Self in Anglo-Saxon England," *Self and Identity*, 1 (2002), 77–97 (p. 85).

58. Harbus, "The Medieval Concept of the Self," p. 83.

59. Ramsden, p. 60.

60. Harbus, *Cognitive Approaches*, pp. 141–142.

61. Ramsden, p. 53.

62. *Ibid.*

63. See Ramsden, pp. 2, 14, and 54.

64. In this way, the mind informs the self. While my definition of the self for this work is not the same as Harbus's, her definition is a recommended starting point for my discussion. Refer to chapter 2. See Antonina Harbus, *The Life of the Mind in Old English Poetry* (Amsterdam: Rodopi, 2002), pp. 155 and 159.

65. Ramsden, p. 57.

66. E.g., when was a more personally autonomous notion of the self more apparent than one of communal attachment, in the literature? And what are the implications of any variation?

67. As cited in Ramsden, p. 22.

68. See my discussion of Satan in *GenB* and the narrator in *Deor*, for instance.

69. Martha Riddiford, "Social Exclusion from Early Medieval Wessex" (Unpublished PhD Thesis, University of Sheffield), 2007, p. 32.

70. These settlements were along the road to Rome, approximately every 12 miles. See *Ibid.*, pp. 40–41.
71. This is precisely my argument for the religious verse cited in chapter 4.
72. *Ibid.*, p. 34.
73. *Ibid.*, pp. 44–45.
74. Charles Radding, "Evolution of Medieval Mentalities: A Cognitive-Structural Approach," *The American Historical Review*, 83, no. 3 (1978), 577–597 (p. 595).
75. This question provides the thrust of inquiry throughout this book.
76. Marilynn Desmond, "The Voice of Exile: Feminist Literary History and the Anonymous Anglo-Saxon Elegy," *Critical Inquiry*, 16, no. 3 (1990), 572–590 (p. 584). For more discussion on this, see Mary Garrison, "An Aspect of Alcuin: *'Tuus Albinus'*—Peevish Egotist? or Parrhesiast?," in *Ego Trouble: Authors and their Identities in the Early Middle Ages*, ed. by Richard Corradini et al. (Austrian Academy of Sciences, 2010), p. 147.

Chapter 1

1. See Peter Burke and Jan Stets, *Identity Theory* (Oxford: Oxford University Press, 2009), p. 132, and Milton Singer, "Pronouns, Persons, and the Semiotic Self," in *Semiotics, Self, and Society*, ed. by Greg Urban and Benjamin Lee (Berlin: Mouton de Gruyter, 1989), pp. 229–298 (p. 255).
2. *Genesis B* (hereafter *GenB*) and *Dream of the Rood* (*DrR*).
3. Burke and Stets, p. 10.
4. See Richard Jenkins, *Social Identity* (New York: Routledge, 2008), p. 17 and p. 64, where he states that society "is a conversation between people; the mind is the internalization of that conversation; the self lies within and between the two." Refer also to Vivien Burr, *Social Constructionism* (London: Routledge, 2003), p. 106.
5. Benjamin Lee and Greg Urban, "Introduction," in *Semiotics, Self, and Society*, ed. Benjamin Lee and Greg Urban (Berlin: Mouton de Gruyter, 1989), 1–14 (p. 2).
6. John Turner, "Towards a Cognitive Redefinition of the Social Group," in *Social Identity and Intergroup Relations*, ed. by Henri Tajfel (Cambridge: Cambridge University Press, 1982).
7. Krinka Petrov, "Memory and Oral Tradition," in *Memory: History, Culture and the Mind*, ed. by Thomas Butler (Oxford: Basil Blackwell, 1989), p. 77.

8. Burke and Stets, p. 127. Here, the discussion is on three main types of identity: a core or "person identity," a "role identity," and a "social identity." The first functions "across situations, across time, across relationships," and is what I would call the "core self," or the basic subjective consciousness of "I" with a negligible—but not absent—influence from culture.
9. Turner, p. 16.
10. Michael Schwalbe and Douglas Mason-Schrock, "Identity Work as Group Process," *Advances in Group Processes*, 13 (1996), 113–147 (p. 121).
11. Although communal in nature, this process does not exclude the possibility for 'unique subjectivities' of individuals on the whole. *Ibid.*, pp. 118 and 122.
12. Elinor Ochs and Lisa Capps, "Narrating the Self," *Annual Review of Anthropology* 25 (1996), 19–43 (p. 30) and also Peter Callero, "The Sociology of the Self," *Annual Review of Sociology*, 29 (2003), 115–133 (p. 121).
13. John Searle, *The Construction of Social Reality* (London: Penguin, 1996), pp. 9 and 12.
14. Jonathan Culler, *The Pursuit of Signs: Semiotics, Literature, Deconstruction* (Ithaca: Cornell University Press, 2001), p. 33.
15. *Ibid.*
16. The authors are referring to an example in Arab law. See Lee and Urban, "Introduction," p. 8. However, Anglo-Saxon law also highlights how community played a role in punishment. The exacting of justice by the victim''s family, for instance, is one example.
17. Charles Taylor, *Sources of the Self: The Making of Modern Identity* (Cambridge: Cambridge University Press, 2010), p. 112.
18. Susan Petrilli, *The Self as a Sign, the World, and the Other: Living Semiotics* (New Brunswick: Transaction Publishers, 2013), p. 59.
19. Thomas Shaw, "The Semiotic Mediation of Identity," *Ethos*, 22 (1994), 83–119 (p. 84).
20. *Ibid.*
21. Refer to Petrilli, p. 61.
22. This is a similar concept to the one that I have termed "actionable identity" in the Introduction.
23. Shaw, p. 113. See also Schwalbe and Mason-Schrock, p. 125, where they refer to each identity as needing to adhere to "local code[s]" in order to assimilate with society.
24. I highlight this process in the following three chapters.
25. Susan Oakdale, "Creating a Continuity

Chapter Notes—1

between Self and Other: First-Person Narration in an Amazonian Ritual Context," *Ethos* 30 (2002), 158–175 (pp. 160–161). Milton Singer even echoes these findings in less-industrialized modern societies, when he states that "a person is not absolutely an individual," since "the man"s circle of society ... is a sort of loosely compacted person." Milton Singer, "Signs of the Self: An Exploration in Semiotic Anthropology," *American Anthropologist*, New Series 82, no. 3 (1980), 485–507 (p. 494).

26. Singer, "Signs of the Self," p. 489.

27. Culler, p. 32.

28. For further reading, see Kenneth Gergen, "Social Constructionist Inquiry: Context and Implications," in *The Social construction of the Person*, ed. by Kenneth Gergen and Keith Davis (New York: Springer-Verlag, 1985), 3–18 (pp. 12–13).

29. In social constructionism, conforming would of course be more prevalent, whereas any deviation would allow us to isolate a more personal, individual iteration of self. See Burke and Stets, p. 5.

30. Callero, p. 123.

31. In contrast to the Editorial "we," which includes the speakers but not the addressee. See Singer, "Pronouns," p. 251.

32. *Ibid.*

33. I depart from fully sanctioning the latter portion of this idea, since the first-person singular pronoun does not always signify a truly personal identity—especially in Old English literature. As we will see, first-person narration in the poetry listed in this chapter almost always refers to the collective. Again, this is to show the contrast with the narration in chapters 2–4.

34. Deborah Schiffrin, "Narrative as Self-Portrait: Sociolinguistic Constructions of Identity," *Language in Society*, 25. 2 (1996), 167–203 (p. 168).

35. Paul Connerton, *How Societies Remember* (Cambridge: Cambridge University Press, 1998), p. 3.

36. See Schiffrin, p. 168 and Connerton, p. 3.

37. Additionally, songs often play the role of reflecting both the current and the past experiences of the participants, creating a kind of symbiosis of identity by allowing for an "appropriation of another's experience as the speaker's." See Oakdale, pp. 166–167.

38. Callero, p. 124.

39. Refer to chapter 2.

40. Peter Burke, "History as Social Memory," in *Memory: History, Culture and the Mind*, ed. by Thomas Butler (Oxford: Basil Blackwell, 1989), 97–113 (p. 98).

41. Ron Eyerman and Jeffrey Jeffrey, "From the Past in the Present: Culture and the Transmission of Memory," in *Collective Memory Reader*, ed. by Vered Vinitzky-Seroussi and Daniel Levy (Oxford: Oxford University Press, 2011), 304–107 (pp. 305–306).

42. See footnote 439, as well.

43. My example from *Wan* and *Seaf* in Chapter 2 explicitly catalogues this process. *Ibid.*, p. 306.

44. Petrov, pp. 86–87.

45. *Ibid.*, pp. 78–79.

46. When referring to the Briton"s repite from war, Bede mentions that "so long as memory of past disaster remained fresh, kings and priests, commoners and nobles kept their proper rank." Here is an early example of how a shared communal memory informed the actions of society members, which also helped to shape identity. See Book I, Chapter 22. Bede, *Ecclesiastical History of the English People* trans. by Leo Sherley-Price (London: Penguin, 1990), p. 72.

47. Eyerman and Olick, p. 305.

48. It is also important to note that French refers to memory as being a "representation [...] of the past," not a perfect reflection. Brigittine French, "The Semiotics of Collective Memories," *Annual Review of Anthropology*, 41 (2012), 337–353 (pp. 339–340).

49. Singer, "Signs of the Self," p. 495.

50. Greg Urban, "The 'I' of Discourse," in *Semiotics, Self, and Society*, ed. by Greg Urban and Benjamin Lee (Berlin: Mouton de Gruyter, 1989), pp. 27–52 (p. 46).

51. I note the effects of exile on the individual in all of the following chapters and its significance on their sense of self.

52. Culler, p. 38.

53. That is to say, whether we speak of the Anglo-Saxons of the conversion period or during the tenth century when the great codices were written and preserved, the influence of either the *scop* or writer would have been similar.

54. Turner, p. 18.

55. In chapter 3, I explore how the *scop* demonstrates both personal and communal identity through his position in society.

56. Culler, p. 29.

57. As I stated earlier, we cannot look for the individual without seeing her in context within wider society. See *Ibid.*, p. 31.

58. Oakdale, p. 169.

59. Urban, pp. 39 and 27.

60. In this case, Urban shows that the "I"

is not the "speaker's everyday identity of self" but an "identity the speaker assumes through the text." See *Ibid.*, pp. 27–28. Additionally, there are times when "personal identity expressed by the pronoun 'I' becomes a feeling of alienation from the collective identity," and therefore it is often used to reflect the plurality of a group. Refer to Singer, "Pronouns," p. 248, who is quoting Levi-Strauss's *L'Homme nu.*

61. Of course, Old English "*scop*" poems like *Deor* and *Widsith*, as well as other verse that peripherally features a minstrel do provide insight into some of these questions, but only imperfect insight.

62. Hugh Magennis, "The Cup as Symbol and Metaphor in Old English Literature," *Speculum* 60, no. 3 (1985), 517–536 (p. 533).

63. Magennis has argued that "the individual is shown ideally as engaged in a communal enterprise," and that "individualism itself can bring community into danger." In communities with strong kinship associations, it is only natural that individualism is often seen as a threat to the status quo, the extended kin group concerns, and the social construction of identity more generally. Hugh Magennis, *Images of Community in Old English Poetry* (Cambridge: Cambridge University Press, 1996), p. 38

64. *Ibid.*, p. 35.

65. See chapter 3 for a full discussion.

66. Ward Parks, "The Traditional Narrator and the 'I Heard' Formulas in Old English Poetry," *Anglo-Saxon England*, 16 (1987), 45–66 (p. 49).

67. Allen Frantzen, "Drama and Dialogue in Old English Poetry: The Scene of Cynewulf's *Juliana*," *Theatre Survey*, 48 (2007), 99–119 (p. 105).

68. Michael Cherniss, "Heroic Ideals and the Moral Climate of *Genesis B*," *Modern Language Quarterly*, 30. 4 (1969), 479–497 (p. 479).

69. R.E. Woolf, "The Devil in Old English Poetry," *The Review of English Studies*, New Series 4, no. 13 (1953), 1–12 (pp. 1–2).

70. Cherniss, pp. 483 and 485.

71. "He ought to have done homage to the lord, he ought to have prized his joys in the heavens, and he ought to have thanked his lord for the bounty he had allotted him in that light." All subsequent references to *GenB*, including editorial practices, come from *Genesis*, in *The Junius Manuscript*, ed. by George Krapp (New York: Columbia University Press, 1931), pp. 3–87.

72. Cherniss, p. 488. Refer also to Paul Cavill, *Anglo-Saxon Christianity: Exploring the Earliest Roots of Christian Spirituality in England* (London: Fount, 1999), p. 128, and Claude Schneider, "Cynewulf's Devaluation of Heroic Tradition in *Juliana*," *Anglo-Saxon England*, 7 (1978), 107–118 (p. 107), for discussion of interpreting Christian characters in terms of the heroic world.

73. *Ibid.*, p. 480. Also see Larry McKill, "Patterns of the Fall: Adam and Eve in the Old English *Genesis A*," *Florilegium*, 14 (1995), 25–41 (pp. 26–27), who speaks of loyalty and "traditional heroic values in *Genesis A*.

74. "Why must I serve for his favor and submit to him in such fealty? I can be a god as well as he. Strong vassals stand by me, who will not fail me in the fight."

75. "Alas! If I had control of my hands, and could for one hour be out of here, for one winter space, then with this company I—But iron fetters surround me, a halter of chains binds me."

76. For further, see Woolf, p. 8.

77. *Ibid.*

78. Janet Ericksen, "Lands of Unlikeness in 'Genesis B,'" *Studies in Philology*, 93 (1996), 1–20 (p. 8).

79. "The one who performs that, for him reward will afterwards be at the ready forever, of such profits as we may gain here inside this fire."

80. P.S. Langeslag, "Doctrine and Paradigm: Two Functions of the Innovations in Genesis B," *Studia Neophilologica* 79, no. 2 (2007), 113–118 (p. 113). See also Cherniss, p. 491.

81. See Cherniss, pp. 491–492 for example, where he says Eve acts to "serve and advise her husband and to protect him."

82. Langeslag, p. 113.

83. "Yet she did it for the sake of loyal intention. She did not know that there would follow so many hurts and sinful woes for mankind, because she took to heart the instruction she heard from that evil messenger; but she thought that she was earning the favour of the heavenly King."

84. Ll. 559b-560b.

85. "Genesis," in *Anglo-Saxon Poetry* trans. and ed. by S.A.J. Bradley (London: Orion Publishing, 1991), p. 28.

86. "What shall it avail you, such hateful contest with your lord"s messenger? We need his favor; he can intercede for us with the Ruler of all, the King of heaven."

87. "Not for me will there be pleasure of giving any service in the world, now that I have lost the favour of my prince."

88. "There is nothing before us to protect againt the storm, nor any provision designated for food, but Mighty God is angry at us."

89. "Lo, Eve! With your wickedness, you have sealed the destiny of our two selves."

90. Eric Jager, "Speech and the Chest in Old English Poetry: Orality or Pectoriality?" *Speculum*, 65. 4 (1990), 845–859 (p. 858).

91. Ericksen, p. 20.

92. As it does with the poems I will look out in the following chapters.

93. McKill, pp. 37–38.

94. Cherniss, p. 495.

95. Woolf, p. 7.

96. "Misery replete will befall the man who does not keep on his guard while he enjoys self-determination." Bradley, p. 30.

97. Andrew Galloway, "Dream-Theory in the *Dream of the Rood* and *The Wanderer*," *The Review of English Studies, New Series* 45, no. 180 (1994), 474–485 (p. 485).

98. Richard Payne, "Convention and Originality in the Vision Framework of *'The Dream of the Rood*,'" *Modern Philology*, 73. 4 (1976), 329–341 (p. 340).

99. "Listen! I want to tell of the best of visions, that I dreamed in the middle of the night when voiceful people lay asleep." This and all subsequent references and editorial practices are taken from "Dream of the Rood," in *The Vercelli Book*, ed. by George Krapp (New York: Columbia University Press, 1932), pp. 61–65.

100. Peggy Samuels, "The Audience Written into the Script of *The Dream of the Rood*," *Modern Language Quarterly* 49, no. 4 (1988), 311–320 (p. 313).

101. Mize also takes note that the dreamer is only, "for the time being," "set [...] apart from community." Britt Mize, "The Mental Container and the Cross of Christ: Revelation and Community in the *Dream of the Rood*," *Studies in Phlology*, 107. 2 (2010), 131–178 (p. 144). See also Samuels, pp. 313 and 315, who says that the dreamer's initial "state of aloneness" moves on to "one of communality" later on, and who "participate[s] in, rather than being the object of, a communal audience."

102. L. 20b.

103. Peri-Nagy Zsuzsanna, "Identity, Authority, Empowering: Another Approach to *The Dream of the Rood*," *Tel* (2012), 1–19 (p. 17). See also Britt Mize, "The Representation of the Mind as an Enclosure in Old English Poetry," 57–90 (pp. 75–76).

104. Adelheid Thieme, "Gift Giving as a Vital Element of Salvation in 'The Dream of the Rood,'" *South Atlantic Review*, 63. 2 (1998), 108–123 (p. 120).

105. Ll. 123b-124a.

106. "It is now my life's hope that I will be allowed to seek the tree of victory alone, more frequently than all other people, and honor it well."

107. "I do not have many powerful friends on earth, but they have departed from here, from the joys of the world and sought the King of glory, they live in heaven with the High Father, and dwell in glory."

108. Mize, "The Mental Container," pp. 144 and 156.

109. Refer to Frantzen and Urban.

110. "I did not then dare, against the Lord's word, to bow or break."

111. "I was raised up as a cross. I lifted the mighty King, Lord of the heavens; I did not dare to lean down."

112. Thieme reminds us that to allow one's lord to die, while his retainer lay passive, "would mean the highest treason, the deepest shame." See Thieme, p. 114.

113. *Bysmeredon hie unc butu ætgædere* (l. 48a). "They degraded us both together."

114. Hugh Magennis, *Images of Community in Old English Poetry* (Cambridge: Cambridge University Press, 1996), p. 23.

115. In Magennis, *Images of Community*, p. 23, he also mentions the bifurcated "highly personal tone" as well as the "fixation on the relationship between the speaker and his lord."

116. Zsuzsanna, p. 5.

117. Samuels, pp. 312 and 314.

118. "All creation wept, mourned the King's death. Christ was on the Cross."

119. L. 34b.

120. "Nevertheless, weeping, we stood [...] in place."

121. The private informs the public, and the individual the communal. See Mize, "The Mental Container" pp. 177–178.

122. See Esther Bernstein, "The Adhesive Nature of Violence: Orality, Violence, and the Communal in *Beowulf* as Opposed to Written Literacy, Emotion, and, and the Individual in "The Dream of the Rood*'*," Paper presented at the Proceedings of the National Conference on Undergraduate Research (NCUR), Ithaca College, New York, March 31-April 2, 2011.

123. Burke and Stets, p. 122.

124. Singer, "Pronouns," p. 284.

Chapter 2

1. See below for discussion, and refer to Hume's quote on perceptions.
2. For instance, Stroud is just one of many philosophers who do not believe that there exists an "invariable and uninterrupted entity that is the self or mind." See Barry Stroud, *Hume* (Abingdon: Routledge, 1977), p. 121.
3. David Wiggins, "Locke, Butler and the Stream of Consciousness: And Men as a Natural Kind," in *The Identities of Persons*, ed. by Amelie Oksenberg Rorty (Berkeley: University of California Press, 1969), pp. 139–173 (p. 168).
4. Quoting Thomas Reid. See John Sutton, *Philosophy and Memory Traces* (Cambridge: Cambridge University Press, 1998), p. 272.
5. X=person 1, y=person 2, t=time, and *iff*= "if and only if." See John W. Carroll and Ned Markosian, *An Introduction to Metaphysics* (Cambridge: Cambridge University Press, 2011), p. 118. See C Jung, *Psychological Types*. trans. by H Baynes (London: Routledge, 1989), p. 448.
6. See C Jung, *Psychological Types*, trans. by H Baynes (London: Routledge, 1989), p. 448.
7. David Hume, "Our Idea of Identity," in *Personal Identity*, ed. by John Perry (Berkeley: University of California Press, 1975), 159–160 (p. 160).
8. See Joseph Butler, "Of Personal Identity," in *Personal Identity*, ed. by John Perry (Berkeley: University of California Press, 1975), 99–105 (p. 99).
9. Wiggins, "Locke," p. 152.
10. Henceforth, all editorial practices and line references will come from Anne L. Klinck, *The Old English Elegies: A Critical Edition and Genre Study* (Montreal: McGill-Queen's University Press, 1992), while I have supplied my own translations. "Often the solitary one waits for honour, the mercy of God, even though for a long time, sad at heart, he has to move with his hands through the ocean's path, the icy-cold sea, to travel the paths of exile: fate is unstoppable."
11. De Lacy is referring to a primary theme in *Wan* that is certainly up for debate—i.e., how much this work is indebted to Christian themes. I briefly address this argument, and how it potentially plays a part in the formation of a new identity below. See Paul De Lacy, "Thematic and Structural Affinities: *The Wanderer* and Ecclesiastes," *Neophilologus*, 82 (1998), 125–137 (p. 127).
12. Klinck, p. 106.
13. See below for a full discussion.
14. Roger Fowler, "A Theme in *The Wanderer*," *Medium Ævum*, 36 (1967), 1–25 (p. 4).
15. "So said the Wanderer, remembering hardships, cruel battle-slaughters, the fall of dear kinsmen."
16. Rosemary Woolf, "*The Wanderer*, *The Seafarer*, and the Genre of *Planctus*," in *Anglo-Saxon Poetry: Essays in Appreciation for John C. McGalliard*, ed. by Lewis E. Nicholson and Dolores Warwick Frese (Notre Dame: University of Notre Dame Press, 1975), 192–207 (p. 207).
17. "Often every dawn, I alone had to lament my sorrows; now there is not one living being to whom I dare to clearly tell my state of mind. I know to be sure that it is a noble custom in a man that he should bind up the treasure of thoughts securely in his breast, let him think as he wishes."
18. The Exeter Book has been variably dated from the late ninth century to no later than 1072. See Klinck, p. 13.
19. S.L. Clark and Julian N. Wasserman, "The Imagery of "The Wanderer," *Neophilologus*, 63 (1979), 291–296 (p. 292).
20. Robert E. Bjork, "Sundor æt Rune: The Voluntary Exile of the Wanderer," *Neophilologus*, 73 (1989), 119–129 (p. 121).
21. Thomas D. Hill, "A Stoic Maxim in 'The Wanderer' and Its Contexts," *Studies in Philology*, 101 (2004), 233–249 (p. 249).
22. "So, often sorrowful, I—separated from my homeland, far from kinsmen—have had to bind my state of mind with fetters, since years ago in the darkness of earth I covered my gold-lord, and I, despondent, travelled away, wintry-minded over the binding of waves, saddened by the loss of a hall, I sought a giver of treasure, whether far or near I could find him who in the mead-hall would acknowledge my love, or would console me in my friendlessness, and entice (me) with good things."
23. Susan Irvine, "Speaking One's Mind in *The Wanderer*," in *Inside Old English: Essays in Honour of Bruce Mitchell*, ed. by John Walmsley (Oxford: Blackwell, 2005), pp. 117–133 (p. 123).
24. *Ibid*.
25. "He who tries it knows how cruel sorrow is as a companion to him who has few beloved confidants. The path of exile holds him, not twisted gold, the frozen heart, not the splendor of the earth; he remembers men of the hall and the receiving of treasure, and how in his youth his gold-lord entertained

him at the banquet—all joy has perished. He understands, therefore, who has to do without his dear lord"s teachings for a long time."

26. This topic is explored in the chapters on communal identity. See James W. Booth, *Communities of Memory: On Witness, Identity, and Justice* (Ithaca: Cornell University Press, 2006), pp. 11–12.

27. See Jon Elster, "Introduction," in *The Multiple Self*, ed. by Jon Elster (New York: Cambridge University Press, 1986), pp. 1–34 (p. 10).

28. A simple yet powerful phrase that includes association with a lord, communion with warriors, and a place within society. See Clark and Wasserman, p. 293.

29. Also see Michelle Z. Rosaldo, "Toward an Anthropology of Self and Feeling," in *Culture Theory: Essays on Mind, Self, and Emotion*, ed. by Richard A. Shweder and Robert A. LeVine (New York: Cambridge University Press, 1992), 137–157 (pp. 139–140).

30. See Grant Gillett, *The Mind and Its Discontents: An Essay in Discursive Psychiatry* (Oxford: Oxford University Press, 1999), p. 335.

31. See Tyler Burge, "Memory and Persons," *The Philosophical Review*, 112.3 (2003), 289–337 (pp. 327–8).

32. "Often when sorrow and sleep simultaneously bind the wretched solitary man, it seems to him in his mind that he is embracing and kissing his lord and laying hands and head on his knee, as in days before he enjoyed the gift throne. Then the friendless man awakes again, sees dark waves in front of him, sea-birds bathing, spreading their wings, falling frost and snow mixed with hail."

33. I.e., an actual memory remembered and not a general idea.

34. Joseph LeDoux, *The Emotional Brain: The Mysterious Underpinnings of Emotional Life* (New York: Phoenix, 1998), p. 209.

35. This explanation is clearly made in *Seaf.* Refer to lines 19–22.

36. See Antonina Harbus, "Deceptive Dreams in 'The Wanderer,'" *Studies in Philology*, 93 (1996), 164–179 (p. 167).

37. Ibid.

38. "Then because of [the loss of] a dear one, the heart's wounds are harder to bear; sorrow is renewed when the memory of kinsmen passes through the mind: he greets his friends with joyous words, eagerly he watches them—the companions of men drift away again; the company of fleeting figures does not bring familiar stories there; sorrow is renewed to him who must very often send his weary spirit over the binding of waves."

39. See Irvine, p. 119.

40. James L. Rosier, "The Literal-Figurative Identity of The Wanderer," *PMLA*, 79 (1964), 366–9 (p. 368).

41. Irvine, p. 120.

42. Thomas Reid, "Of Identity," in *Personal Identity*, ed. by John Perry (Berkeley: University of California Press, 1975), 107–112 (p. 108).

43. "Therefore, I cannot think why in this world my mind does not grow dark when I consider the life of men—how they, spirited noble thanes, have suddenly left the hall. Just so this middle-earth declines and falls each and every day."

44. Elizabeth A. Hait, "The Wanderer's Lingering Regret: A Study of Patterns of Imagery," *Neophilologus*, 68 (1984), 278–291 (p. 279).

45. John L. Selzer, "'The Wanderer' and the Meditative Tradition," *Studies in Philology*, 80 (1983), 227–237 (p. 233).

46. This typology, or "schema" of identity, is explored in detail in chapter 3.

47. "Therefore, a man cannot become wise before he has lived many winters in the worldly kingdom. A wise man must be patient, not too angry, nor too hasty of speech, nor too weak in combat, nor too careless, nor too fearful, nor too joyful, nor too eager, nor too greedy for wealth, nor ever too desirous of making a boast before he sufficiently understands. A man must wait before he states a pledge until that person of bold spirit is fully aware of the way the thinking of his mind wants to go. A wise man must understand how eerie it will be when all this world's wealth stands ruined, as even now randomly throughout this middle-earth, walls stand, wind-blown, covered with hoarfrost, snow-swept buildings. The wine-halls are crumbling; the rulers are lying dead, deprived of joy; the whole proud noble band has fallen beside the wall. Some battle took and carried away along the long road; a bird carried one off over the deep sea; one the gray wolf dismemebered in death; one a sad-faced warrior buried in a grave in the earth. Thus, the creator of men devastated this world, until lacking the sounds of town-dwellers, the old giant structures stood empty."

48. John C. Pope, "Dramatic Voices in *The Wanderer* and *The Seafarer*," in *Medieval and Linguistic Studies: In Honor of Francs Peabody Magoun, Jr.*, ed. by Jess B. Bessinger, Jr., and Robert P. Creed (London: George Allen and Unwin Ltd., 1965), pp. 165–193 (p. 173).

Chapter Notes—2

49. "Then he who has wisely pondered upon this foundation and deeply thinks about this dark life, wise of heart, from afar often remembers a multitude of slaughters and says these words."
50. Woolf, p. 201.
51. Hait, p. 284.
52. David H. Demo, "The Self-Concept Over Time: Research Issues and Directions," *Annual Review of Sociology*, 18 (1992), 303–326 (p. 316).
53. For more on this motif, see Woolf, p. 200 and Klinck, p. 124.
54. "Where did the horse go? Where went the kinsman? Where did the treasure-giver go? Where went the feast seats? Where are the hall-joys? Oh, bright cup! Oh, mail-shirted warrior! Oh, the majesty of the ruler!"
55. "Everything in earth"s kingdom is full of hardship; the dispenser of destiny causes change in the world under the heavens. Here treasure is transitory, a friend is transitory, man is transitory, a kinsman is transitory. All this foundation of earth becomes empty." Also, De Lacy claims that in *Wan*, "there is an overwhelming sense of the transitory nature of existence." I would emend this to "the nature of community/society." Throughout the poem, there is only the briefest reference to the natural world, and none at all to one's soul dying. See especially lines 64–88. See De Lacy, p. 129.
56. See Eilnor Ochs and Lisa Capps, "Narrating the Self," *Annual Review of Anthropology*, 25 (1996), 19–43 (p. 29).
57. "Thus spoke the wise man in his mind, as he sat apart in thought. Good is he who keeps his faith; a man must never reveal his anxieties from his heart too quickly, unless the man beforehand knows the remedy and how to bring it about with zeal. It will be good for him who seeks honour, consolation from the Father in Heaven, where all security lies for us."
58. See Pope, p. 170.
59. De Lacy, p. 130.
60. Augustine is here quoted in Selzer, p. 230, as is the John Burnaby quote that follows.
61. James F. Doubleday, "The Three Faculties of the Soul in The Wanderer," *Neophilologus*, 53 (1969), 189–194 (pp. 189–193).
62. *Ibid.*
63. Selzer, p. 228.
64. James F. Doubleday, "The Limits of Philosophy: A Reading of 'The Wanderer,'" *Notre Dame English Journal*, 7 (1972), 14–22 (p. 18).
65. See above for our definition of the self. Harbus, "Deceptive," pp. 164–165.
66. Rosier, p. 366.
67. Bjork, p. 123.
68. Fowler provides a nice description of this, when he says that this section shows "the hardship of homelessness, of one who has lost his place [identity/selfhood?] in heroic society; exile exemplified in the personal narrative of an *eardstapa*." Fowler, p. 7.
69. The concept of the communal self based on a Christian community was also explored in chapter 1.
70. "I can tell a true tale about my own self, and speak of experiences—how in days of toil I often endured hardship, how I have endured bitter anxiety at heart and experienced many abodes of anxiety in a ship, and the tossing of horrible waves, where the perilous night-watch often came upon me at the prow of the ship when it jostles by the cliffs. My feet were oppressed by the cold, bound by the frost with cold chains, while sorrows sighed hot around my heart. Hunger tore within the heart of the sea-weary one. This the man does not know, who on land is most fairly suited, how I, wretchedly sad, have for years dwelt on the ice-cold sea in winter, on the paths of exile, deprived of kinsmen, hung about with icicles; hail flew in storms."
71. See Frederick S. Holton, "Old English Sea Imagery and the Interpretation of 'The Seafarer,'" *The Yearbook of English Studies*, 12 (1982), 208–217 (p. 211).
72. See H.P. Grice, "Personal Identity," in *Personal Identity*, ed. by John Perry (Berkeley: University of California Press, 1975), pp. 73–95 (p. 85).
73. *Ibid.*
74. More discussion on this is provided below.
75. "There I could not hear anything except for the roaring of the sea—the ice-cold wave. At times, I took for myself the swan's song as entertainment, the gannet's cry and the curlew's sound of in place of the laughter of men, the seagull singing in place of the mead-drink. There, storms beat on the stony cliffs while the the icy-feathered tern answered them; very often the eagle cried out in response, wet-feathered. No supportive kinsman could comfort the destitute soul."
76. "Indeed, he who has experienced life's joys in cities, and few terrible experiences—proud and flushed with wine—little believes how I, often weary, had to endure on the sea-path. The shadow of night grew dark, it snowed from the north, hoar-frost bound the

land, hail fell upon the earth, the coldest of grains."

77. Indeed, I also show its prevelance in the characters of *Widsith, Deor, Wife,* and *Wulf* (and to a lesser extent, *GenB, DrR,* and *Elene*) in chapters 1, 2 and 3. See Juienne H. Empric, "'The Seafarer': An Experience in Displacement," *Notre Dame English Journal,* 7 (1972), 23–33 (p. 31).

78. Gillett, p. 336.

79. Refer also to chapter 3, where I investigate the "schema of self" in *Deor* and *Widsith*.

80. Jeffrey K. and Joyce Robbins, Olick, "From 'Collective Memory' to the Historical Sociology of Mnemonic Practices," *Annual Review of Sociology* 24 (1998), p. 122.

81. "Now the thoughts of my heart are in conflict that I should try the experience of the high tossing of salty waves for myself; the soul's desire at all times urges the spirit to travel, that far from here I should seek the land of foreigners." For further discussion on the possible meanings behind the concepts of land and sea in Old English, see Dee Dyas, "Land and Sea in the Pilgrim Life: The *Seafarer* and the Old English *Exodus*," *English Language Notes*, 35.2 (1997), 1–9 (pp. 2 and 7), who says that "land and sea can be seen to be imbued with considerable spiritual significance, the former representing worldly joys and security, the latter signifying abandonment to the will of God." Suffice it to say that I agree with Dyas's analysis that land implies spiritual death, while sea can refer to those who are on a spiritual pilgrimage. "The Seafarer," in *Elegies*, p. 80.

82. The exchange of identity schema in the audience and the narrator is given special consideration in chapter 3.

83. E.g., lines 55b-57 in Wan: *cearo bið geniwad þam þe sendan sceal swiþe / geneahhe ofer waþema gebind werigne sefan.*

84. Refer to I.L. Gordon,"Traditional Themes in *The Wanderer* and *The Seafarer*," *The Review of English Studies*, New Series, 5.17 (1954), 1–13 (p. 3). See also lines 19–29 in *Wan*, for comparison.

85. Stanley B. Greenfield, "Attitudes and Values in 'The Seafarer,'" *Studies in Philology*, 51.1 (1954), 15–20 (p. 16).

86. We have already discussed how in lines 1–17 the seafarer is showing us this division of self; and here likewise *sylf* separates two aspects of the seafarer. See Empric, p. 30.

87. "because there is not any man on Earth so confident in tempermant, nor so generous of his gifts, nor so keen in his youth, nor in his deeds so brave, nor his lord so gracious to him, that he never worries about his sea voyage, as to what the Lord wishes to provide for him."

88. See Greenfield, pp. 19–20.

89. "He will not have a thought for the harp, nor for the ring-giving ceremony, nor the joy of a woman, nor worldly hope, nor about anything else, apart from the tossing of the waves; but he who sets out on the water always has the yearning. Groves take on blossoms; cities become beautiful; the meadows become beautiful; the world hastens onwards. All these urge the spirit of one eager of mind to the journey, whoever intends thus, to travel far on the ocean's paths. Likewise, the cuckoo announces by its mournful voice, the keeper of summer sings, foretells bitter sorrow in the heart. That man, the man blessed with bounty, does not understand this—what those people endure who travel the paths of exile most widely."

90. Demo, p. 322.

91. Refer to chapters 1 and 3 for a discussion on the audience's role in preserving a communal self-concept.

92. "For this reason, now my mind moves beyond the confines of my breast; my mind moves far and wide with the sea over the whale's home, over the face of the Earth; it then comes back to me, eager and fierce; the lone flier cries and urges the spirit irresistibly over the whale's path, over the expanse of waters; because for me the joys of the Lord are more urgent (hotter) than this dead life, fleeting life on land."

93. Vivian Salmon, "'The Wanderer' and 'The Seafarer,' and the Old English Conception of the Soul," *The Modern Language Review*, 55 (1960), 1–10 (pp. 1–2).

94. *Ibid.*

95. See Holton, p. 212, who has identified this in the Old English *physiologus.*

96. Neil Hultin, "The External Soul in 'The Seafarer' and 'The Wanderer,'" *Folklore*, 88 (1977), 39–45 (p. 44).

97. *Ibid.*

98. Greenfield, p. 15.

99. See M.R. Godden, "Anglo-Saxons on the Mind," in *Learning and Literature in Anglo-Saxon England: Studies Presented to Peter Clemoes on the Occasion of His Sixty-Fifth Birthday*, ed. by Michael Lapidge and Helmut Gneuss (Cambridge: Cambridge University Press, 2009), pp. 271–295 (p. 295).

100. "I do not believe at all that for him the riches of the earth stand eternal; one of

three things will always fall into doubt before his death: disease or old age or sword-hate will tear away life from the doomed man."

101. "The days have departed, all the pomp of the kingdom of Earth; now there are no kings, nor Caesars, nor gold-giveing lords such as there were long ago, when they performed the most wonderful deeds of glory among themselves and lived in a most noble renown. This noble band has perished; the joys have departed. The inferior remain and possess the world, through toil they enjoy it. Prosperity has been brought down; the Earth's nobility grows old and withers, just like all men now throughout middle-earth."

102. "Old age advances on him, his face grows pale; gray-haired he laments; he knows his friends of old, the sons of princes, have been consigned to the Earth. Then when life is lost to him, his body will not be able to taste sweet, nor feel pain, nor raise a hand, nor think with the mind."

103. See Eli Hirsch, *The Concept of Identity* (New York: Oxford University Press, 1982), pp. 206–207 and 210.

104. *Ibid.*

105. See John Locke, "Of Identity and Diversity," in *Personal Identity*, ed. by John Perry (Berkeley: University of California Press, 1975), pp. 33–52 (pp. 35, 39, and 44).

106. *Ibid.*

107. "Great is the awesomeness of the ordaining Lord, before which this earth will turn away; he established the solid grounds, the face of the Earth and the sky above."

108. "Foolish is he who does not fear his Lord: death will come upon him unpremeditated. Blessed is he who lives in humility: to him will come grace from the heavens. The ordaining Lord will make stable his heart, because he trusts in his might. A man must steer a willful heart and keep it fixed upon stable points; and, worthy of men's trust and pure in his ways, each man must conduct himself with moderation through happiness and through adversity, in joy and in affliction, even if the Lord wills to prove to him, permeated by fire, or assay, smelted in the flame, the friend he has made. Fate is stronger, the ordaining Lord mightier, than the mind of any man. Let us think where we have a home and then consider how we may come to be there, and also let us strive so that we may be allowed in eternal bliss, where life is dependent on the Lord's love, hope in the heavens." I have used Bradley's translation here from lines 106–116, as I feel that it accurately and concisely lays out the conclusion of the verse. "The Seafarer," in *Anglo-Saxon Poetry*, ed. by S.A.J. Bradley (London: Orion Publishing Group, 1991), p. 334.

109. Georgiana Donavin, "A Preacher's Identity: Allusions to Jonah in 'The Seafarer,'" *The Yearbook of English Studies*, 22 (1992), 28–37 (pp. 36–37).

110. Refer to *Ibid.* and Dorothy Whitelock, "The Interpretation of *The Seafarer*," *The Early Cultures of North-West Europe (H.M. Chadwick Memorial Studies)*, ed. by Sir Cyril Fox and Bruce Dickins (Cambridge: Cambridge University Press, 1950), pp. 261–271 (p. 263).

111. Holton, p. 213.

112. Pope, p. 178.

113. Greenfield, p. 17.

114. Antonina Harbus, *The Life of the Mind in Old English Poetry* (Amsterdam: Rodopi, 2002), p. 130.

115. Harbus, *Life of the Mind*, p. 129.

116. This is highly significant for my discussion in chapters 3 and 4 especially. See Pope, p. 188.

117. James F. Doubleday, "Two-Part Structure in Old English Poetry," *Notre Dame English Journal*, 8.2, pp. 75 and 77.

118. Helen T. Bennett, "Exile and the Semiosis of Gender in Old English Elegies," in *Class and Gender in Early English Literature*, ed. by Britton J. Harwood and Gillian R. Overing (Bloomington: Indiana University Press, 1994), pp. 43–58 (p. 44).

119. W.F. Klein, "Purpose and the "Poetics' of *The Wanderer* and *The Seafarer*," in *Anglo-Saxon Poetry: Essays in Appreciation for John C. McGalliard*, ed. by Lewis E. Nicholson and Dolores Warwick Frese (Notre Dame: University of Notre Dame Press, 1975), pp. 208–223 (p. 212).

120. Edward B. Irving, Jr., "Images and the Meaning in the Elegies," in *Old English Poetry: Fifteen Essays*, ed. by Robert P. Creed (Providence: Brown University Press, 1967). Harbus, *The Life of the Mind*, p. 121.

121. Peter Stockwell, *Cognitive Poetics: An Introduction* (London: Routledge, 2002), p. 87.

122. Patrick J. Geary, *Phantoms of Remembrance: Memory and Oblivion at the End of the First Millennium* (Princeton: Princeton University Press, 1994), pp. 26, 29.

123. So too does it affect the person[s] doing the listening/reading. Refer to chapter 1 for a discussion of this. LeDoux, p. 210.

124. Antonio Damasio, *Self Comes to Mind: Constructing the Conscious Brain* (London: Vintage, 2012), p. 133.

125. The topic of the communal self is discussed in greater detail in the following chapters, and chapters 1 and 3 particularly. See Shaun Gallagher and Dan Zahavi, *The Phenomenological Mind*, 2nd ed. (Abingdon: Routledge, 2012), p. 94.

126. See Peter L. Callero, "The Sociology of the Self," *Annual Review of Sociology*, 29 (2003), 115–133 (p. 123). Pierce puts this another way, saying that the "self is thus both a product and an agent" of communication via an "outreaching identity," meaning that our ideas and thoughts express themselves into the wider community, which is how a social consciousness of a society can be stable over many generations. A community keeps these general ideas about itself over many years, and this relays to new generations, cycle after cycle. Amazingly, in *Wan* and *Seaf* we find evidence of this process.

127. Cited in *Ibid.*

128. Roderick M. Chisholm, "The Loose and Popular and the Strict and Philosophical Senses of Identity," in *Perception and Personal Identity: Proceedings of the 1967 Oberlin Colloquium in Philosophy*, ed. by Norman S. Care and Robert H. Grimm (Cleveland: Case Western Reserve University Press, 1969), p. 103.

129. John Perry, "The Problem of Personal Identity," in *Personal Identity*, ed. by John Perry (Berkeley: University of California Press, 1975), pp. 3–30 (p. 10).

Chapter 3

1. I.e., at least at the time of composition of the *Exeter Book*.

2. See Roberta Frank, "Germanic Legend in Old English Literature," in *The Cambridge Companion to Old English Literature*, ed. by Malcolm Godden and Michael Lapidge (Cambridge: Cambridge University Press, 1991), pp. 88–106 (p. 91) and Bede, *Ecclesiastical History of the English People*, trans. by Leo Sherley-Price (London: Penguin, 1990), p. 248.

3. *Ibid.*

4. In later Norse sagas, we may find such sentiment, as an "independence and pride in being a member of that [professional poet] profession." See William Lawrence, "Structure and Interpretation of 'Widsith,'" *Modern Philology*, 4.2 (1906), 329–374 (p. 329).

5. Lisa M. Horton, "Singing the Story: Narrative Voice and the Old English Scop," *The Hilltop Review*, 4 (2010), 45–57 (pp. 47–48).

6. John D. Niles, *Homo Narran: The Poetics and Anthropology of Oral Literature* (Philadelphia: University of Pennsylvania Press, 1999), p. 69.

7. Frank, p. 98.

8. The time here refers to the recording of *Deor* and *Widsith* in the *Exeter Book*, in the tenth century. Leonard Forster and George Anderson also note that, particularly in *Deor*, there is an obvious "comparing of misfortunes" of the *scop* with "more notable" Germanic characters. Refer to Morton W. Bloomfield, "The Form of *Deor*," *PMLA*, 79.5 (1964), 534–541 (p. 534).

9. Morton W. Bloomfield and Charles W. Dunn, *The Role of the Poet in Early Societies* (Cambridge: D.S. Brewer, 1992), p. 24 and Emily V. Thornbury, *Becoming a Poet in Anglo-Saxon England* (Cambridge: Cambridge University Press, 2014), p. 134.

10. "I want to say this about myself, that for a time I was the scop of the Heodeningas, dear to [my] lord; my name was Deor. For many years I had a good position, a kind lord, until now Heorrenda, a man skilled in songs, received the land that the protector of men formerly gave to me. That passed away; so may this also."

11. "Welund, that single-minded man, endured exile, suffered hardships among snakes. For a companion he had sorrow and sadness, wintery-cold misery."

12. Thomas T. Tuggle, "The Structure of 'Deor,'" *Studies in Philology*, 74 (1977), 229–242 (p. 238).

13. Edward I. Condren, "Deor"s Artistic Triumph," *Studies in Philology*, 78.5 (1981), 62–76 (p. 65).

14. Jerome Mandel, "Exemplum and Refrain: The Meaning of 'Deor,'" *The Yearbook of English Studies*, 7 (1977), 1–9 (p. 2).

15. Tuggle, p. 238.

16. "For Beadohild, her brother's death was not as painful in her soul as her own matter, in that she had clearly perceived that she was with child."

17. Condren, p. 68.

18. Physical isolation does also play a key role in the emotions of exile, as chapter 2 identified. I also discuss this in chapter 4.

19. Condren, p. 68.

20. Her son, Widia, is mentioned in both *Widsith* and *Waldere*. See Mandel, p. 3.

21. "ruled the city of the Mæringas for thirty years. That was known to many."

22. Tuggle, p. 236. Frankis is a notable

exception to this argument, claiming that Theodric's section could just as easily go with the fifth stanza, where Eormanric's rule showcases a tyrant's abuse of his people. See P.J. Frankis, "'Deor' and 'Wulf and Eadwacer': Some Conjectures," *Medium Aevum*, 31 (1962), 161–175 (p. 164). Additionally, Mandel makes the argument that in Theodric, we are witnessing "a good man suffering in his separation from his rightful place in society," and in Eormanric, a "physical separation" "in spirit of a king and his people." See Mandel, p. 5.

23. Condren, p. 73.
24. "Sat shackled with sorrows, with the expectation of troubles, and often wished that this kingdom would be conquered."
25. Condren, p. 2.
26. Frank, p. 99.
27. In fact, I gave this question special consideration in chapter 1, arguing that the reading/listening to stories solidified and helped sustain the shema, or idea of the communal-self in the Anglo-Saxon world of the tenth century.
28. Morton and Bloomfield, p. 6.
29. *Ibid.*, p. 7.
30. Niles, p. 128.
31. See Bloomfield and Dunn, p. 101 and Thornsbury, pp. 101 and 134 specifically.
32. Mandel, p. 7.
33. Bloomfield, p. 534.
34. Frankis, pp. 166–167.
35. Niles, p. 70.
36. *Ibid.*, p. 165. See also W.H. French, "Widsith and the Scop," *PMLA*, 60, 3 (1945), 623–630 (p. 623).
37. For an early defense of the latter, see William Witherle Lawrence, "The Song of Deor," *Modern Philology*, 9 (1911), 23–45 (p. 7). Contrasting this reading, Mandel sees it as a didactic work that expounds upon "some general human concern outside the poem itself and not to Deor's misfortune which he describes at the end of the poem." He also makes it a point to note the various "connotation[s] of isolation" in the poem. Refer to Mandel, p. 1.
38. "He sits sorrowful, deprived of joy, his mind darkens, [and] he thinks [his] share of hardships to be unending. Then he may think that throughout this world, the wise lord often [causes] changes; to many a nobleman he shows mercy, certain prosperity, [and] to others a share of troubles."
39. See Bloomfield and Dunn, p. 97 and Niles, p. 87.
40. Refer to Tuggle, p. 240 and Mandel, p. 7.

41. Frankis, p. 167.
42. Condren, p. 64. Again, this was included in chapter 1, and it plays an essential role in semiotics and the social construction of the self.
43. For further reading, see Bloomfield and Dunn, p. 24 and Roberta Frank, "The Search for the Anglo-Saxon Oral Poet," *Bulletin of the John Rylands University Library of Manchester*, 75 (1993), pp. 11–36 (p. 28).
44. Norman E. Eliason, "The Story of Geat and Mæðhild in 'Deor,'" *Studies in Philology*, 62 (1965), 495–509 (p. 496).
45. See Frank, *Germanic Legend*, p. 91.
46. For Old English poetry especially, we have a discourse surrounding so-called "transitional" poetry, but this study does not depend on the veracity of any of these concepts, so they will not be approached in any detail here. Additionally, there has been much scholarly work done on the orality of literature in society (both past and modern, and both equally pertinent to Old English literature, since even modern societies with a strong oral tradition continue from a past tradition that often spans centuries or millennia).
47. Alan Jabbour, "Memorial Transmission in Old English Poetry," *The Chaucer Review*, 3.3 (1969), 174–190 (pp. 177–178).
48. *Ibid.*, p. 178.
49. *Ibid.*
50. See Francis P. Magoun, "Bede"s Story of Caedman: The Case History of an Anglo-Saxon Oral Singer," *Speculum*, 30 (1955), 49–63 (p. 52).
51. *Ibid.*
52. This opens up the possibility of further research that would consider hundreds of years of literature and statistically highlight the themes and paradigms that we may consider salient to the study of identity. We could then compare these themes with the historical period and see how identity changed for a society over time.
53. Kemp Malone, "Widsith and the Critic," *ELH*, 5 (1938), 49–66 (pp. 59–60).
54. I.e., the date of composition in *Exeter Book*.
55. "I was with the Huns and the Glory-Goths, with the Swedes, the Geats and the South-Danes. I was with Wenlas and with Waerne and with the Wicingas...," etc. Subsequent references and editorial practices of *Widsith* come from *The Exeter Anthology of Old English Poetry*, ed. by Bernard Muir, 2 vols. (Exeter: University of Exeter Press, 1994).

56. Margaret Schlauch, "Widsith, Vithforull, and Some Other Analogues," *PMLA*, 46.4 (1931), 969–987 (p. 977).
57. Frankis, p. 165.
58. Peter Stockwell, *Cognitive Poetics: An Introduction* (London: Routledge, 2002), p. 77.
59. "[Offa] being in his youth, first conquered the greatest kingdom of men."
60. "So I travelled through many foreign lands over the spacious world. I experienced good and evil there, deprived of [my] family, far from [my] kinsmen, I served far and wide. Hence, I am able to narrate and tell a tale, recite it in the presence of a host [of men] in the meadhall, how these noble benefactors were kind to me."
61. Stockwell, p. 165.
62. *Ibid.*, pp. 79–80.
63. *Ibid.*
64. *Ibid.*, p. 83.
65. Clare Walsh, "Schema Poetics and Crossover Fiction," in *Contemporary Stylistics*, ed. by Peter Stockwell and Marina Lambrou (London: Continuum, 2010), pp. 106–117 (p. 108). See also Guy Cook, *Discourse and Literature: The Interplay of Form and Mind* (Oxford: Oxford University Press, 1995) for the original reference.
66. This is of course also evident in *Wan* and *Seaf*, as this disruption occurs as they are in exile.
67. Walsh, p. 108.
68. While the subject cannot be broached here, a self-study spanning several centuries would benefit by looking at the schema of self in societies, in order to discover subtle changes and so determine how the concept of the personal-self manifested in society over time.
69. "Yet in all this I wish to have courage and to rejoice and hope for myself, adorn myself for the spiritual path and set myself to that journey which I must undertake, prepare my soul and endure all this myself for God with a happy mind, now that I am firmly resolved in my heart. Indeed the Lord knows of certain sins of mine that I do not know to perceive wisely myself." Refer to Antonina Harbus, *Cognitive Approaches to Old English Poetry* (Cambridge: D.S. Brewer, 2012), p. 157.
70. Walsh, p. 114.
71. Horton, p. 51. See also W.H. French, "Widsith and the Scop," *PMLA* 60, 3 (1945), 623–630 (p. 623).
72. Various examples apply here. For instance, Eormanric's giving of a ring to Widsith (*se me beag forgeaf, burgwarena fruma*), and Gunther"s *glædlicne mappum / songes to leane*, and Ealhild, *the goldhrodene cwen giefe bryttian*, for example.
73. Horton, pp. 55 and 50, respectively.
74. Stephen Evans, *The Heroic Poetry of Dark-Age Britain: An Introduction to Its Dating, Composition, and Use as a Historical Source* (Lanham: University Press of America, 2002), p. 12.
75. "So wandering, the fated minstrels of men move throughout creation and many lands, they declare their needs and speak their thanks, always, south or north, they meet someone knowledgeable of songs, liberal with gifts, who wants his fame raised up before his people, to attain valor, until everything falls apart, light and life together; he earns praise, has perpetual glory under heaven."
76. Evans, p. 14.
77. I would qualify this statement and say that the *scop* was the main source of history for the common person. Lewis Anderson, *The Anglo-Saxon Scop* (Milton Keynes: Lightning Source UK, 2012), pp. 15, 17, and 23.
78. Bloomfield and Dunn, p. 111 and Niles, p. 75.
79. A possible implication of this idea comes in *Deor*, as Frederick Biggs' article powerfully suggests a theme of admonition toward his lord. See Frederick M. Biggs, "Deor"s Threatened 'Blame Poem,'" *Studies in Philology*, 94.3 (1997), 297–320 (pp. 297–320). Other commentators, however, do not subscribe to this. Evans remarks that "it would have been unlikely (if not impossible) for a poet to criticize his own lord," while Horton comments that the "scop was duty-bound to record only such events as bring no dishonor to his employer." See Evans, p. 14, and Horton, p. 49. Of course, it is possible that *Deor* could be read as a passive-aggressive warning to the would-be lord who would disregard his loyal *scop*.
80. Niles, p. 76.
81. Bloomfield and Dunn, p. 7.
82. See French, p. 625, and Anderson, p. 30.
83. Evans, p. 16.
84. "Every mouth needs food; meals should come on time. Gold befits a man"s sword, glorious victory-blade, jewels on a queen, a good poet for men...." "Maxims (B)," in *The Exeter Anthology*, p. 254, ll. 124a-27a.
85. Frank, *The Search*, p. 35.
86. Lawrence, p. 333.

Chapter 4

1. Clifford Davidson, "Erotic 'Women's Songs' in Anglo-Saxon England," *Neophilologus*, 59 (1975), 451–462 (p. 460).
2. The term "high individuality" refers to one's sense of self that is nearly completely disassociated (independent) from any communal role, societal function, or group structure. The implication is that the personal-self is not exclusively derived from any external source(s).
3. Helen Bennett, Gillian Overing, and Clare A. Lees, "Anglo-Saxon Studies: Gender and Power: Feminism and Old English Studies," *Medieval Feminist Forum,* 10 (1990), 15–23 (p. 17).
4. Helen Damico and Alexandra Olsen, "Introduction: Old English Literature in the University Curriculum," in *New Readings on Women in Old English Literature,* ed. by Alexandra Olsen and Helen Damico (Bloomington: Indiana University Press, 1990), pp. 1–28 (p. 4).
5. Edith Williams, "What's So New About the Sexual Revolution? Some Comments on Anglo-Saxon Attitudes Toward Sexuality in Women Based on Four Exeter Book Riddles," in *New Readings on Women in Old English Literature,* ed. by Helen Damico and Alexandra Olsen (Bloomington: Indiana University Press, 1990), pp. 137–145 (p. 144).
6. Jane Chance, *Woman as Hero in Old English Literature* (Syracuse: Syracuse University Press, 1986), p. xiv.
7. Refer to chapter 3, and Guy Cook's discussion previously.
8. See Berit Astrom, "The Politics of Tradition: Examining the History of the Old English Poems *The Wife's Lament* and *Wulf and Eadwacer*" (unpublished doctoral thesis, Universitet Umea, 2002), pp. 31–2.
9. *Ibid.*
10. The scope of this chapter does not allow for a thorough examination of the debates surrounding this topic, of which there is much variety. We need only to limit our discussion to generalities that will allow us to make observations regarding a potential individualized self for women. Refer to Elizabeth Judd, "Women Before the Conquest: Women in Anglo-Saxon England," *Anglo-Saxon England,* 1 (1974), 127–148 (p. 127), and also Helen Bennett, "Medieval Women in Modern Perspective," in *Women's History in Global Perspective*, ed. by Bonnie Smith (Champaign: University of Illinois Press, 2005), pp. 139–186 (pp. 153–154).
11. See below for a discussion of this in *Juliana* and *Elene*. See also Bennett, "Medieval Women," p. 146.
12. See Pat Belanoff, "The Fall (?) of the Old English Female Poetic Image," *PMLA*, 104.5 (1989), 822–831 (p. 822).
13. See Helene Scheck, "Seductive Voices: Rethinking Female Subjectivities in *The Wife's Lament* and *Wulf and Eadwacer,*" *Literature Compass,* 5.2 (2008), 220–227 (pp. 223–224) and Shari Horner, *The Discourse of Enclosure: Representing Women in Old English Literature* (Albany: State University of New York Press, 2001), p. 46.
14. *Ibid.*
15. See Belanoff, "Female Poetic Image," p. 828.
16. *Ibid.*
17. Scheck, p. 224.
18. My argument in chapters two and three explicitly counter this position.
19. Citing Elaine Tuttle Hansen. See Helen Bennett, "The Female Mourner at Beowulf's Funeral: Filling in the Blanks/Hearing the Spaces," *Exemplaria,* 4 (1992), 35–50 (pp. 41–2).
20. Marilynn Desmond, "The Voice of Exile: Feminist Literary History and the Anonymous Anglo-Saxon Elegy," *Critical Inquiry* 16, no. 3 (1990), 572–590 (p. 585).
21. Carol Clover writes here specifically on the concept of revenge in Anglo-Saxon society. See Bennett, "The Female Mourner," p. 43.
22. Damico et al., "University Curriculum," in *New Readings,* p. 12.
23. Specifically, the female mourner at Beowulf's funeral. Joyce Hill, "Þæt Wæs Geomuru Ides: A Female Stereotype Examined," in *Readings on Women in Old English Literature,* ed. by Helen Damico and Alexandra Olsen (Bloomington: Indiana University Press, 1990), 235–247 (p. 242).
24. Melanie Heyworth, "Nostalgic Evocation and Social Privilege in the Old English Elegies," *Studia Neophilologica,* 76 (2004), 3–11 (p. 3).
25. *Ibid.*, p. 4
26. For a discussion, see Hugh Magennis, "Gender and Heroism in the Old English *Judith,*" in *Writing Gender and Genre in Medieval Literature: Approaches to Old and Middle English Texts,* ed. by Elaine Treharne (Cambridge: D.S. Brewer, 2002), pp. 5–18 (p. 13).
27. *Ibid.*
28. Heyworth, p. 3.
29. Alexandra Olsen, "Cynewulf's

Chapter Notes—4

Autonomous Women: A Reconsideration of *Elene* and *Juliana*," in *New Readings on Women in Old English Literature*, ed. by Helen Damico and Hennessey Olsen, Alexandra (Bloomington: Indiana University Press, 1990), pp. 222–234 (p. 222). See also Anne Klinck, "Female Characterization in Old English Poetry and the Growth of Psychological Realism: *Genesis B* and *Christ I*," *Neophilologus*, 63. 4 (1979), pp. 597–610.

30. Desmond, p. 585.
31. E.g., lamenting the loss of a husband in *Wife*, or recalling a ring-giving ceremony in *Wan*. This knowledge also aids us in understanding the predominance of exile as a theme in the elegies in general. See Belanoff, "Female Poetic Image," p. 822.
32. Pat Belanoff, "Women's Songs Women''s Language: Wulf and Eadwacer and *The Wife's Lament*," in *New Readings on Women in Old English Literature*, ed. by Alexandra Olsen and Helen Damico (Bloomington: Indiana University Press, 1990), 146–156 (p. 153).
33. See *Ibid.*, p. 146 and (citing Kemp Malone) Susan Schibanoff, "Medieval Frauenlieder: Anonymous Was a Man?," *Tulsa Studies in Women's Literature*, 1. 2 (1982), 189–200 (pp. 189–91).
34. Desmond, p. 583.
35. See Schibanoff, p. 191 and especially Ann McMillan, "Fayre Sisters Al: The Flower and the Leaf and The Assembly of Ladies," *Tulsa Studies in Women's Literature*, 1 (1982), 27–42.
36. Scheck, p. 222.
37. Astrom claims that since no mention of a female *scop* exists from the Anglo-Saxon period, it is assumed that a male minstrel would simply "imitate a woman" in the lyrics. Unfortunately, as it stands now, there is no way to be sure either way. See Berit Astrom, "The Creation of the Anglo-Saxon Woman," *Studia Neophilologica*, 70 (1998), 25–34 (p. 30).
38. *Ibid.*
39. The female mourner at Beowulf's funeral and Hildeburh's unwanted pregnancy in *Deor*, for example.
40. Horner, p. 29.
41. Belanoff, *"Women's Songs,"* p. 149.
42. Scheck, p. 220.
43. Horner, p. 30.
44. Christine Fell, Cecily Clark, and Elizabeth Williams, *Women in Anglo-Saxon England and the Impact of 1066* (London: British Museum Publications, 1984), p. 67.
45. Berit Astrom, "The Creation of the Anglo-Saxon Woman."
46. Belanoff, "Women's Songs," p. 152.
47. See Horner, p. 31.
48. The obvious problem with this position is that it gives us a stereotyped image of women, genderized in the literature certainly by a male poet, and almost never voiced—at least ostensibly—by women themselves. See Richard Burton, "Woman in Old English Poetry," *The Sewanne Review*, 4 (1895), 1–14 (p. 3).
49. Fell, et al., p. 70.
50. William Lawrence, "The Banished Wife's Lament," *Modern Philology*, 5.3 (1908), p. 11.
51. There is, of course, some variation in the scholarship in the rigidity of these views. For instance, I read the poem as having a clear four-part structure, not three, and the notion of the narrator's unhappiness being the result of her separation from a man I find undeveloped (i.e., what are the larger implications of this separation in terms of highlighting her sense of identity? The latter is one of the foci of this section). Alain Renoir, "A Reading Context for *The Wife's Lament*," in *Anglo-Saxon Poetry: Essays in Appreciation for John C. McGalliard*, ed. by Dolores Frese and Lewis Nicholson (Notre Dame: University of Notre Dame Press, 1975), 224–241 (p. 238).
52. "I make this tale, very sad about me—about the journey of myself. I can say what miseries I have experienced, since I grew up—new or old—no more than now; I have ever struggled [with] the torture of my exile." Henceforth, OE and editorial practices come from *The Wife's Lament*, *The Exeter Anthology of Old English Poetry*, ed. by Bernard Muir, 2 vols. (Exeter: Short Run Press, 2000).
53. See Barrie Straus, "Women's Words as Speech: Speech as Action in The Wife's Lament," *Texas Studies in Literature and Language* 23, no. 2 (1981), 268–285 (pp. 269–272).
54. This concept and what it means for the expression of individuality is explored more fully below, particularly as it applies to the ending. See *Ibid.*
55. For instance, there are three in *Wulf*, eight in *Wan*, and nine in *Seaf*.
56. E.g., refer to *ongeat þa geomormod godes sylfes sið* ("the man of a sorrowing mind recognized the coming of God"s own self," line 52 in *The Descent Into Hell*) "Hwæt, þu Eue, hæfst yfele gemearcod uncer sylfra sið ("Lo, Eve! With your wickedness, you have sealed the destiny of our two selves'—line 791–792a in *Genesis*), and Huru, ðæs beho-

fað hæleða æghwylc *þæt he his sawle sið sylfa gebence* ("Truly, it is necessary for each warrior to consider for himself the journey his soul will have to make," ll. 1–2 in *Soul and Body I*). *The Descent Into* Hell, "The Exeter Anthology," p. 343, *Genesis*, "The Junius Manuscript," ed. by George Philip Krapp (New York: Columbia University Press, 1931), p. 27, and *Soul and Body I*, "The Vercelli Book," ed. by George Philip Krapp (New York: Columbia University Press, 1932), p. 54. In chapter 1 I discuss this phrase in *GenB*.

57. Jane Curry, "Approaches to a Translation of the Anglo-Saxon *The Wife's Lament*," *Medium Aevum* 35, no. 3 (1966), 187–198 (pp. 194–5).

58. "I had few dear ones in this place—(few) loyal friends." See lines 16–17a.

59. Schibanoff, p. 192.

60. "Therefore, my mind is sad, since I found a man fully suitable for me—an unhappy, miserable man—concealing his mind, considering crimes (against me)."

61. "A man commanded me to live in a wood grove, under an oak tree in an earth cave. Ancient is this earth-hall; I am all consumed with longing, the valleys are dark, the mountains high; the bitter towns are overgrown with briars—a dwelling without joys. Here very often my lord's departure has angrily overtaken me. There are friends living on Earth, beloved ones sharing a bed, while I alone wander at dawn under an oak tree, around this cave. There I must sit throughout the summer-long day; there I can weep over the journey of my exile—my miseries. Therefore, I cannot ever rest from this anxiety of mine and all this longing that in this life has beset me."

62. See Michael Lapidge, "The Comparative Approach," in *Reading Old English Texts*, ed. by Katherine O'Brian O'Keefe (Cambridge, 1997), 20–38 (p. 34) and Alaric Hall, "The Images and Structure of *The Wife's Lament*," *Leeds Studies in English*, 33 (2002), 1–29 (p. 1).

63. Brookbanks, p. 27.

64. Of course, the goal of this research is to find counter examples to this, so that we may discover that Anglo-Saxons indeed had a sense of personal identity and autonomy in certain circumstances. In chapter 1, I investigated the common representation of identity in OE poetry (i.e., the social-self).

65. Curry, p. 194.

66. Davidson, p. 459.

67. "Ever shall a young man be sad, hard in the thought of his heart; likewise he must have a joyous comportment, and also have heart-misery—a multitude of sorrows. Let all his worldly joy depend on his own self; let him be flung far into hostile nations, so that my friend, my miserable friend, sits under a stone-slope, frozen by the storm, surrounded by water in a dreary hall. Let him suffer great anxiety; often he remembers a more joyful dwelling. Woe it is to him who must, out of longing, wait for a loved one."

68. John Niles, "The Problem of the Ending of the Wife's 'Lament,'" *Speculum* 78, no. 4 (2003), 1107–1150 (p. 1115).

69. Brookbanks, p. 25.

70. See Niles, p. 1135.

71. Brookbanks, p. 25.

72. Niles, p. 1143.

73. *Ibid*.

74. Albano also suggests that in *Beowulf*, Hildeburh participated in vengeance through her speech in the Finn Episode. See Robert Albano, "The Role of Women in Anglo-Saxon Culture: Hildeburh in *Beowulf* and a Curious Counterpart in the *Volsunga Saga*," *English Language Notes*, 32 (1994), 1–10 (pp. 7–9).

75. Elinor Lench, "The Wife's Lament: A Poem of the Living Dead," *Comitatus: A Journal of Medieval and Renaissance Studies*, 1 (1970), 3–22 (p. 20).

76. Stanley Greenfield, "The Wife's Lament Reconsidered," *PMLA*, 68. 4 (1953), 907–912 (pp. 907–8) and Barrie Straus, "Women's Words as Speech: Speech as Action in The Wife's Lament," *Texas Studies in Literature and Language*, 23.2 (1981), 268–285 (p. 278). See Belanoff, "Women's Songs," p. 149.

77. Belanoff, "Women's Songs," p. 149.

78. Karl Wentersdorf sees this in "striking contrast to the upbeat conclusion of ... *The Wanderer*." Karl Wenterdorf, "The Situation of the Narrator in the Old English Wife's Lament," *Speculum*, 56.3 (1981), 492–516 (p. 516). See also Niles, p. 1149, who also makes it clear that the narrator in *Wife* does not have the same "supernal consolations that are implicit" in *Wan* and *Seaf* to hold on to.

79. Herein lies a prime example of both the public and private.

80. Ashby Kinch, "The Ethical Agency of the Female Lyric Voice: 'The Wife's Lament' and 'Catullus 64,'" *Studies in Philology*, 103.2 (2006), 121–152 (p. 145).

81. Dolores Frese, "Wulf and Eadwacer: The Adulterous Woman Reconsidered," *Notre Dame English Journal*, 15 (1983), 1–22 (p. 3).

82. Dolores Frese, "*Wulf and Eadwacer*: The Adulterous Woman Reconsidered," in *New Readings on Women in Old English Lit-*

erature, ed. by Helen Damico and Alexandra Olsen (Bloomington: Indiana University Press, 1990), 273–291. This is an updated version of the 1983 article.

83. "I followed tracks of exile in hopes for my Wulf; then it was rainy weather and I, tearful, sat." I have used Muir's edition throughout.

84. Desmond, p. 587.

85. See Frese, "The Adulterous Woman," p. 278 and Peter Baker, "The Ambiguity of 'Wulf and Eadwacer,'" *Studies in Philolgy* 78, no. 5 (1981), p. 49.

86. "Wulf! My Wulf, it was not a lack of food, but my expectations of you—your seldom visiting—that caused my sorrowful mind."

87. "To my people, it is as if one gives them a gift; they will receive him if he approaches with a troop. It is different for us."

88. Frese, p. 11.

89. Baker, p. 40 and Frese, p. 17.

90. Emily Jensen, "Narrative Voice in the Old English 'Wulf,'" *The Chaucer Review*, 14 (1979), p. 376.

91. Horner, p. 43.

92. *Ibid.*, p. 48.

93. Chance, p. 90.

94. Horner, p. 49.

95. That it is indeed gendered is, of course, the basis of argument for this chapter.

96. Emily Jensen, "Narrative Voice in the Old English 'Wulf,'" *The Chaucer Review*, 13.4 (1979), 373–383 (p. 380).

97. Chance, p. 94.

98. Jensen, p. 375.

99. Baker, p. 48.

100. Jensen, p. 380.

101. Davidson, p. 460.

102. "That one easily tears asunder which was never joined—our song together."

103. Jensen, p. 373, Baker, p. 50, and Frese, p. 8. See also Donald Fry, "'Wulf and Eadwacer': A Wen Charm," *The Chaucer Review*, 5 (1971), p. 247.

104. Frese, p. 3.

105. *Ibid.*

106. Also, because of comparison and space considerations, I have included only a brief sample size. This is by no means exhaustive. *Elene*, for instance, is full of first-person (indirect) speech that I would argue is entirely based on community and her place in society.

107. "Her brothers' death was not as painful in her soul as her own matter, in that she had clearly perceived that she was with child."

108. Magennis, p. 7.

109. Elaine Hansen, "From *Freolicu Folccwen* to *Geomuru Ides*: Women in Old English Poetry Reconsidered," *Michigan Academian*, 9 (1973), 109–117 (p. 114).

110. Astrom, p. 3. See also Chance, p. 92.

111. Martin Camargo, "The Finn Episode and the Tragedy of Revenge in Beowulf,'" *Studies in Philology*, 78.5 (1981), 120–134 (pp. 129–30).

112. Dorothy Porter, "The Social Centrality of Women in *Beowulf*: A New Context," *The Heroic Age*, 5 (2001), 1–6 (p. 5).

113. See Albano, p. 5.

114. "That was a sad woman." Hill also astutely compares this with an earlier passage that represents the heroic male stereotype (*þæt wæs god cyning*) in line 11b. See Joyce Hill, "þæt Wæs Geomuru Ides: A Female Stereotype Examined," in *Readings*, p. 241.

115. What can be recovered from the text, however, clearly describes a woman, a song, and sad sorrows. This, without further interpretation, is enough to make our case. See Bennett, "The Female Mourner," p. 36.

116. *Ibid.*, p. 46.

117. Mary Catherine Davidson, "Speaking of Nostalgia in Beowulf," *Modern Philology*, 103 (2005), p. 149. See also Burton, pp. 149 and 151.

118. Hansen, p. 117.

119. Horner, pp. 54–55.

120. See Heyworth, p. 3 and Desmond, p. 585.

121. Renoir, p. 235.

122. Niles, p. 1149.

123. Desmond, p. 588. See also Horner, p. 30.

124. Scheck, p. 222.

Conclusion

1. Richard Shweder and Joan Miller, "The Social Construction of the Person: How Is It Possible?" in *The Social Construction of the Person*, ed. by Keith Davis and Kenneth Gergen (New York: Springer-Verlag, 1985), p. 69.

2. See Richard Jenkins, *Social Identity* (New York: Routledge, 2008), who argues that "the self [is] an individual's reflexive sense of her or his own particular identity, constituted *vis-à-vis* others in terms of similarity and difference, without which she or he wouldn't know who they are and hence

wouldn't be able to act," p. 49 and Deborah Schiffrin, "Narrative as Self-Portrait: Sociolinguistic Constructions of Identity," *Language in Society* 25, no. 2 (1996), 167–203 (p. 170), who says that "our identities as social beings emerge as we construct our own individual experiences as a way to position ourselves in relation to social and cultural expectations."

3. Jonathan Culler, *The Pursuit of Signs: Semiotics, Literature, Deconstruction* (Ithaca: Cornell University Press, 2001), p. 8.

4. Paul Cavill, *Anglo-Saxon Christianity: Exploring the Earliest Roots of Christian Spirituality in England* (London: Fount, 1999), p. 49.

5. John Searle, *The Construction of Social Reality* (London: Penguin, 1996) p. 134.

Bibliography

Editions and Translations

Bede, *Ecclesiastical History of the English People*, trans. by Leo Sherley-Price (London: Penguin, 1990).
Bradley, S.A.J, *Anglo-Saxon Poetry*, ed. by S.A.J Bradley (London: Orion Publishing, 1991).
Elene, Calder, D.G., and Allen, M.J.B., *Sources and Analogues of Old English Poetry: The Major Latin Sources in Translation*, trans. by D.G. Calder and M.J.B. Allen (Cambridge: DS Brewer, 1976), pp. 60–68.
Heaney, Seamus, *Beowulf: Bilingual Edition* (London: Faber & Faber, 1999).
Klinck, Anne L., *The Old English Elegies: A Critical Edition and Genre Study* (Montreal and Kingston: McGill-Queen's University Press, 1992).
Krapp, George, *The Junius Manuscript* (New York: Columbia University Press, 1931).
____, *The Vercelli Book*, ed. by George Krapp (New York: Columbia University Press, 1932).
Muir, Bernard, *The Exeter Anthology of Old English Poetry* (Exeter: Short Run Press, 2000).

Historical Studies

Baldwin, Geoff, "Individual and Self in the Late Renaissance," *The Historical Journal*, 44.2 (2001), 341–364.
Bandel, Betty, "The English Chroniclers' Attitude Toward Women," *Journal of the History of Ideas*, 16 (1955), 113–118.
Bedos-Rezak, Brigitte Miriam, "Medieval Identity: A Sign and a Concept," *The American Historical Review*, 105.5 (2000), 1489–1533.
Bennett, Helen, "Medieval Women in Modern Perspective," in *Women's History in Global Perspective*, ed. by Bonnie Smith (Champaign: University of Illinois Press, 2005), pp. 139–186.
Bloomfield, Morton W., and Dunn, Charles W., *The Role of the Poet in Early Societies* (Cambridge: D.S. Brewer, 1992).
Bossy, Michel-Andre, "Medieval Debates of Body and Soul," *Comparative Literature*, 28.2 (1976), 144–163.
Burkitt, Ian, *Social Selves: Theories of Self and Society* (Los Angeles: SAGE, 2009).
Bynum, Caroline, "Did the Twelfth Century Discover the Individual?" *The Journal of Ecclesiastical History*, 31 (1980), 1–17.
____, *Jesus as Mother: Studies in the Spirituality of the High Middle Ages* (Berkeley: University of California Press, 1982).
Cavill, Paul, *Anglo-Saxon Christianity: Exploring the Earliest Roots of Christian Spirituality in England* (London: Fount, 1999).

Bibliography

Dietrich, Sheila, "An Introduction to Women in Anglo-Saxon Society (C. 600–1066)," in *The Women of England: From Anglo-Saxon Times to the Present* (Hamden: The Shoe String Press, 1980), pp. 32–56.

Fell, Christine, Clark, Cecily, and Williams, Elizabeth, *Women in Anglo-Saxon England and the Impact of 1066* (London: British Museum Publications, 1984).

Frank, Roberta, "The Search for the Anglo-Saxon Oral Poet," *Bulletin of the John Rylands University Library of Manchester*, 75 (1993), 11–36.

Garrison, Mary, "An Aspect of Alcuin: 'Tuus Albinus'—Peevish Egotis? or Parrhesiast?" in *Ego Trouble: Authors and their Identities in the Early Middle Ages*, ed. by Richard Corradini et al. (Vienna: Austrian Academy of Sciences, 2010), pp. 137–152.

Guenther, Kelly, "Defining and Shaping the Moral Self in the Ninth Century: Evidence from Baptismal Tracts and the Reception of Augustine's *De Trinitate*" (unpublished doctoral thesis, University of York), 2006.

Judd, Elizabeth, "Women Before the Conquest: Women in Anglo-Saxon England," *Anglo-Saxon England*, 1 (1974), 127–148.

Lancaster, Lorraine, "Kinship in Anglo-Saxon Society—I," *The British Journal of Sociology*, 9.3 (1958), 230–250.

McMillan, Ann, "Fayre Sisters Al: The Flower and the Leaf and the Assembly of Ladies," *Tulsa Studies in Women's Literature*, 1 (1982), 27–42.

McNamara, Jo Ann, and Wemple, Suzanne, "The Power of Women through the Family in Medieval Europe: 500–1100," *Feminist Studies*, 1 (1973), 126–141.

Meyer, Marc, "Land Charters and the Legal Position of Anglo-Saxon Women," in *The Women of England: From Anglo-Saxon Times to the Present*, ed. by Barbara Kanner (London: Mansell, 1979), pp. 57–82.

Miles, Margaret R., *Carnal Knowing: Female Nakedness and Religious Meaning in the Christian West* (Boston: Beacon, 1989).

Niles, John D., *Homo Narran: The Poetics and Anthropology of Oral Literature* (Philadelphia: University of Pennsylvania Press, 1999).

Penelope, Julia, and McGowan, Cynthia, "Woman and Wife: Social and Semantic Shifts in English," *Papers in Linguistics*, 12.3–4 (1979), 491–502.

Radding, Charles, "Evolution of Medieval Mentalities: A Cognitive-Structural Approach," *The American Historical Review*, 83.3 (1978), 577–597.

―――, *A World Made by Men: Cognition and Society, 400–1200* (Chapel Hill: University of North Carolina Press, 1985).

Riddiford, Martha, "Social Exclusion from Early Medieval Wessex" (unpublished doctoral thesis, University of Sheffield, 2007).

Rivers, Theodore, "Widows' Rights in Anglo-Saxon Law," *American Journal of Legal History*, 19 (1975), 208–215.

Scammell, Jean, "Freedom and Marriage in Medieval England," *The Economic History Review*, 27.4 (1974), 523–537.

Schulenburg, Jane, "Female Sanctity: Public and Private Roles, ca. 500–1100," in *Women and Power in the Middle Ages*, ed. by M. Koweleski and M. Erler (Athens: University of Georgia Press, 1988), pp. 102–125.

Searle, Eleanor, "Freedom and Marriage in Medieval England: An Alternative Hypothesis," *The Economic History Review*, 29.3 (1976), 482–486.

Stenton, Doris, *The English Woman in History* (London: George Allen & Unwin, Ltd., 1957).

Thornbury, Emily V., *Becoming a Poet in Anglo-Saxon England* (Cambridge: Cambridge University Press, 2014).

Ullmann, Walter, *The Individual and Society in the Middle Ages* (London: Methuen & Co., Ltd., 1967).

Bibliography

Self and Identity Studies

Booth, James W., *Communities of Memory: On Witness, Identity, and Justice* (Ithaca: Cornell University Press, 2006).

Burge, Tyler, "Memory and Persons," *The Philosophical Review*, 112.3 (2003), 289–337.

———, "Perception, and Memory," *Philosophical Studies: An International Journal for Philosophy in the Analytic*, 86.1 (1997), 21–47.

Burke, Peter, "History as Social Memory," in *Memory: History, Culture and the Mind*, ed. by Thomas Butler (Oxford: Basil Blackwell, 1989), pp. 97–113.

———, and Stets, Jan, *Identity Theory* (Oxford: Oxford University Press, 2009).

Burr, Vivien, *Social Constructionism* (London: Routledge, 2003).

Butler, Joseph, "Of Personal Identity," in *Personal Identity*, ed. by John Perry (Berkeley: University of California Press, 1975), pp. 99–105.

Callero, Peter L., "The Sociology of the Self," *Annual Review of Sociology*, 29 (2003), 115–133.

Carroll, John W., and Markosian, Ned, *An Introduction to Metaphysics* (Cambridge: Cambridge University Press, 2011).

Cerulo, Karen, "Identity Construction: New Issues, New Directions," *Annual Review of Sociology*, 23 (1997), 385–409.

Chandler, Daniel, *Semiotics: The Basics* (London: Routledge, 2007).

Chisholm, Roderick M., "The Loose and Popular and the Strict and Philosophical Senses of Identity," in *Perception and Personal Identity: Proceedings of the 1967 Oberlin Colloquium in Philosophy*, ed. by Norman S. Care and Robert H. Grimm (Cleveland: Case Western Reserve University Press, 1969), pp. 82–106.

Connerton, Paul, *How Societies Remember* (Cambridge: Cambridge University Press, 1998).

Cook, Guy, *Discourse and Literature: The Interplay of Form and Mind* (Oxford: Oxford University Press, 1995).

Culler, Jonathan, *The Pursuit of Signs: Semiotics, Literature, Deconstructio* (Ithaca: Cornell University Press, 2001).

Damasio, Antonio, *Self Comes to Mind: Constructing the Conscious Brain* (London: Vintage, 2012).

Decety, Jean, and Sommervile, Jessica A., "Shared Representations Between Self and Other: A Social Cognitive Neuroscience View," *Trends in Cognitive Sciences*, 7.12 (2003), 527–533.

Demo, David H., "The Self-Concept Over Time: Research Issues and Directions," *Annual Review of Sociology*, 18 (1992), 303–326.

Descartes, Rene, *Meditations on First Philosophy: With Selections from the Objections and Replies*, trans. by Michael Moriarty (Oxford: Oxford University Press, 2008).

Dewey, John, *Democracy and Education* (London: Macmillan Company, 1916).

Eco, Umberto, *Semiotics and the Philosophy of Language* (Bloomington: Indiana University Press, 1984).

Elster, Jon, "Introduction," in *The Multiple Self*, ed. by Jon Elster (New York: Cambridge University Press, 1986), pp. 1–34.

Eyerman, Ron, and Olick, Jeffrey, "From the Past in the Present: Culture and the Transmission of Memory," in *Collective Memory Reader*, ed. by Vered Vinitzky-Seroussi and Daniel Levy (Oxford: Oxford University Press, 2011), pp. 304–307.

Faulkner, Paul, "The Social Character of Testimonial Knowledge," *The Journal of Philosophy*, 97.11 (2000), 581–601.

French, Brigittine, "The Semiotics of Collective Memories," *Annual Review of Anthropology*, 41 (2012), 337–353.

Gallagher, Shaun, and Zahavi, Dan, *The Phenomenological Mind*, 2nd ed. (Abingdon: Routledge, 2012).

Bibliography

Geary, Patrick J., *Phantoms of Remembrance: Memory and Oblivion at the End of the First Millennium* (Princeton: Princeton University Press, 1994).
Gergen, Kenneth, "Social Constructionist Inquiry: Context and Implications," in *The Social construction of the Person*, ed. by Kenneth Gergen and Keith Davis (New York: Springer-Verlag, 1985), pp. 3–18.
Gertler, Brie, *Self-Knowledge* (New York: Routledge, 2011).
Gillett, Grant, *The Mind and its Discontents: An Essay in Discursive Psychiatry* (Oxford: Oxford Unversity Press, 1999).
Grice, H.P., "Personal Identity," in *Personal Identity*, ed. by John Perry (Berkeley: University of California Press, 1975), pp. 73–95.
Hart, Elizabeth F., "The Epistemology of Cognitive Literary Studies," *Philosophy and Literature*, 25.2 (2001), 314–334.
Harter, Susan, *The Construction of the Self: A Developmental Perspective* (New York: Guilford, 1999).
Hinchman, Lewis P., "The Idea of Individuality: Origins, Meaning, and Political Significance," *The Journal of Politics*, 52.3 (1990), 759–781.
Hirsch, Eli, *The Concept of Identity* (New York: Oxford University Press, 1982).
Holland, Norman, "Unity Identity Text Self," *PMLA*, 90.5 (1975), 813–822.
Horwitz, Murray, and Rabbie, Jacob, "Individuality and Membership in the Intergroup System," in *Social Identity and Interoup Relations*, ed. by Henri Tajifel (Cambridge: Cambridge University, 2010), pp. 241–274.
Hume, David, "Of Personal Identity," in *Personal Identity*, ed. by John Perry (Berkeley: University of California Press, 1975), pp. 161–172.
Jackson, Tony E., "Literary Interpretation and Cognitive Literary Studies," *Poetics Today*, 24.2 (2003), 191–205.
Jenkins, Richard, *Social Identity* (New York: Routledge, 2008).
Jung, C., *Psychological Types*, trans. by H. Baynes (London: Routledge, 1989)
Kelly, W.M., et al., "Finding the Self? An Event-Related fMRI Study," *Journal of Cognitive Neuroscience*, 14.5 (2002), 785–794.
Kemp, Simon, *Cognitive Psychology in the Middle Ages* (Westport: Greenwood Press, 1996).
Kim, Jaegwon, *Philosophy of Mind*, 3rd ed. (Boulder: Westview Press, 2011).
Kitayama, Hinobu, and Park, Jiyoung, "Cultural Neuroscience of the Self: Understanding the Social Grounding of the Brain," *SCAN*, 5 (2010), 111–129.
Klein, Stanley B., Rozendal, Keith, and Cosmides, Leda, "A Social-Cognitive Neuroscience Analysis of the Self," *Social Cognition*, 20.2 (2002), 105–135.
Lackey, Jennifer, "Testimonial Knowledge and Transmission," *The Philosophical Quarterly*, 49.197 (1999), 471–490.
LeDoux, Joseph, *The Emotional Brain: The Mysterious Underpinnings of Emotional Life* (New York: Phoenix, 1998).
Lee, Benjamin, and Urban, Greg, "Introduction," in *Semiotics, Self, and Society*, ed. by Benjamin Lee and Greg Urban (Berlin: Mouton de Gruyter, 1989), pp. 1–14.
Lindholm, Charles, "Does the Sociocentric Self Exist? Reflections on Markus and Kitayama's 'Culture and the Self,'" *Journal of Anthropological Research*, 53.4 (1997), 405–422.
Locke, John, "Of Identity and Diversity," in *Personal Identity*, ed. by John Perry (Berkeley: University of California Press, 1975), pp. 33–52.
Luckmann, Thomas, and Berger, Peter, *The Social Construction of Reality: A Treatise in the Sociology of Knowledge* (New York: Doubleday, 1966).
McCready, Amy, "The Ethical Individual: An Historical Alternative to Contemporary Conceptions of the Self," *The American Political Science Review*, 90 (1996), 90–102.
Morris, Colin, *The Discovery of the Individual 1050–120.* (London: SPCK, 1972).

Bibliography

Murray, D.W., "What Is the Western Concept of the Self? On Forgetting David Hume," *Ethos* 21 (1993), 3–23.
Oakdale, Susan, "Creating a Continuity between Self and Other: First-Person Narration in an Amazonian Ritual Context," *Ethos* 30 (2002), 158–175.
Ochs, Elinor, and Capps, Lisa, "Narrating the Self," *Annual Review of Anthropology*, 25 (1996), 19–43.
Olick, Jeffrey K., and Robbins, Joyce, "From 'Collective Memory' to the Historical Sociology of Mnemonic Practices," *Annual Review of Sociology*, 24 (1998), 105–140.
Palmer, Alan, "Storyworlds and Groups," in *Introduction to Cognitive Cultural Studies*, ed. by Lisa Zunshine (Baltimore: Johns Hopkins University Press, 2010), pp. 176–192.
Perry, John, "The Problem of Personal Identity," in *Personal Identity*, ed. by John Perry (Berkeley: University of California Press, 1975), pp. 3–30.
Petrilli, Susan, *The Self as a Sign, the World, and the Other: Living Semiotics* (New Brunswick: Transaction Publishers, 2013).
Petrov, Krinka, "Memory and Oral Tradition," in *Memory: History, Culture and the Mind*, ed. by Thomas Butler (Oxford: Basil Blackwell, 1989).
Reicher, Stephen, "The Determination of Collective Behaviour," in *Social Identity and Intergroup Relations*, ed. by Henri Tajifel (Cambridge: Cambridge University Press, 2010), pp. 41–86.
Reid, Thomas, "Of Identity," in *Personal Identity*, ed. by John Perry (Berkeley: University of California Press, 1975), pp. 107–112.
Richardson, Alan, "Literature and the Cognitive Revolution: An Introduction," *Poetics Today*, 23.1 (2002), 1–20.
Rosaldo, Michelle Z., "Toward an Anthropology of Self and Feeling," in *Culture Theory: Essays on Mind, Self, and Emotion*, ed. by Richard A. Shweder and Robert A. LeVine (New York: Cambridge University Press, 1992), pp. 137–157.
Schelling, Thomas C., ed., "The Mind as a Consuming Organ," in *The Multiple Self*, ed. by Jon Elster (New York: Cambridge University Press, 1986), pp. 177–195.
Schiffrin, Deborah, "Narrative as Self-Portrait: Sociolinguistic Constructions of Identity," *Language in Society* 25, no. 2 (1996), 167–203.
Schwalbe, Michael, and Mason-Schrock, Douglas, "Identity Work as Group Process," *Advances in Group Processes*, 13 (1996), 113–147.
Searle, John R., *The Construction of Social Reality* (London: Penguin, 1996).
———, "Social Ontology and the Philosophy of Society," *Analyse & Kritik*, 20 (1998), 143–158.
Shaffer, Jerome A., *Philosophy of Mind* (Englewood Cliffs: Prentice-Hall, 1968).
Shaw, Thomas, "The Semiotic Mediation of Identity," *Ethos* 22 (1994), 83–119.
Shweder, Richard, and Miller, Joan, "The Social Construction of the Person: How Is It Possible?" in *The Social Construction of the Person*, ed. by Keith Davis and Kenneth Gergen (New York: Springer-Verlag, 1985), pp. 41–72.
Silver, Maury, and Sabini, John, "Sincerity: Feelings and Constructions in Making a Self," in *The Social Construction of the Person*, ed. by Keith Davis and Kenneth Gergen (New York: Springer-Verlag, 1985), pp. 191–202.
Singer, Milton, "Pronouns, Persons, and the Semiotic Self," in *Semiotics, Self, and Society*, ed. by Greg Urban and Benjamin Lee (Berlin: Mouton de Gruyter, 1989), pp. 229–296.
———, "Signs of the Self: An Exploration in Semiotic Anthropology," *American Anthropologist*, 82, no. 3 (1980), 485–507.
Stockwell, Peter, *Cognitive Poetics: An Introduction* (London: Routledge, 2002).
Strawson, Galen, "The Sense of the Self," in *From Soul to Self*, ed. by M. James C. Crabbe (London: Routledge, 1999), pp. 126–152.

Bibliography

Stroud, Barry, *Hume* (Abingdon: Routledge, 1977).
Sutton, John, *Philosophy and Memory Traces* (Cambridge: Cambridge University Press, 1998).
Swann, William, Jr., *Resilient Identities: Self-Relationships and the Construction of Social Reality* (New York: W.H. Freeman and Company, 1999).
Taylor, Charles, *Sources of the Self: The Making of Modern Identity* (Cambridge: Cambridge University Press, 2010).
Tuan, Yi-Fu, "Community, Society, and the Individual," *Geographical Review*, 92.3 (2002), 307–318.
Turner, John, "Towards a Cognitive Redefinition of the Social Group," in *Social Identity and Intergroup Relations*, ed. by Henri Tajfel (Cambridge: Cambridge University Press, 1982), pp. 15–40.
Urban, Greg, "The 'I' of Discourse," in *Semiotics, Self, and Society*, ed. by Greg Urban and Benjamin Lee (Berlin: Mouton de Gruyter, 1989), pp. 27–52.
Van Meijl, Toon, "Culture and Identity in Anthropology: Reflections on 'Unity' and 'Uncertainty' in the Dialogical Self," *International Journal for Dialogical Science*, 3.1 (2008), 165–190.
Walsh, Clare, "Schema Poetics and Crossover Fiction," in *Contemporary Stylistics*, ed. by Peter Stockwell and Marina Lambrou (London: Continuum, 2010), pp. 106–117.
Wiggins, David, "Locke, Butler and the Stream of Consciousness: And Men as a Natural Kind," in *The Identities of Persons*, ed. by Amelie Oksenberg Rorty (Berkeley: University of California Press, 1969), pp. 139–173.
Williams, C.J.F., *Being, Identity, and Truth* (Oxford: Clarendon Press, 1992).
Zunshine, Lisa, "Lying Bodies of the Enlightenment: Theory of Mind and Cultural Historicism," in *Introduction to Cognitive Cultural Studies*, ed. by Lisa Zunshine (Baltimore: Johns Hopkins University Press, 2010), pp. 115–133.

Textual Studies

Acker, Paul, "Horror and the Maternal in 'Beowulf,'" *Modern Language Association* 121, no. 3 (2006), 702–716.
Adams, John, "'Wulf and Eadwacer': An Interpretation," *Modern Language Notes*, 73 (1958), 1–5.
Albano, Robert, "The Role of Women in Anglo-Saxon Culture: Hildeburh in *Beowulf* and a Curious Counterpart in the *Volsunga Saga*,'" *English Language Notes* 32 (1994), 1–10.
Anderson, Lewis, *The Anglo-Saxon Scop* (Toronto: Librarian, 1903).
Anscombe, Alfred, "The Historical Side of the Old English Poem of 'Widsith,'" *Transactions of the Royal Historical Society*, Third Series 9 (1915), 23–165.
Astrom, Berit, "The Creation of the Anglo-Saxon Woman," *Studia Neophilologica*, 70 (1998), 25–34.
_____, "The Politics of Tradition: Examining the History of the Old English Poems *The Wife's Lament* and *Wulf and Eadwacer*" (unpublished doctoral thesis, Universitet Umea, 2002).
Baker, Peter, "The Ambiguity of 'Wulf and Eadwacer,'" *Studies in Philology* 78, no. 5 (1981), 39–51.
Bandel, Betty, "The English Chroniclers' Attitude Toward Women," *Journal of the History of Ideas* 16, no. 1 (1955), 113–118.
Belanoff, Pat, "The Fall(?) of the Old English Female Poetic Image," *PMLA* 104, no. 5 (1989), 822–831.
_____, "Women's Songs Women's Language: Wulf and Eadwacer and The Wife's Lament,"

in *New Readings on Women in Old English Literature*, ed. by Alexandra Olsen and Helen Damico (Bloomington: Indiana University Press, 1990), pp. 193–203.
Bennett, Helen T., "Exile and the Semiosis of Gender in Old English Elegies," in *Class and Gender in Early English Literature*, ed. by Britton J. Harwood and Gillian R. Overing (Bloomington: Indiana University Press, 1994), pp. 43–58.
_____, "The Female Mourner at Beowulf's Funeral: Filling in the Blanks/Hearing the Spaces," *Exemplaria*, 4 (1992), 35–50.
_____, "From Peace Weaver to Text Weaver: Feminist Approaches to Old English Studies," *Old English Newsletter*, 15 (1989), 23–42.
_____, Overing, Gillian, and Lees, Clare A., "Anglo-Saxon Studies: Gender and Power: Feminism and Old English Studies," *Medieval Feminist Forum* 10 (1990), 15–23.
Bernstein, Esther, "The Adhesive Nature of Violence: Orality, Violence, and the Communal in *Beowulf* as Opposed to Written Literacy, Emotion, and the Individual in 'The Dream of the Rood,'" Paper presented at The National Conference on Undergraduate Research (NCUR), 2011, Ithaca College, New York, March 31-April 2, 2011.
Biggs, Frederick M., "Deor's Threatened 'Blame Poem,'" *Studies in Philology*, 94.3 (1997), pp. 297–320.
Bjork, Robert E., "*Sundor æt Rune*: The Voluntary Exile of the Wanderer," *Neophilologus*, 73 (1989), 119–129.
Bloomfield, Morton W., "The Form of *Deor*," *PMLA*, 79.5 (1964), 534–541.
Brookbanks, Jennifer, "The Participation of Women in the Anglo-Saxon World: *Judith* and *The Wife's Lament*," *Innervate* 1 (2008), 25–31.
Burton, Richard," Woman in Old English Poetry," *The Sewane Review*, 4 (1895), 1–14.
Camargo, Martin, "The Finn Episode and the Tragedy of Revenge in 'Beowulf,'" *Studies in Philology* 78, no. 5 (1981), 120–134.
Chance, Jane, *Woman as Hero in Old English Literature* (Syracuse: Syracuse University Press, 1986).
Cherniss, Michael, "Heroic Ideals and the Moral Climate of *Genesis B*," *Modern Language Quarterly* 30, no. 4 (1969), 479–497.
Clark, S.L., and Wasserman, Julian N., "The Imagery of 'The Wanderer,'" *Neophilologus*, 63 (1979), 291–296.
Condren, Edward I., "Deor's Artistic Triumph," *Studies in Philology*, 78.5 (1981), 62–76.
Curry, Jane, "Approaches to a Translation of the Anglo-Saxon *The Wife's Lament*," *Medium Aevum* 35, no. 3 (1966), 187–198.
Damico, Helen, "The Valkyrie Reflex in Old English Literature," in *New Readings on Women in Old English Literature*, ed. by Helen Damico and Alexandra Hennessey Olsen (Indiana University Press, 1990), pp. 176–192.
_____, and Olsen, Alexandra, "Introduction: Old English Literature in the University Curriculum," in *New Readings on Women in Old English Literature*, ed. Alexandra Olsen and Helen Damico (Bloomington: Indiana University Press, 1990, pp. 1–28.
Davidson, Clifford, "Erotic 'Women's Songs' in Anglo-Saxon England," *Neophilologus*, 59 (1975), 451–462.
Davidson, Mary Catherine, "Speaking of Nostalgia in Beowulf," *Modern Philology*, 103 (2005), 143–155.
De Lacy, Paul, "Thematic and Structural Affinities: *The Wanderer* and Ecclesiastes," *Neophilologus*, 82 (1998), 125–137.
Desmond, Marilynn, "The Voice of Exile: Feminist Literary History and the Anonymous Anglo-Saxon Elegy," *Critical Inquiry* 16, no. 3 (1990), 572–590.
Dockray-Miller, Mary, "Female Community in the Old English Judith," *Studia Neophilologica* 70, no. 2 (1998), 165–172.

Bibliography

Donavin, Georgiana, "A Preacher's Identity: Allusions to Jonah in 'The Seafarer,'" *The Yearbook of English Studies*, 22 (1992), 28–37.

Doubleday, James F., "The Limits of Philosophy: A Reading of 'The Wanderer,'" *Notre Dame English Journal*, 7 (1972), 14–22.

____, "The Three Faculties of the Soul in *The Wanderer*," *Neophilologus*, 53 (1969), 189–194.

____, "Two-Part Structure in Old English Poetry," *Notre Dame English Journal*, 8.2 (1973), 71–79.

Dyas, Dee, "Land and Sea in the Pilgrim Life: *The Seafarer* and the Old English *Exodus*," *English Language Notes*, 35.2 (1997), 1–9.

Eliason, Norman E., "The Story of Geat and Mæðhild in 'Deor,'" *Studies in Philology*, 62 (1965), 495–509.

____, "Two Old English Scop Poems," *PMLA*, 81.3 (1966), 185–192.

Empric, Julienne H., "The Seafarer: An Experience in Displacement," *Notre Dame English Journal*, 7 (1972), 23–33.

Ericksen, Janet, "Lands of Unlikeness in Genesis B," *Studies in Philology*, 93 (1996), 1–20.

Evans, Stephen, *The Heroic Poetry of Dark-Age Britain: An Introduction to Its Dating, Composition, and Use as a Historical Source* (Lanham: University Press of America, 2002).

Fowler, Roger, "A Theme in *The Wanderer*," *Medium Ævum*, 36 (1967), 1–14.

Frank, Roberta, "Germanic Legend in Old English Literature," in *The Cambridge Companion to Old English Literature*, ed. by Malcolm Godden and Michael Lapidge (Cambridge: Cambridge University Press, 1991), pp. 82–100.

Frankis, P.J., "Deor and Wulf and Eadwacer: Some Conjectures," *Medium Aevum*, 31 (1962), 161–175.

Frantzen, Allen, "Drama and Dialogue in Old English Poetry: The Scene of Cyewulf"s *Juliana*," *Theatre Survey*, 48 (2007), 99–119.

French, W.H., "Widsith and the Scop." *PMLA* 60, 3 (1945), pp. 623–30.

Frese, Dolores, "Wulf and Eadwacer: The Adulterous Woman Reconsidered," *Notre Dame English Journal*, 15 (1983), 1–22.

____, "*Wulf and Eadwacer*: The Adulterous Woman Reconsidered," in *New Readings on Women in Old English Literature*, ed. by Helen Damico and Alexandra Olsen (Bloomington: Indiana University Press, 1990), pp. 273–291.

Fry, Donald, "Finnsburh: A New Interpretation," *The Chaucer Review*, 9 (1974), 1–14.

____. "'Wulf and Eadwacer': A Wen Charm," *The Chaucer Review*, 5 (1971), 247–263.

Galloway, Andrew, "Dream-Theory in the *Dream of the Rood* and *The Wanderer*," *The Review of English Studies*, New Series 45, no. 180 (1994), 475–485.

Gameson, Richard, and Fiona Gameson, "*Wulf and Eadwacer*, *The Wife's Lament*, and the Discovery of the Individual in Old English Verse," in *Studies in English Language and Literature: "Doubt Wisely"—Papers in Honour of E.G. Stanley*, ed. by M.J Toswell and E.M Tyler (London: Routledge, 1996), pp. 457–475.

Ganze, Ronald, "From *Anhaga* to *Snottor*: The Wanderer's Kierkegaardian Epiphany," *Neophilologus*, 89 (2005), 629–640.

Godden, M., "Anglo-Saxons on the Mind," in *Learning and Literature in Anglo-Saxon England: Studies Presented to Peter Clemoes on the Occasion of His Sixty-Fifth Birthday*, ed. by Michael Lapidge and Helmut Gneuss (Cambridge: Cambridge University Press, 2009), pp. 271–299.

____, "Biblical Literature: The Old Testament," in *The Cambridge Companion to Old English Literature*, ed. by Michael Lapidge and Malcom Godden (Cambridge: Cambrdige University Press, 2002), pp. 206–226.

Gordon, I.L., "Traditional Themes in *The Wanderer* and *The Seafarer*," *The Review of English Studies*, New Series, 5.17 (1954), 1–13.

Bibliography

Greenfield, Stanley B., "Attitudes and Values in 'The Seafarer,'" *Studies in Philology*, 51.1 (1954), 15–20.
____, "The Wife's Lament Reconsidered," *PMLA* 68, no. 4 (1953), 907–912.
Hait, Elizabeth A., "The Wanderer's Lingering Regret: A Study of Patterns of Imagery," *Neophilologus*, 68 (1984), 278–291.
Hall, Alaric, "The Images and Structure of *The Wife's Lament*," *Leeds Studies in English*, 33 (2002), 1–29.
Hansen, Elaine, "From *Freolicu Folccwen* to *Geomuru Ides*: Women in Old English Poetry Reconsidered," *Michigan Academian*, 9 (1973), 109–117.
Harbus, Antonina, *Cognitive Approaches to Old English Poetry* (Cambridge: D.S. Brewer, 2012).
____, "Cognitive Studies of Anglo-Saxon Mentalities," *Pareron* 27, no. 1 (2010), 13–26.
____, "Deceptive Dreams in 'The Wanderer,'" *Studies in Philology*, 93 (1996), 164–179.
____, *The Life of the Mind in Old English Poetry* (Amsterdam: Rodopi, 2002).
____, "The Medieval Concept of the Self in Anglo-Saxon England," *Self and Identity* (2002), 77–97.
Heyworth, Melanie, "Nostalgic Evocation and Social Privilege in the Old English Elegies," *Studia Neophilogica*, 76 (2004), 3–11.
Hill, Joyce, "þæt Wæs Geomuru Ides: A Female Stereotype Examined," in *Readings on Women in Old English Literature*, ed. by Helen Damico and Alexandra Olsen (Bloomington: Indiana University Press, 1990), pp. 235–247.
Hill, Thomas D., "A Stoic Maxim in 'The Wanderer' and Its Contexts," *Studies in Philology*, 101 (2004), 233–249.
Holton, Frederick S., "Old English Sea Imagery and the Interpretation of 'The Seafarer,'" *The Yearbook of English Studies*, 12 (1982), 208–217.
Horner, Shari, *The Discourse of Enclosure: Representing Women in Old English Literature* (Albany: State University of New York Press, 2001).
____, "Spiritual Truth and Sexual Violence: The Old English 'Juliana,' Anglo-Saxon Nuns, and the Discourse of Female Monastic Enclosure," *Signs* 19, no. 3 (1994), 658–675.
Horton, Lisa M., "Singing the Story: Narrative Voice and the Old English Scop," *The Hilltop Review*, 4 (2010), 45–57. http://www.mun.ac/mst/heroicage/issues/5/porter1.html [accessed 07 August 2013] (1–8).
Hultin, Neil, "The External Soul in 'The Seafarer' and 'The Wanderer,'" *Folklore* 88 (1977), 39–45.
Irvine, Susan, "Speaking One"s Mind in *The Wanderer*," in *Inside Old English: Essays in Honour of Bruce Mitchell*, ed. by John Walmsley (Oxford: Blackwell, 2005), pp. 117–133.
Irving, Edward B., Jr., "Images and the Meaning in the Elegies," in *Old English Poetry: Fifteen Essays*, ed. by Robert P. Creed (Providence: Brown University Press, 1967), pp. 153–165.
Jabbour, Alan, "Memorial Transmission in Old English Poetry," *The Chaucer Review*, 3.3 (1969), 174–190.
Jager, Eric, "Speech and the Chest in Old English Poetry: Orality or Pectoriality?" *Speculum* 65, no. 4 (1990), 845–859.
Jensen, Emily, "Narrative Voice in the Old English 'Wulf,'" *The Chaucer Review*, 13, no. 4 (1979), 373–383.
Kinch, Ashby, "The Ethical Agency of the Female Lyric Voice: The Wife"s Lament and Catullus 64," *Studies in Philology*, 103, no. 2 (2006), 121–152.
Klein, Stacy, "Reading Queenship in Cynewulf"s Elene," *Journal of Medieval and Early Modern Studies*, 33 (2003), 47–89.
Klein, W.F., "Purpose and the 'Poetics' of *The Wanderer* and *The Seafarer*," in *Anglo-Saxon Poetry: Essays in Appreciation for John C. McGalliard*, ed. by Lewis E. Nichol-

Bibliography

son and Dolores Warwick Frese (Notre Dame: University of Notre Dame Press, 1975), pp. 208–223.

Klinck, Anne, "Female Characterization in Old English Poetry and the Growth of Psychological Realism: *Genesis B* and *Christ I*," *Neophilologus*, 63, no. 4 (1979), 597–610.

Langeslag, P.S., "Doctrine and Paradigm: Two Functions of the Innovations in Genesis B," *Studia Neophilologica*, 79, no. 2 (2007), 113–118.

Lapidge, Michael, "The Comparative Approach," in *Reading Old English Texts*, ed. by Katherine O"Keefe (Cambridge, 1997), pp. 20–38.

Lawrence, William, "The Banished Wife"s Lament," *Modern Philology*, 5, no. 3 (1908), 387–405.

____, "The Song of Deor," *Modern Philology*, 9 (1911), 23–45.

____, "Structure and Interpretation of 'Widsith,'" *Modern Philology*, 4.2 (1906), 329–374.

Lench, Elinor, "*The Wife's Lament*: A Poem of the Living Dead," *Comitatus: A Journal of Medieval and Renaissance Studies*, 1 (1970), 3–22.

Lionarons, Joyce, "Cultural Syncretism and the Construction of Gender in Cynewulf"s *Elene*," *Exemplaria*, 10 (1998), 51–68.

Lockett, Leslie, *Anglo-Saxon Psychologies in the Vernacular and Latin Tradition* (Toronto: University of Toronto Press, 2011).

____, "Corporeality in the Psychology of the Anglo-Saxons" (Unpublished PhD Thesis, University of Notre Dame, 2004).

Magennis, Hugh, "The Cup as Symbol and Metaphor in Old English Literature," *Speculum* 60, no. 3 (1985), 517–536.

____, "Gender and Heroism in the Old English *Judith*," in *Writing Gender and Genre in Medieval Literature: Approaches to Old and Middle English Texts*, ed. by Elaine Treharne (Cambridge: D.S. Brewer, 2002), pp. 5–18.

____, *Images of Community in Old English Poetry* (Cambridge: Cambridge University Press, 1996).

Magoun, Francis P., "Bede's Story of Caedman: The Case History of an Anglo-Saxon Oral Singer," *Speculum*, 30 (1955), 49–63

Malone, Kemp, "Alliteration in *Widsith*," *ELH*, 2.4 (1935), 291–293

____, "Exemplum and Refrain: The Meaning of '*Deor*,'" *The Yearbook of English Studies*, 7 (1977), 1–9.

____, "The Myrgingas of *Widsith*," *Modern Language Notes*, 55.2 (1940), 141–142.

____, "The Suffix of Appurtenance in Widsith," *The Modern Language Review*, 28.3 (1933), 315–325.

____, "Two Notes on *Widsith*," *Modern Language Notes*, 47.6 (1932), 367–371.

____, "Widsith: Addenda and Corrigenda," *The Modern Language Review*, 31.4 (1936), 547–579.

____, "*Widsith* and the Critic," *ELH*, 5 (1938), pp. 49–66.

____, "The With-Myrgings of 'Widsith,'" *The Modern Language Review*, 39 (1944), 55–6.

Mandel, Jerome, "Contrast in Old English Poetry," *The Chaucer Review*, 6.1 (1971), 1–13.

McKill, Larry, "Patterns of the Fall: Adam and Eve in the Old English *Genesis A*," *Florilegium*, 14 (1995), 25–41.

McKinney, Windy, "Creating a *gens Anglorum*: Social and Ethnic Identity in Anglo-Saxon England through the Lens of Bede"s *Historia Ecclesiastica*" (Unpublished PhD Thesis, University of York, Centre for Medieval Studies, 2011).

Mize, Britt, "The Mental Container and the Cross of Christ: Revelation and Community in the *Dream of the Rood*," *Studies in Phlology*, 107 (2010), 131–178.

____, "The Representation of the Mind as an Enclosure in Old English Poetry," *Anglo-Saxon England* (2006), 57–90.

Bibliography

Moffat, Douglas, "Anglo-Saxon Scribes and Old English Verse," *Speculum*, 67 (1992), 805–827.
Nash, Walter, "An Anglo-Saxon Mystery," *Language and Literature*, 19 (2010), 99–112.
Niles, John, "The Problem of the Ending of the Wife's Lament," *Speculum*, 78, no. 4 (2003), 1107–1150.
Norman, F., "Deor: A Criticism and an Interpretation," *The Modern Language Review*, 32.3 (1937), 374–381.
Olsen, Alexandra, "Cynewulf's Autonomous Women: A Reconsideration of Elene and Juliana," in *New Readings on Women in Old English Literature*, ed. by Helen Damico and Hennessey Olsen, Alexandra (Bloomington: Indiana University Press, 1990), pp. 222–234.
Orton, Peter, "An Approach to Wulf and Eadwacer," *Proceedings of the Royal Irish Academy. Section C: Archaeology, Celtic Studies, History, Linguistics, Literature*, 85 (1985), 223–258.
Palmer, R, "Characterization in the Old English Juliana," *South Atlantic Bulletin*, 41, no. 4 (1976), 10–21.
Parks, Ward, "The Traditional Narrator and the "I Heard" Formulas in Old English Poetry, *Anglo-Saxon England*, 16 (1987), 45–66.
Payne, Richard, "Convention and Originality in the Vision Framework of 'The Dream of the Rood,'" *Modern Philology*, 73, no. 4 (1976), 329–341.
Phipps, Charles, "A Feminist Critique of *Beowulf*: Women as Peace-Weavers and Goaders in Beowulf's Courts" (Unpublished Master's Thesis, Marshall University, 2012) http://mds.marshall.edu/cgi/viewcontent.cgi?article=1297&context=etd [accessed 07 August 2013].
Pope, John C, "Dramatic Voices in *The Wanderer* and *The Seafarer*," in *Medieval and Linguistic Studies: In Honor of Francs Peabody Magoun, Jr.*, ed. by Jess B. Bessinger, Jr., and Robert P. Creed (London: George Allen and Unwin, Ltd., 1965), pp. 165–193.
Porter, Dorothy, "The Social Centrality of Women in *Beowulf*: A New Context," *The Heroic Age*, 5 (2001), 1–6.
Ramsden, Alexandra, "Anglo-Saxon Conceptions of the Inner Self: An Exploration of Traditions and Innovation in Selected Cynewulfian and Alfredian Texts" (Unpublished PhD Thesis, University of York, Centre for Medieval Studies, 2008).
Renoir, Alain, "A Reading Context for *The Wife's Lament*," in *Anglo-Saxon Poetry: Essays in Appreciation for John C. McGalliard*, ed. Dolores Frese and Lewis Nicholson (Notre Dame: University of Notre Dame Press, 1975), pp. 224–241.
Rosier, James L., "The Literal-Figurative Identity of *The Wanderer*," *PMLA*, 79 (1964), 366–369.
Salmon, Vivian, "'The Wanderer' and 'The Seafarer,' and the Old English Conception of the Soul," *The Modern Language Review*, 55 (1960), 1–10.
Samuels, Peggy, "The Audience Written into the Script of *The Dream of the Rood*," *Modern Language Quarterly*, 49, no. 4 (1988), 311–320.
Scheck, Helene, "Seductive Voices: Rethinking Female Subjectivities in *The Wife's Lament* and *Wulf and Eadwacer*," *Literature Compass*, 5, no. 2 (2008), 220–227.
Schibanoff, Susan, "Medieval *Frauenlieder*: Anonymous Was a Man?" *Tulsa Studies in Women's Literature*, 1, no. 2 (1982), 189–200.
Schlauch, Margaret, "Widsith, Vithforull, and Some Other Analogues," *PMLA*, 46.4 (1931), 969–987.
Schneider, Claude, "Cynewulf"s Devaluation of Heroic Tradition in *Juliana*," *Anglo-Saxon England*, 7 (1978), 107–118.
Selzer, John L., "'The Wanderer' and the Meditative Tradition," *Studies in Philology*, 80 (1983), 227–237.

Bibliography

Singh, Stephanie, "The Importance of Women in Anglo-Saxon Society as Portrayed Through Literature," *The Compass*, 1 (2015) http://scholarworks.arcadia.edu/cgi/viewcontent.cgi?article=1010&context=thecompass [accessed May 23, 2016]

Sklute, John, "*Freothuwebbe* in Old English Poetry," in *New Readings on Women in Old English Poetry*, ed. by Alexandra Olsen and Helen Damico (Bloomington: Indiana University Press, 1990), pp. 204–210.

Smith, A.H., "þeodric in "Widsith" and the Rok Inscription," *The Modern Language Review*, 26.3 (1931), 330–332.

Straus, Barrie, "Women"s Words as Speech: Speech as Action in The Wife's Lament." *Texas Studies in Literature and Language*, 23, no. 2 (1981), 268–285.

Tampierova, Helena, "*The Dream of the Rood*—A Blend of Christian and Pagan Values," *South Bohemian Anglo-American Studies*, 1 (2007), 47–51.

Thieme, Adelheid, "Gift Giving as a Vital Element of Salvation in The Dream of the Rood," *South Atlantic Review*, 63, no. 2 (1998), 108–123.

Tuggle, Thomas T., "The Structure of 'Deor,'" *Studies in Philology*, 74 (1977), 229–242.

Tupper, Jas W., "Deor"s Complaint," *Modern Language Notes*, 10.2 (1895), pp. 63–4.

Wentersdorf, Karl, "The Situation of the Narrator in the Old English *Wife's Lament*," *Speculum*, 56, no. 3 (1981), 492–516.

Whitelock, Dorothy, "The Interpretation of *The Seafarer*," in *The Early Cultures of North-West Europe (H.M. Chadwick Memorial Studies)*, ed. by Sir Cyril Fox and Bruce Dickins (Cambridge: Cambridge University Press, 1950), pp. 261–272.

Williams, Edith, "What's So New About the Sexual Revolution? Some Comments on Anglo-Saxon Attitudes Toward Sexuality in Women Based on Four Exeter Book Riddles," in *New Readings on Women in Old English Literature*, ed. by Helen Damico and Alexandra Olsen (Bloomington: Indiana University Press, 1990), pp. 137–145.

Wittig, Joseph, "Figural Narrative in Cynewulf's *Juliana*," *Anglo-Saxon England*, 4 (1975), 37–55.

Woolf, R.E., "The Devil in Old English Poetry," *The Review of English Studies*, New Series, 4, no. 13 (1953), 1–12.

_____, "*The Wanderer, The Seafarer*, and the Genre of *Planctus*," in *Anglo-Saxon Poetry: Essays in Appreciation for John C. McGalliard*, ed. by Lewis E. Nicholson and Dolores Warwick Frese (Notre Dame: University of Notre Dame Press, 1975), pp. 192–207.

Zsuzsanna, Peri-Nagy, "Identity, Authority, Empowering: Another Approach to the *Dream of the Rood*," *Tel* (2012), 1–19.

Index

Adam 48–51; *see also* Eve
Aelfric 21
Alcuin 26–27, 100
Alexander 113
Ambrose 89
Atilla 113
Augustine 22, 78

The Battle of Brunanburh 16
The Battle of Maldon 16, 21
Beadohild 103–105, 109, 111, 113, 148
Bede 41, 89, 100
Beowulf 38, 52, 134, 144, 158–152
Boethius 22

Cædmon 100
Caesar 113
Cartesian 6; *see also* Descartes
Chaucer 132
cognitive cultural studies 17
Confessions 22
Consolation of Philosophy 22
Cynewulf 127

Deor 28, 76, 86, 99, 101–121, 128, 123, 134, 142, 144, 146, 148, 150–152, 154–155
Descartes 9; *see also* Cartesian
developmental psychology 11
The Dream of the Rood (DrR) 28, 51–53, 55–57

Elene 124
Elene 57, 124, 127, 132
Eormanric 105, 109, 111, 113
Eve 48–51; *see also* Adam
Exeter Book 22, 96, 103, 114, 149, 154

Finn 149–150
Freawaru 148
Freudian 8

Genesis B (GenB) 28, 39, 45–46, 48, 51–52, 57, 151

Gregory the Great 89
Guthlac A 21

Heoden 101
Heorrenda 101, 104–105, 109
Hildeburh 124, 148–150, 152
Historia Ecclesiastica 41
Hrothgar 38, 144
Hume, David 10, 59, 62
Hygd 148

Judith 124, 130, 132
Juliana 124, 127, 130, 132

King Alfred 22

Locke, John 91–92, 127

Marxism 8
Maxims I 120

neuroscience 8–9, 17
nostalgia 39, 130

Offa 115
Old Norse 103, 140
Ostrogoth 105

peregrini pro Christo 26
Plato 10

Resignation B 117

Satan 45–51, 57, 89,
scop 28, 35, 39, 41–45, 99–108, 111–114, 116–121, 126, 128–129, 133, 142, 150–151, 154–155
The Seafarer (Seaf) 1, 9, 13, 35, 47, 52–53, 59–62, 81–99, 101–104, 110, 123, 125, 128, 136–137, 140–141, 145–147, 151–152, 154
self-development 7
self-schema 9–10, 53, 99, 114–116, 118, 120–121

Index

self-script 115
situational-self protocols 6
social constructionism 7–8, 28, 34, 37, 47
sociological self 8
Soliloquies 22
Soul 2, 9–10, 19, 20–21, 24–25, 59–60, 71, 79, 81, 83, 89–90, 93–94, 117, 136

Theodric 105, 109, 113

The Wanderer (Wan) 1, 9, 13, 21, 35, 47, 53, 59–92, 94–99, 101–103, 104, 110, 114, 117, 123, 125, 128, 136–137, 140–141, 145–147, 151–152,
Wealhtheow 130, 148
Welund 102–105, 109, 111, 113
Widsith 28, 39, 99, 101, 108–109, 111, 113–121, 123, 144, 150, 154
Wife of Bath 132
The Wife's Lament (Wife) 29, 123, 125, 127, 128, 132–152, 155
Wulf and Eadwacer (Wulf) 29, 123, 125, 127–128, 132–134, 142–149, 151–152, 155

www.ingramcontent.com/pod-product-compliance
Lightning Source LLC
Chambersburg PA
CBHW032102300426
44116CB00007B/850